Assembling Flann O'Brien

Maebh Long

D1518745

BLOOMSBURY

LONDON • NEW DELHI • NEW YORK • SYDNEY

Bloomsbury Academic

An imprint of Bloomsbury Publishing Plc

50 Bedford Square	1385 Broadway
London	New York
WC1B 3DP	NY 10018
UK	USA

www.bloomsbury.com

Bloomsbury is a registered trade mark of Bloomsbury Publishing Plc

First published 2014

© Maebh Long, 2014

British Library Cataloguing-in-Publication Data

A catalogue record for this book is available from the British Library.

ISBN: HB: 978-1-4411-8705-5
PB: 978-1-4411-9020-8
ePDF: 978-1-4411-6030-0
ePub: 978-1-4411-1335-1

Library of Congress Cataloging-in-Publication Data

A catalog record for this book is available from the Library of Congress.

Typeset by Deanta Global Publishing Services, Chennai, India
Printed and bound in India

CONTENTS

Acknowledgements vi
Abbreviations viii

Introduction 1

1 Fragments of palimpsests 9

2 Driven to repeat 57

3 Ireland on trial 107

4 A hard life for women 149

5 Archival fantasies 191

Bibliography 225
Index 239

ACKNOWLEDGEMENTS

All extracts from Brian O'Nolan's work are quoted with the kind permission of the Brian O'Nolan estate. Unpublished letters, manuscripts and other papers quoted are courtesy of the John J. Burns Library, Boston College and the Special Collections Research Centre, Morris Library, Southern Illinois University, Carbondale. My thanks to the staff at both special collections, in particular, Justine Sundaram of Boston College: when my house was broken into a few months before the book was due, and my laptop and some backups stolen, she very kindly sent me scans of the most important files.

Without funding from the School of Language, Arts and Media, and the Faculty of Arts, Law and Education at the University of the South Pacific, the archival component of this book could not have been undertaken, and I thank the School and the Faculty for their assistance. From USP I'd like to wholeheartedly thank Sudesh Mishra and Matthew Hayward, and Russell Smith while he was with us on leave from ANU.

I am indebted, as always, to Timothy Clark of Durham University, and I'm most grateful for those in Durham who read and commented on drafts: Marc Botha, Ann-Marie Einhaus, Beth Hannon and Emily Ridge. I would also like to thank James Quick, Sarah Jackson, Phil Leonard, John Phillips and, as ever, Graham Allen.

Paul Fagan and Ruben Borg of the International Flann O'Brien Society, and other Flanneurs Jonathan Ó Néill, Adam Winstanley and Jennika Baines have all been extremely helpful, and I would particularly like to thank Carol Taaffe for being so generous with her time and expertize.

Thanks also to David Avital, Laura Murray, Andrew Wardell and Mark Richardson at Continuum, now Bloomsbury, for their assistance along the way.

I'd like to thank my grandparents for their support, and in particular, my grandfather for painstakingly cutting out and posting every recent mention of Brian O'Nolan in the *Irish Times*. Eileen O'Brien and Peter Curran for being constants, and the Longs – Áine, Finbarr, Ciara – for well, everything. Finally, love and thanks to Tom, for having to listen to it all!

ABBREVIATIONS

Books

AB   Myles na gCopaleen. *An Béal Bocht*. Dublin: Mercier Press, 1999.

AS   Flann O'Brien. *At Swim-Two-Birds*. London: Penguin, 2001.

HL   Flann O'Brien. *The Hard Life*. London: Paladin, 1990.

PM   Flann O'Brien. *The Poor Mouth*. London: Flamingo, 1993.

RS   Flann O'Brien. *Rhapsody in Stephen's Green*. Ed. Robert Tracy. Dublin: Lilliput Press, 2011.

SP   Flann O'Brien. *Stories and Plays*. London: Paladin, 1991.

TP   Flann O'Brien. *The Third Policeman*. London: Harper Perennial, 2006.

Archives

BC   Flann O'Brien Papers, MS1997–27, John J. Burns Library, Boston College, Boston, US.

SIUC   Brian O'Nolan papers, 1914–66, ID: 1/4/MSS 051, Special Collections, Southern Illinois University, Carbondale, US.

Introduction

'*Writing is not quite the word. Assembly, perhaps,*
is better – or accretion'.

FLANN O'BRIEN, *THE DALKEY ARCHIVE*

From the chaotic collage that was *Blather*, through the fragments of *At Swim-Two-Birds*, the footnotes of *The Third Policeman*, the 'assembly belt'[1] and disjointed apostrophes of *Cruiskeen Lawn*, the Gaelic borrowings of *An Béal Bocht*, and the thefts, appropriations and visitations of the last novels, Brian O'Nolan's works are acts of assembly, writing as a performance of conjunction and interruption, quotation and pastiche. O'Nolan himself is no different; he is a throng, a congregation of identities producing an anarchic and sprawling corpus of work. His pseudonymic writings and intimations of further, unknown works have left his oeuvre open and undetermined, and his masks cause the voices in his texts to multiply into a cacophony, a menagerie containing Myles na gCopaleen, Flann O'Brien, An Broc, Brother Barnabas, George Knowall, John James Doe, Count Blather, Matt Duffy and occasionally Brian O'Nolan. This profusion of names is further multiplied by internal divisions, as Flann O'Brien is divided by two periods of authorship misrepresented by a common name, and Myles na gCopaleen is a mélange of radically differing roles and histories, often within a single piece a multiple, self-interrupting disorder of opinions and voices:

I have received a number of letters (*ha-ha-ha!*) from users (*God help them!*) of my patent fishing rods (*patent swindle rods!*) made from pressed slack. These readers are delighted with them (*lies, lies lies!*) and swear that they are superior (*show the letters, show the letters!*) to the timber article. (*Why don't you shut up?*) I (*who are you?*) am glad that my researches are appreciated. In this unhappy world (*why don't you leave it and make it better?*) it is, indeed, heartening to know that one's poor efforts (*listen to the poor idiot!*) are meeting with approbation. It's pleasing to know that the public looks up to me (*wait till they have you strung up on a lamp-post?*) and (*they'll look up to you then!*) admit my pre-eminence in the field of invention. (*Ho-ho-ho!*) My other experiments are proceeding (*how about the T. D.'s wife?*) and I hope to be in a position to report shortly (*are you sure you won't be found out?*)

I am going to close down for a moment. But be assured that I have a powerful apparatus to deal with this Ghost Voice. All will be well tomorrow.[2]

Even Brian O'Nolan's 'real' identity is a scrapbook of alternative histories, the most famous of which is his supposed marriage to Clara Ungerland, the blonde, violin-playing daughter of a Cologne basket-weaver.

The assemblage that was O'Nolan reflects an Ireland struggling to find an identity, and O'Nolan's protean plurality – albeit a plurality strongly pre-disposed towards the white, male, educated Dubliner – represents the writer's response to what he felt to be an oppressive and cynically constructed 'Keltanschauung',[3] a supposedly 'natural' identity and outlook concocted from the spurious myth, invention and prejudice proffered by the Gaelic Revivalists, the government and, although rarely directly targeted by O'Nolan, the Church. As a more playful Myles wrote,

> if you are Irish, write and tell me about it. . . . State at what age you first realised you were an Irish person. When did you have your first fight? At what age did you make your first brilliant "Irish" witticism? At what age did you become a drunkard? Please tell me all, because there can be no cure until the pathological background has been explored. If you conceive yourself to be a cultural chauvin, please state whether your fixations are concerned with footballs, hoses [sic], folk dances, political frontiers or mere languages. . . . Remember that I too was Irish. Today I am cured. I am no longer Irish. I am merely a person.[4]

As an alternative to the 'drunk, truculent, witty, celtic, dark, desperate, amorous'[5] Irish Paddy, O'Nolan assembled a new crowd of Irish men – and occasionally women – to replace the stage Irishman he detested. While these new characters substituted urban pre-occupations for the rural lives most commonly shown on the Abbey stage – to name one of Myles's *bêtes noires* – O'Nolan's early work in particular was a reaction to the Gaelic Revivalists' belief – as O'Nolan depicted it – that 'poverty and savage existence on remote rocks was a most poetical way for people to be, provided they were other people'.[6] For O'Nolan, Ireland was a disjointed assembly too often repeating the same refrain, and he worked, particularly in the early *Cruiskeen Lawn*, to call attention to this ongoing chorus:

> our national heritage mumble mumble mumble our tradition for artistic endeavour mumble mumble respite from politics mumble mumble maintaining our world-wide reputation for mumble mumble mumble the case of the Lane pictures mumble mumble emigration of all our greatest writers mumble mumble necessity for those who care for artistic things to get together mumble mumble repeal of Censorship Act mumble mumble mumble cheapening influence of the cinema on human values mumble mumble mumble mumble.[7]

O'Nolan's clamorous response to the Church, State and stage's attempted ventriloquism act was a series of fragmentary texts ruptured by a polyphony of voices, subversive structures, dark protagonists, grimy lives, black humour and cutting invective. His works combine original text with 'found-object' fragments, that is, extracts from encyclopaedia entries, recipe books, old tomes, letters, newspaper articles, political gossip or writings which simply provoked or amused. O'Nolan's texts are ensemble pieces, collections of literary plunder that subvert concepts of structure, originality and the generic conventions of journalism and the novel. Supplementing his technique of performance plagiarism is an attention to syntactic and semantic detail whose often obsessive focus and rigour is belied by a greater commitment to provocation or humour. That is, while O'Nolan was genuine in his dismissal of poor literary craft – 'I *hate* loose writing'[8] – behind much of his literary or linguistic analysis is the sense that, as Lewis Carroll's

Duchess says, 'he only does it to annoy, because he knows it teases'. O'Nolan's texts thus exhibit a certain uneasy relationship to literary pretensions, knowledge and the art of writing itself. Manus of *The Hard Life*, for example, is a master of conveyor-belt publication, representing everything that is wrong with the treatment of knowledge as commodity. By wholly disrespecting intellectual property rights, Manus amasses and sells purloined and repackaged learning under the guise of a pseudo-democratic, assembly-line approach to education: the 'mass-production of knowledge, human accomplishment and civilization', he claims, would turn the world into one 'of sophisticated and genial people, all well-to-do, impatient with snivellers, sneaks and politicians on the make' (HL 102). This sanctimonious profiteering from the research of others fakes its learning and its sources, claiming expertize and qualifications where none exist. And yet, while Manus appears in every way to be a charlatan, he does learn to walk the tightrope, manages, albeit imperfectly, to impart that skill to others, and has his team create a miracle cure for rheumatism which, despite certain complications, does work. His counterfeiting of knowledge does not cancel its quality or effects; the knowledge he mines is legitimate, simply stolen. While throughout O'Nolan's works there is a distaste for those who copy and fabricate, and while characters' literary endeavours contain elements of the parasitic and corrupt, the 'art' of assemblage is a consistent feature of his own writings.

In *The Myth of Sisyphus*, Albert Camus writes that 'The mind's first step is to distinguish what is true from what is false. However, as soon as thought reflects on itself, what it first discovers is a contradiction'. If, he continues, quoting Aristotle, we assert 'that all is true we assert the truth of the contrary assertion and consequently the falsity of our own thesis (for the contrary assertion does not admit that it can be true)'. Similarly, if we assert that all is false, then the statement immediately defeats itself. And if we say that all statements other than our own are false, we are obliged to admit an infinite number of true and false statements, 'For the one who expresses a true assertion proclaims simultaneously that it is true, and so on *ad infinitum*'. 'This vicious cycle', Camus asserts, 'is but the first of a series in which the mind that studies itself gets lost in a giddy whirling'.[9] The joy of giddy whirling through the paradoxes of logic and language is precisely what marks O'Nolan's early works, and is lost in his later, but this pleasure doesn't preclude constant doubt about knowledge and learning. The freedom offered in the confusion of *The Third Policeman* – '*Anything can be said in this place and it will be true and will have to be believed*' (TP 88) – is also its danger. Both Flann O'Brien and Myles na gCopaleen embraced erudition, pedantry and close reading while remaining highly suspicious of, as Myles put it, 'intellectsects';[10] early Myles played the sophistic philistine with aplomb, while O'Brien's first, experimental novels contained educated and bookish protagonists who were egotistic, arrogant and somewhat inept. This ambivalence towards learning and Irish society is rather nicely represented in a lapsarian fable recounted by Kant, in which Eden is a world composed of a

> garden with ample trees richly provided with splendid fruits, whose digested residue, after the couple's enjoyment of them, vanished through an unnoticed evaporation; the exception was a single tree in the middle of the garden, which bore a fruit which was delicious but did not dry up in this way. As it now happened, our first parents now lusted after it, despite the prohibition against tasting it, and so there was no other way to keep heaven from being polluted except to take the advice of one of the angels who pointed out to them the distant earth, with the words: "There is the toilet of the whole universe", and then carried them there in order to relieve themselves, but then flew back to heaven leaving them behind. That is how the human race is supposed to have arisen on earth.[11]

Adam and Eve's desires condemned them to a life surrounded by the filth that is the run-off of pleasure and learning, as only a single tree, the tree of desire – which by extension is the tree of lost innocence and knowledge – produces real waste. Knowledge and desire lead to filth, and while O'Nolan was no believer in a Rousseauian state of nature, within his works desire is dangerous and learning is tainted by ordure: 'I know one Cork intellectual who always calls his septic tank "the library"'.[12] Anthony Cronin, O'Nolan's biographer, refers to O'Nolan's period in University College Dublin as a 'baptism in the squalor of which he would be the exegete',[13] but this sense of life's grime does not, however, preclude humour; it demands it. As O'Brien wrote of Joyce, 'With a laugh he palliates the sense of doom that is the heritage of the Irish

Catholic. True humour needs this background urgency: Rabelais is funny, but his stuff cloys. His stuff lacks tragedy' (SP 175). It is this sense of dark laughter that makes O'Nolan's work 'bitterly funny'[14] – with emphasis on the 'bitter' – for as O'Nolan aged and his talents were awarded with neither real respect nor financial reward, he turned towards social commentaries, political diatribes, laboured novels and clichéd scripts that he thought would generate more income than avant-garde works which had, as his literary agents said of *At Swim-Two-Birds*, 'almost every possible defect from a commercial point of view'.[15] It was the failure of Irish society to recognize the talent exhibited in his early novels and journalistic output with proper financial reward that caused his brother to write:

> Brian's personal story in the end was full of sadness. Fame and recognition came too late to do him any good. Fortune came not at all. The world saw to it that this master in the precise use of words was never able to extend his mastery (as he himself puts it) to the simple act of writing his name "in little books called cheque books".[16]

O'Nolan once wrote that certain audiences were 'very hard to amuse – they look for overtones, undertones, subtones, grunts and "philosophy", they assume something very serious is afoot. It's disquieting for a writer is [sic] only, for the moment, clowning'.[17] *Assembling Flann O'Brien* is a series of incursions into Brian O'Nolan's novels, plays, short stories, articles and archival documents that looks at overtones, undertones, subtones, grunts and 'philosophy', and does not presume that humour can be used as a defence against intellectual engagement, or to deny content which is contentious, provocative or of interest to a theoretical analysis. It also presumes, following the centenary of O'Nolan's birth and the articles, special issues, conferences, collected editions and performances this provoked, that the body of work on O'Nolan has reached the point of critical mass whereby an interconnected scholarly corpus exists. This means that academic engagements can be now thought of as elaborating or commenting on a disciplinary area rather than introducing each time a marginal author, and for that reason this work does not re-present summaries of O'Nolan's texts, repeat biographical information or reiterate now-canonical quotations. Instead it engages in an analysis of O'Nolan's works – prioritizing the novels, but incorporating other writings, published and unpublished – and assembles a host of theorists, thinkers and philosophers with which to challenge and elucidate certain thematic or structural patterns and events within O'Nolan's texts. When certain subjects recur these patterns of repetition cross the work's chapters, but rather than prioritizing a single leitmotif running across O'Nolan's work, context or biography, *Assembling Flann O'Brien* is primarily concerned with engaging with each work as a singularity. While attitudes towards sexuality and women are a consistent thread, different chapters address different issues arising from each novel. Thus, *At Swim-Two-Birds* is read through its fragmentary structure and treatment of procreation, *The Third Policeman*'s hellish recurrences as a repetition of the structures of desire and the death drive, *An Béal Bocht* as an engagement with Agamben's 'bare life' and the proper name, *The Hard Life* as a nexus for O'Nolan's representations of women and *The Dalkey Archive* as an archive of tensions with knowledge, Joyce and autobiography.

In the case of a man so fond of pen names – indeed, O'Nolan once speculated on the possibility of 'a pen-face'[18] – academic referencing is difficult. Given that there are marked differences between the character, or, as Brooker puts it, style[19] that is Myles na gCopaleen and the author Flann O'Brien, and that O'Nolan cannot be naively conflated with his authorial personae, an extra layer of framing and distance must be added to the usual progression: the opinions of the characters are not those of the narrator, the opinions of the narrator not those of the author and the opinions of the author not those of Brian O'Nolan. Hence, as has been the case in this introduction, when a specific text is referred to, it will be attributed to the author credited for that work, and O'Nolan will be referred to only when points encompassing his different roles are made or when biographical/archival detail is referred to. This by no means allows O'Nolan deniability for the undercurrents in his work, particularly those that engage with sexuality and gender, but complicates any picture that presumes to easily equate the man and his character authors. Finally, *Assembling Flann O'Brien* takes its name from the technique of assemblage so frequently employed by O'Nolan, but uses 'O'Brien' to establish not only its predominant engagement with the novels, but also to move away from any sense of a psychobiographical focus.

Notes

1   Myles na gCopaleen, Cruiskeen Lawn, *Irish Times* (hereafter referred to as CL) 5 June 1942.
2   CL 27 October 1941.
3   CL 4 July 1953.
4   CL 31 May 1943.
5   CL 6 September 1943.
6   CL 4 October 1954.
7   CL 16 August 1941.
8   CL 5 October 1944.
9   Albert Camus, *The Myth of Sisyphus*, trans. Justin O'Brien (London: Penguin, 2000), 22.
10 CL 20 May 1942.
11 Immanuel Kant 'The End of All Things' *Religion and Rational Theology*, trans. and ed. Allen W. Wood and George D. Giovanni (Cambridge: Cambridge University Press, 2001), 224–5.
12 F. O'Brien, Letters to the Editor, *Irish Times*, 2 August 1940.
13 Anthony Cronin, *No Laughing Matter: The Life and Times of Flann O'Brien* (New York: Fromm International Publishing Company, 1998), 71.
14 Brian O'Nolan (hereafter BON) to Timothy O'Keeffe (hereafter TOK) 27 November 1963. Brian O'Nolan papers, 1914–66, ID: 1/4/MSS 051, Special Collections, Southern Illinois University, Carbondale, US. Hereafter SIUC.
15 Patricia Ross of A. M. Heath to BON, 11 July 1938, SIUC.
16 Gearoid O'Nolan to L. H. Stevens, NSW, Australia, undated, Flann O'Brien Papers, MS1997–27, John J. Burns Library, Boston College, Boston, US. Hereafter referred to as BC.
17 BON to Gerald Gross, 16 January 1962, SIUC.
18 BON to TOK, 19 August 1961, SIUC.
19 Joseph Brooker, *Flann O'Brien* (Tavistock: Northcote, 2005), 90.

1

Fragments of palimpsests

That *At Swim-Two-Birds* is a fragmented text is a generally accepted truism – Keith M. Booker employs its 'complex, multistylistic collage of fragments from a variety of different cultural domains'[1] to support a Bakhtinian reading of polyphony and Menippean satire, David Cohen calls its 'disruptive and fragmentary quality'[2] exemplary of postmodernism, while for Joshua D. Esty, *At Swim-Two-Birds* shows O'Brien to be 'the inventor of a wilfully fragmentary postcolonial form'.[3] Joseph Brooker reads it as 'a collection of fragments, disjointed almost by design . . . open to chance and contingency',[4] while for Dennell Downum its fragments position it as a late modernist text eschewing 'Joycean notions of artistic genius and unity, openly embracing instead an aesthetic based on literary borrowings and fragmentation'.[5] For Peter Childs, the fragments of *At Swim-Two-Birds* make it the perfect text with which to conclude his Routledge guide to Modernism, as its interlocking units see the

> omniscient perspective of the realist text . . . broken up into fragments as narrative styles, from literary history and life, are juxtaposed with each other. . . . Published in the year the war began, *At Swim-Two-Birds* can serve as one marker of the end of the Modernist revolution. . . . Through formal and linguistic experimentation the Modernists had overturned previous modes of representation, thereby laying the foundations for postmodernist writers to undermine the very categories of "character," "representation," "reality" and even "literature."[6]

The fragments that *At Swim-Two-Birds* has shored against its ruins share with Eliot's *The Waste Land* a radical aesthetics, structural experimentation, unconventional chronology, scepticism towards a coherent identity, varied quotation and allusion, uncertain narrative frames, contaminated planes of reality and a tendency to do everybody in different voices. But while the fragments of Eliot's poem may be understood as the splintering and piecemeal reassembling of society, O'Brien's novel presents the fragments of a whole that never existed. This is not to argue that Eliot presumes that English pre-war society was a closed, ordered monad, but that for O'Nolan modern Irish society was always already a collection of fragments, and as such his particles pertain to the absence of a pre-existing totalized, independent unit. For Eliot, fragments represent a modern dissolution; O'Brien's fragments more radically point to the permanent absence of any form of meaningful identity or totality. Irish society was being assembled from reactions to colonialism, the propaganda of revivalism, the strictures of Catholicism, the vibrancy of international modernism and the values of Victorianism, and O'Nolan and his friends were themselves caught between despising the 'Catholic triumphalism, the pious philistinism, the Puritan morality and the peasant or *petit bourgeois* outlook of the new state'[7] and being unable to shake themselves free of Catholicism or Ireland. There was no stable whole from which modern Ireland had come, and the past(s) it was drawing upon to create an identity were – arguably – diverse fictions.

The fragments of *At Swim-Two-Birds* are and are not colloquial fragments; they are not the shards produced by the rupturing of a pre-existing totality, as while they are the result of extensive editing and abridging, the earliest draft does not represent a stable, composite, completed whole. Rather, the fragmentation found in *At Swim-Two-Birds* is a plural speech of dissymmetry and irreversibility. It is a non-progressive series of beginnings that never present a secure foundation as there is always something that came before. It is a non-linear series of endings that never offer closure as there is always something more to come. Each fragment is both wholly independent as it functions as a separate aside, and absolutely part of a whole, as it is a section in a larger work. It is the fragmentation of a work in progress, where process is privileged over product, as there can be no static result. Thus, vignettes take precedent over plot, and narrative is a disordered series of snapshots. Contexts, spaces, temporality, genres, frames, form, themes, references, quotations all become contaminated, revealing not a homogeneous mess, but a deep interconnectedness, paradoxicality and philosophical complexity to the 'story-teller's book web' (AS 19) and to Ireland itself. Thus the mode of fragmentation that O'Brien uses in *At Swim-Two-Birds* can be seen to be a modernist reworking of the German Romantic Fragment.

Fragments

As Friedrich Schlegel famously pronounced, and as O'Nolan would have no doubt agreed: 'It is equally fatal for the mind to have a system and to have none. It will simply have to decide to combine the two'.[8] The German Romantic work was the hyphenation of poetry and philosophy, system and non-system, reason and chaos, the playful and the earnest, the objective and the subjective, the real and the ideal. Schlegel argued that of necessity the world cannot be presented in logical, rational arguments – 'Verily, it would fare badly with you if . . . the whole world were ever to become wholly comprehensible in earnest'[9] – and as a result the work must reflect this chaotic excess. But while espousing the paradoxical, the romantic work must also be what Derrida termed a poetico-literary performativity or contaminated performative/ constative, that is, a work which describes/critiques itself as it presents itself, that is, always, in 'artist reflection and beautiful self-mirroring . . . simultaneously poetry and the poetry of poetry'.[10] In performing what it describes and reflecting on itself, the romantic, ironic work was not simply a production, but an enactment of production, a reflexive autoproduction or *autopoiesis*. However, the reflexivity or self-consciousness of the romantic work operates through a concave lens – it does not tend towards a single point, but diverges out in excess. In other words, the text does not circle in on itself in a closed loop, but expands outwards in each reading. As such, while *At Swim-Two-Birds* is a work that is deliberately, chaotically resistant to clear exposition, it is also a text that theorizes on what a work should be – offering manifestoes, explanations, commentaries and exegeses. But the formula that this 'self-evident sham' (AS 25) proffers does not enable the reader to plumb the depths of the text and rationalize it to the point of completing any necessary critical elucidation. Instead, it emphasizes the complexity that is to come, showing the task of the reader not to be the solving of a logical puzzle, but its extension.

In his manifesto, the student narrator complains that the novel overly apes realism and is, therefore, 'inferior to the play inasmuch as it lack[s] the outward accidents of illusion, frequently inducing the reader to be outwitted in a shabby fashion and caused to experience a real concern for the fortunes of illusory characters' (AS 25). So the narrator writes novel-as-Brechtian-play, with the fragments providing the appropriate *Verfremdungseffekt*. The fragments explaining tropes employed and describing particular foodstuffs, denials, chuckles, tones, noises, exclamations and so on operate in order to provide not only an interpretative exegesis of an action, and thereby satisfy the German Romantic wish for a fragmentary work to contain self-reflection, but also stage directions whose undercutting of novelistic conventions shatters the effects of realism.

The perfect Romantic work was a work of fragments, so much so that the fragment became 'the romantic genre *par excellence*'.[11] It was, however, the perfect genre because a fragment is ostensibly not a genre at all; a fragment can be any length, style or structure. The fragment is thus a form of multiplicity and contamination, or, like the Good Fairy, a formless form, a 'form that, being all forms – that is, at the limit, being none at all – does not realise the whole, but signifies it by suspending it, even breaking it'.[12] Comprising discrete sections, a fragmentary text is a cacophony, a plural speech of dissymmetry and irreversibility without unifying core or centralizing structure. To write in fragments is to write so that 'the continuity of the movement of writing might let interruption as meaning, and rupture as form, intervene fundamentally'.[13] *At Swim-Two-Birds* is thus a stately pleasure dome which contains the interruption of Coleridge's fevered writing by the man from Porlock, rather than explaining it in the preface. It is the form of a delimited limitlessness where the lines between generic distinctions, stylistic conventions and narrative frames break down. The stylistic mutability of the fragmentary text resonates throughout *At Swim-Two-Birds* – Clissman notes thirty-six different styles within the text[14] – as we move from the alliteration and assonance of Middle Irish verse – 'The arms to him were like the necks of beasts, ball swollen with their bunched-up brawnstrings and blood-veins' (AS 14–15) – to the self-consciously formal – 'my dim room rang with the iron of fine words and the names of great Russian masters were articulated with fastidious intonation' (AS 24). We step between *Bildungsroman*, Western, courtroom drama, mythological saga, fairy tale, modernism, naturalism and realism, in a text comprising extracts, quotations, myths, dialogues, high and low artistic forms. Sweeping throughout the text is the shape-shifting man-bird Sweeny, whose form is never clear: a man wholly transformed into a bird, or a man with the powers of a bird? His is a text of different fragments, different dates and different sources, a text reused and rewritten throughout *At Swim-Two-Birds*. *At Swim-Two-Birds* is not merely a novel of intertextual connections, but a novel of fragments that interrogate and question form and genre. These differing styles and voices, be they representative of a post-modern refusal of metanarratives, a post-colonial rejection of imperial decree, a Marxist denunciation of capitalist commodity fetish or a Bakhtinian polyphony, are collected through the open, non-hierarchical form of the fragment. This is not to argue that *At Swim-Two-Birds* is non-judgemental and non-partisan, but rather that the refusal of a fragmentary text to absolutely or finally position itself enables O'Brien – and Myles in *Cruiskeen Lawn* – to be judgemental and partisan from all sides. As Anthony Cronin wrote, accidentally elucidating the fragmentary: 'Myles na gCopaleen will usually be found on several sides of a question at once'.[15]

Echoing the name under which various sections of *Finnegans Wake* were first published, *At Swim-Two-Birds* is referred to as a 'work in progress' by the majority of critics.[16] A work in constant progress it undeniably is, both for O'Nolan, who wrote fragments and showed them to Niall Sheridan, and for the narrator, who wrote fragments and showed them to Brinsley. For the German Romantics, a work written in fragments always took this form, as discrete units were constantly shaped into a protean, chimerical whole: '*work in progress* henceforth becomes the infinite truth of the [fragmentary] work'.[17] As the totality that the fragments created was always open and changing, what was prioritized was not the creation of a static finished artefact, but instead the act of production – *poiesis* – itself. The German Romantics emphasized the process rather than the product, as neither the act of writing nor of reading generates a permanent, unchanging object. This privileging of process rather than product is performed with increasing hyperbole in *At Swim-Two-Birds* and throughout the *Cruiskeen Lawn*. Within the relative realism of the narrator's autobiographical fragments it means that the narrator doesn't enjoy re-reading his work, unless it is to garner praise from his friends: 'My literary or spare-time compositions, written not infrequently with animation and enjoyment, I always found tedious of subsequent perusal. This sense of tedium is so deeply seated in the texture of my mind that I can rarely suffer myself to endure the pain of it' (AS 60). As his year meanders, so too does his text, until it ends – at the level of the Trellis saga – quite arbitrarily, in a way that perfectly performs the process/ product hierarchy: Teresa burns Trellis's manuscript, and the work is unworked.

The trope of a writing that produces not product but immediate effect is taken to greater extreme in the torture of Trellis, where persecution and writing about that persecution become identical; writing is the production not of text but of manifest effects, and as such writing has immediate physical and ontological implications. Writing is radically performative rather than constative, that is, productive rather than descriptive, as it is a series of stage directions that create the action described, and which are thereby subject to temporal progression. The act of writing becomes an act of directing that has immediate effect; should writing cease, or focus on a different event/character, the subject of the former passage may rest during what appears to function as 'real' time. Furthermore, once written, events cannot be re-read. Hence, when Orlick takes a break from writing and leaves the room, Shanahan, Lamont and Furriskey are troubled by the delay, as they feel that it will allow Trellis momentary respite – 'Gentlemen, said Shanahan, we're taking all the good out of it by giving him a rest, we're letting him get his wind. Now that's a mistake' (AS 181). So they take up the pen, and beginning where Orlick ceased, subject Trellis to prosaic and unliterary torture until he returns. To prevent Orlick from discovering their actions, they write: 'the Pooka worked more magic till himself and Trellis found themselves again in the air in their own bodies, just as they had been a quarter of an hour before that, none the worse for their trying ordeals' (AS 183). As the characters have been thus repositioned, Orlick is unable to discern the events of the preceding period and continues writing. In a phantasmagorical mode of literary creativity, and as a manifestation of the 'work in progress', this writing creates not just words on a page but 'living' characters and 'real' events that are materialized in the act of writing.[18]

The most important characteristic of the fragment is its paradoxical status of incomplete completion. The romantic fragment is not an unfinished work or a section torn from a totalized whole, but a deliberate form simultaneously sovereign while calling to an indeterminate completion. As one of Schlegel's most quoted fragments states, 'a fragment, like a miniature work of art, has to be entirely isolated from the surrounding world and be complete in itself like a hedgehog'.[19] The fragment must be totalized, independent and autonomous. Thus, each fragment must be its own example, and as a romantic work theorize and comment upon itself. Its uniqueness rejects an example other than itself, and it is thereby itself and representation of itself, whole and internally fragmented, one and divided. It is a form of limits and limitlessness, a mode of interruption and borders whose margins generate excess: 'A work is cultivated when it is everywhere sharply delimited, but within those limits limitless and inexhaustible; when it is completely faithful to itself, entirely homogeneous, and nonetheless exalted above itself'.[20] The fragments of At Swim-Two-Birds exist in isolation; the letter from the English bookie, the extracts from novels, the story of Sweeny, the tales of Finn, the torture of Trellis, the cowboy anecdotes, the student's drinking sagas, and the dialogue between the Pooka and the Good Fairy all operate as discrete units. And yet they are also clearly interconnected, not only in terms of a conventional narrative development, but as repetitions and reworkings of each other. Thus, Finn tells the story of Sweeny, Sweeny appears and tells his own story, and Orlicks's torture narrative/act rewrites it. A joke told to the unreceptive Kelly is repeated, to greater acclaim, to Brinsley and Donaghy. Orlick takes on characteristics of the narrator, and Trellis comes to represent the uncle. The narrator's sore tooth is Furriskey's threatening cavity. The narrator's friend Brinsley is twice introduced as if for the first time – 'A friend of mine, Brinsley' (AS 23, 34) – and the narrator's uncle is described and redescribed (AS 10, 30, 92, 132, 215), not only enabling the reader to chart the narrator's feelings towards the uncle, but also enabling each biographical reminiscence to stand alone.

The fragment is a thought that is both complete and incomplete, an instance of a single supposition that exists complete in itself, and yet is simultaneously part of a greater whole. Each fragment is a project, a 'fragment of the future',[21] a calling to what comes next and what will, even with each addition, remain indeterminate. Three times in *At Swim-Two-Birds,* we are presented with synopses, 'being a summary of what went before, FOR THE BENEFIT OF NEW READERS' (AS 60 et passim). Each synopsis is concluded with three words – 'Now read on'. In fragmentation, in texts that are permanent becomings, projections into the future, one never definitely begins. One simply reads on. The fragments form a whole which is not the sum of their parts, and which is neither greater nor lesser than each individual fragment. They cannot be read solely as aphoristic totalized wholes, nor as paragraphs that conjoin to form a greater whole, but as a form that is simultaneously both (and neither); that which 'makes possible new relations that except themselves from unity, just as they exceed the whole'.[22] Fragments are a writing of discontinuity on which continuity is imposed, a force of alternating, ironic energy in which 'every whole can be a part and every part really a whole'.[23] The fragments of *At Swim-Two-Birds* do not create a solid, consistent unit, but a protean, shifting web of fragments that can be read in numerous sequences to countless results. While any text may produce a near infinite amount of readings, the fragmentary mode forces the reader to structure the fragments into a coherent work, while knowing the transient nature of this reading.

The serial (il)logic of the fragment means that, as Derrida writes, each 'in the series can come before or after the other, before *and* after the other – and in the other series'.[24] Each fragment is centre of a series and the border of (another) series, the death knell and morning bell for every other fragment, and the fragmentary thus introduces a spatial and temporal exigency. Each fragment is before and after every other fragment, in wholly different time frames, and yet they could not exist 'without the promise of a now in common',[25] a space in which and from which comparisons and conjunctions can be made.[26] Thus, the narrator's texts are not written in a notebook, but on pieces of paper kept in a portfolio, 'an article composed of two boards of stout cardboard connected by a steel spine containing a patent spring mechanism' (AS 50). The text physically comprises fragments held loosely together, easily vulnerable to loss and of impermanent order. We begin with three somewhat arbitrary extracts from his portfolio, are given a section of the trial before we are aware that Orlick has been born (AS 42), are provided with the section explaining Trellis's obsession with green books (AS 98) after the concept has already been introduced (AS 36), skip sections and are told that passages have been lost. We are presented not just with a text in fragments, but a text whose fragments are already deliberately disordered.[27]

Fragments – 'unfinished separations'[28] – position the sujet over the fabula, that is, narrative (and narrative form) over the underlying, chronological story, but emphasize the sujet's polyvalent and protean nature. When reading a fragmentary text, one does not work to *solve* it: one cannot uncover the fabula concealed beneath the twisting fragments of the narrative, as there is no single, stable story or plot, but a multitude of potential combinations of fragments producing myriad sujets. The act of reading imposes a system on the unsystematic, and independent events are structured into a narrative. Connections are made between themes, allusions, characters, actions and language, and each reading proposes an argument, thesis or plot. Reading as the forging of connections is unavoidable; but while one may read for *a* plot, one does not read for *the* plot. For Peter Brooks plot is 'the principle of interconnectedness and intention which we cannot do without in moving through the discrete elements – incidents, episodes, actions – of a narrative' that 'allows us to connect a whole'.[29] Plots, he argues, are not just outlines, skeletons that organize and support, but 'intentional structures, goal-orientated and forward moving'.[30] Reading for the plot pursues the teleological and the systematic; while this is generally problematic, in the case of the fragmentary text it is directly antithetical. If plot, like a plot of land, demarcates and encloses, in a fragmentary work the fragments subdivide plot, turning the story into a series of vignettes, a literary Rundale system. This is not to say that the fragmentary text is of necessity *plotless*, but that it is an anarchistic revolt against the concept of a linear succession of events that have a stable beginning, a section of development and complication, and a definite ending.

Because of the relative insignificance of the plot, even that which is 'required by the ramification of the plot or argument' (AS 60) can be replaced with a quick synopsis. Deciding to extract eleven pages detailing the birth of Orlick and the death of his mother, the narrator writes: 'the omission of several pages at this stage does not materially disturb the continuity of the story' (AS 145). What, one wonders, would have to be lost in order to do so? In *At Swim-Two-Birds,* the traditional elements of a plot – exposition, conflict, climax, dénouement – are presented in fragments that are quantitatively fewer and shorter than those that are unrelated to action and conclusion, so that temporal and narrative flow becomes wholly secondary to the individual vignettes presented by the fragments. The decisions made by the narrator on what to include and withhold seem based on wholly arbitrary judgements and situations. The majority of the book comprises long lists, retellings of middle Irish texts, press reports, seemingly irrelevant anecdotes, rambling dialogues, letters and extracts from texts on alcohol, tobacco, tea, poetry, road safety, betting, daily regimes and advice columns. From the book which arguably forms the core of the *At Swim-Two-Birds*, and is the motivator for the entirety of the plot of the narrator's writings – Trellis's green book on sin – we receive not a single extract. The actions of the characters are motivated by a book we never read, and which arguably is never written; missing this nucleus, the text is always fragmented, being the shards of a whole that (arguably) does not and did not exist.

Ethics by numbers

During the course of the Pooka and the Good Fairy's discussion(s), the 'contrapuntal character of Bach's work' (AS 110) is mentioned as a 'delight', with the Good Fairy adding that 'Counterpoint is an odd number' (AS 110), and therefore good and true. Counterpoint is a counter-point, that is, an antithetical statement, and a (harmonious) relation between independent voices. It is a working in unison and a working against, and each fragment is always in contretemps, in countertime or counterpoint with all the other fragments. Throughout *At Swim-Two-Birds* we are presented with an Ireland out of time with itself, attempting to force a harmony from cacophony, but each time confronted and confounded by a plurality of counter-points, beating in counter-time. This offbeat, where any rhythm can take sway at any time, also points to the absence of a primary time frame that is circled by proleptic or analeptic steps. As Sheridan writes, paraphrasing O'Nolan's early descriptions of *At Swim-Two-Birds* and calling to the work of Dunne in *The Third Policeman* and *The Dalkey Archive*: 'Conventional notions of Time would be scorned. Past, present and future would be abolished, and the work would exist in a supra-Bergsonian continuum – communicating simultaneously on several planes of consciousness and also on various subliminal levels'.[31] While a fragmentary text may have a narrative that is linear, meaning that the fragments are ordered in adherence with the passing of progressive, narrative time, the fragmentary form emphases the fact that individual vignettes are of far more importance than the development of the plot. Schlegel's fragmentary novel, *Lucinde*, follows the normal passage of time, but the fact that the fragments are temporally consecutive is nigh irrelevant. Their import is to be found in their individual moments, and in the fact that they create shifting, kaleidoscopic patterns.

Through contrapuntal conversation, the ethicality of odd and even numbers is repeatedly stressed by the Pooka and the Good Fairy, and summarized in the text's ultimate Pythagorean conclusion: 'Evil is even, truth is an odd number, and death is a full stop' (AS 216). If death is final stasis, evil is a closed dialectic of thesis and antithesis: a binary, uniform and homogeneous and neat. Truth, on the other hand, is messy and unclear. One always has to suffer the 'odd truth' (AS 114) of a veracity in motion, a Hegelian dialectic of thesis, antithesis and synthesis, truth as an open triad. Derrida writes that 'Three is the first figure of repetition'[32] as it escapes the closure of a simple – duplicitous – duplication, and thus 'The infinite is doubtless neither one, nor empty, nor innumerable. It is of a ternary essence'. The ultimate conclusion to the text, with its obsessive attention to triads, thus concludes in truth and openness. Truth is an awkward multiplicity against the tidy plurality of evil. And yet, truth, as an odd number, is also singular, as truth is one. Truth is, therefore, fragmentation: singular and plural, independent and relative, complete in itself and always awaiting further explication. Hence, 'Minus One, Zero and Plus One are the three insoluble riddles of the Creation' (AS 190): the 'first' and opposing singularities of odd truths clustered around zero, both a number and the absence of a number. Evil lies in the belief in stable origins, absolute truths and truisms, discrete totalities, and as such, while O'Brien may invert the numbers used by Nietzsche in aphorism 260 of *The Gay Science* – '*One times one.* – One is always wrong; but with two, truth begins'[33] – the odd truth of multiplicity and alterity is the same.

The Pooka, with a neat, ordered and therefore evil mind, has the practice of inquiring as to the 'oddity or otherwise of the last number' (AS 109), as on this last number the fate of the world hangs: 'will it be an odd one and victory for you and your people, or an even one and the resolution of heaven and hell and the world in my favour' (AS 109). But, as befits O'Nolan's *Weltanschauung*, the final numeral that ends the struggle between good and evil will not be an archangel on a white horse, nor a fearsome, seven-headed dragon, but a force so diluted as to end the distinction. Evil is produced in response to good, good in response to evil, but each act of production gives issue to a weaker and feebler force, until the last numeral is one whose 'chief characteristics must be anaemia, ineptitude, incapacity, inertia and a spineless dereliction of duty' (AS 110). In the end, there are no winners, and the world dies, not with a bang but a whimper.

One might, in fact, surmise that the apocalypse is already at hand, since the evil of the Pooka seems in doubt, and the goodness of the reagent, apparently secure in the mirroring of proper name and ontological category – 'My correct name is Good Fairy, said the Good Fairy. I am a good fairy' (AS 104) – is equally dubious. In manner the Good Fairy is selfish, judgemental and petty. The apparent sophistication evinced by his dialogue with the Pooka rapidly deteriorates on the walk, as he threatens to kick Slug Willard in the face, taunts Jem Casey and disparages the 'working man' for striking – 'They have the country crippled with their strikes. . . . Holidays with full pay if you please. No wonder the moneyed classes are leaving the country. Bolshevism will be the next step' (AS 120). He refuses to take a message to Casey's wife, damns Sweeny for being a drunk – 'I don't believe in wasting my sympathy on sots' (AS 127) – and later proposes to gag him. He demands to be included in the poker game, insists on his word of honour he has money when he has none, loses, and finally forsakes the soul of Orlick to avoid public condemnation for his misdeeds. The supposedly good fairy is thus narrow-minded, conservative, aggressive, a bigot and a cheat. The devil pooka, on the other hand, is civilized, tolerant and peaceful. He presents himself as an individual respecting moderation: open-minded yet distrustful of vulgarity, fond of alcohol but not drunkenness, educated but not part of the distant elite, and possessing 'great admiration for the worker' (AS 120). Good, it seems, is represented by a small-time charlatan, while evil by poised, considerate intelligence.[34] But lest we presume that O'Brien presents no more than a simple inversion – one that would be evil in its straightforwardness – a little more attention needs to be paid to the actions of the Pooka.

The Good Fairy gives no sign of immorality while in the Pooka's house; it is while he rests in the Pooka's pocket that he grows increasingly belligerent. When cards are suggested by Shorty Andrews, it is the Pooka who paraliptically raises the topic of gambling – 'I don't hold with gambling' (AS 139) – and then proceeds, face averted, to quietly reinforce the idea: 'Of course a small stake to keep one's interest from flagging, . . . there is no great harm in that' (AS 139). When the others object to the Good Fairy's involvement, under the grounds of respect and civility the Pooka insists that the spirit be allowed to play. The Pooka then talks incessantly while he deals the even number of cards, continuing to speak while everyone checks their cards – the Good Fairy asking for the evil number of two – muttering on while everyone plays, and finally bests the distracted crowd. The Good Fairy, having lied to partake, is thus indebted to him, and Orlick's fate is sealed. Evil is two-faced and double-dealing; seeing the odd truth involves seeing beyond the Pooka's calm, civilized charm to recognize the way in which he tricks the fairy, and also realizing that good and evil are not simple, uninvolved opposites but complicated contaminations. Eva Wäppling notes that Pooka, from the Irish *púca*, has always been a mixture of good and evil,[35] and the devil Pooka and the Good Fairy defy an easy binary of good versus evil. They are other to a clear ethical or moral opposition, and inasmuch as their physical form is indeterminate, so too is their character. While O'Nolan might have wished to avoid the accusations of blasphemy that the original names of good spirit or good angel might have caused, his choices give a far richer contamination and complexity to his text, one of whose possible names was *Truth is an Odd Number*.

Beginnings and endings

A fragment must be thought of as a non-originary origin; even should it commence a series of numbered fragments, its position is not static. A fragment is always disordered, always potentially first and last and somewhere in between. Intertextuality means that no text ever fundamentally and unambiguously begins on its first page – as Blanchot wrote, 'If the book could for a first time really begin, it would, for one last time, long since have ended'[36] – but in the case of fragments the chaos of the impossibility of beginning is radicalized.

At Swim-Two-Birds begins without beginning: it opens with the impossibility of making any firm first step, and thereby begins, *in medias res*, by commenting on the multiplicity and arbitrariness of origins. As the narrator writes,

> One beginning and one ending for a book was a thing I did not agree with. A good book may have three openings entirely dissimilar and interrelated only in the prescience of the author, or for that matter one hundred times as many endings. (AS 9)

Thus, the narrator presents three different openings, each describing one of the characters of his text(s) – the courtly devil Pooka MacPhellimey, John Furriskey and Finn Mac Cool, the mythical hero of old Ireland. But preceding these fragments is a further fragment explaining the need for multiple beginnings, and thus we are presented with four separate, related and yet unrelated beginnings that move through differing narrative layers. The first stems from the narrator's autobiographical frame tale, while the subsequent three belong to the frame of the narrator's fiction. What the narrator lists as the first opening is already preceded by the narrator's autobiographical opening and is, therefore, both the first opening and the second opening. The second/third opening begins (through) a further frame tale, as John Furriskey is one of the characters of Trellis's book. The second/third opening therefore begins, in a sense, without having begun, as the frame tale of Trellis's text has not been introduced. It thus operates out of synchronization, out of time, beginning before the beginning of its sequence and out of its own narrative space. In counterpoint to its proleptic movement is the intertextually analeptic use of the Irish hero Fionn MacCumhaill, which throws the third/fourth opening back to the mythological cycle of the Fianna, and thus begins having begun *fadó, fadó* – a long, long time ago.[37] Or rather recently, to the work of O'Nolan's brother: Ciaran Ua Nuallain wrote 'The Return of Finn' in *Comhthrom Féinne* in 1935, in which Finn MacCumhaill 'is keeping body and soul together with difficulty in a slatternly Rathmines boarding-house'.[38] The four beginnings do not begin in the same narrative space, but begin at different times and in different frame tales, that is, in different narrative realities. They present four different, independent openings that are nonetheless conjoined and contaminated. The narrator's openings are dependent on the frame tale, or narrative space, of the narrator having begun. They begin having thus already begun in the narrator. But a stable, non-fragmented point of origin cannot be located in the narrator's autobiographical frame tale, as it begins following the author's epigraph, a quotation from Euripides' *Heracles*: 'Ἐξίσταται γὰρ πάντ' ἀπ' ἀλλήλων δίχα' [For all things change, making way for each other]. Each beginning of *At Swim-Two-Birds* refers to another beginning, and all refer to change, to making way, to moving elsewhere, to digressing. Each beginning is preceded by another beginning, another text, another reference – back to Old Ireland, back to Ancient Greece – and so *At Swim-Two-Birds* is always a fragment within a greater textual web.

   At Swim-Two-Birds begins with Chapter 1, but never proffers Chapter 2. Similarly, when Orlick commences his writing of the torture of Trellis he begins with 'Part One. Chapter One' (AS 164), but despite rewriting and changes of direction neither Chapter 2 nor Part 2 is ever forthcoming. These false monuments to traditional progression are derided, not only by the multiple beginnings, but also by the multiple endings offered by *At Swim-Two-Birds*. This triad of conclusions appears to finish the text without loose ends; Todd Comer, for example, writes that in the end 'the narrator's writing turns conservative',[39] while David Cohen writes that '*At Swim-Two-Birds* [is] a novel about a man seduced by the power of authority, and, as such, a completely conventional novel. The three endings defy their labels and become the climax, denouement, and conclusion'.[40] The antepenultimate and penultimate conclusions have disappointed a number of critics, as they appear to outline how the narrator, on achieving an honours degree and winning the approval of his uncle, no longer needs to pen tales of rebellion against authority figures, and so ends the characters' torture of Trellis. But while the general contentment pervading the narrator's house following his examination success and his resultant positive '*Description of my uncle*: Simple, well-intentioned; pathetic in humility; responsible member of large commercial concern' (AS 215) appears to lead directly to Trellis's salvation and the narrator's adoption of his uncle's bourgeois values, the situation is far from unambiguous. The narrator's uncle presents him with a watch to mark the occasion of his graduation from student life, a gift that places the student within staid, responsible adult society. The watch supposedly signifies the closure of the fragments and the movement of the student away from the flights of fancy that caused him to write such experimental work. Yet, while walking up the stairs to his room the narrator hears the bells of the Angelus – which chime at 6 a.m. and 6 p.m. – ring out while the watch reads 5.54. The two timepieces, the personal wristwatch and the bells of the greater community, still fail to ring in time. On the narrator's wrist, the watch keeps a different time, operates in a different frame and is out of synchronization. O'Nolan, who went from UCD to work in the civil service, knew of the impossibility of truly fitting in with a society of bureaucracy and middle-class complacency, and so the penultimate conclusion ends while beating a different time.

Similarly, the ending to the antepenultimate conclusion refuses to conclude without openness, ambiguity and the indication of further fragments. The torture of Trellis ends because his servant, Teresa, burns pages of his novel, particularly 'the pages which made and sustained the existence of Furriskey and his true friends' (AS 215–16). Thus, as is most commonly assumed, the narrator's novel resolves itself peaceably for Trellis, as the narrator no longer requires a scapegoat on which to displace the feelings of exasperation generated by his uncle. But not all the characters involved in the torture and trial of Trellis were created by him. Lamont, Shanahan and Finn MacCool were hired hands (AS 61). His supposed defence lawyers, the deaf and dumb Timothy Danaos and Dona Ferentes, do not exist in his book, but figure in the independent lives led by Lamont and Shanahan while he was asleep.[41] Of those involved in the trial, Slug Willard was employed by Trellis, neither Sweeny, the Good Fairy nor Jem Casey figure in his book, Mr Tracy was a fellow author, Shorty Andrews, Red Kiersay and Supt. Clohessy had worked for Tracy, not Trellis, while Mr Lamphall is mentioned for the first time at the trial. Thus, the only characters created by Trellis are Furriskey, the Pooka, Sheila Lamont and, as a result of his rape of Sheila, Orlick. When the manuscript is burned, then arguably these characters cease to exist, but the others are either wholly unaffected or simply left *unemployed*, as the narrative in which they were employed no longer exists. Burning, so superstition goes, wholly destroys, but Sweeny goes on to figure in the next fragment. If Sweeny exists, then so too must the other characters borrowed by Trellis, and the supposed finality of death on the pyre is interrupted by the potential for a further 'now read on', a fragment in which

Lamont and Shanahan, furious at the death of their friend, find a new way to exact revenge. The end is not an ending, but simply a pause or interlude before the next fragment.[42]

Contradictions and purity

The form of the fragment is such that while acknowledging the impossibility of reading without imposing a system, it actively resists definitive order. The lacunae that figure between fragments and aphorisms are paths that allow for an infinite number of routes to be taken between fragments, and hence an infinite possibility of readings. At the same time, however, the caesuras present an unbridgeable abyss between fragments; the fragments are too isolated to be in opposition or contradiction. A collection of aphorisms presents ideas that radically contradict or consolidate an argument; these agreements or resistances are not, however, part of a set system, and any attempt to systematize them should recognize that the system is imposed and wholly born from the act of reading. One might compare the difference between the fragments to Lyotard's problem of the differend, in which a case between parties 'cannot be equitably resolved for lack of a rule applicable to both arguments':[43] their particularity is such that no general rule can do them justice. As Blanchot writes:

> Fragmentary speech does not know contradiction, even when it contradicts. Two fragmentary texts may be opposed: they are simply posed one after another, one without relation to the other, or related one to another by this indeterminate blank that neither separates nor unites them but brings them to the limit they designate, which would be their meaning – if, precisely, they did not thereby, hyperbolically, escape a speech of signification. . . . [The fragmentary is there] where opposition does not oppose but rather juxtaposes, where juxtaposition gives together what escapes all simultaneity, without becoming a succession.[44]

The independence and complicity of the fragments is performed in the relation between Trellis and Orlick. While Trellis is a separate entity, and supposedly on a different – higher – ontological plane than the characters, he is able to cross these boundaries and rape

Sheila Lamont. This impossible movement across planes of reality is exemplary of a contamination between fragments that are wholly separate. The result of this impossible association is a son, another fragment, who then further mixes fragments by writing his father into another fragment. These involvements twist planes of reality, narrative frames, subject and object, author and character, until each fragment – each character – can declaim, 'I am my own father and my own son. I am every hero from the crack of time' (AS 19). The relations between the – wholly independent – fragments are so impossibly implicated that teasing out contradictions and associations must be based on the knowledge that no stable logic can be applied.

The subordinating of context and logical or realistic interaction is perfectly demonstrated in the narrator's virtuoso use of style. In the long, oneiric section listing the songs sung and fruits picked as the Pooka, Good Fairy and friends walk to the Red Swan to celebrate Orlick's birth, not only are all able to sing songs from Ireland, England, America, Cuba, Germany, Italy, France and Austria, they are also able to pluck flowers from a Chinese Magnolia tree, pick coconuts, yams and melons and drink from jungle springs. In other words, during this dream-like sequence not only is their knowledge of music and languages not limited to what they, as prototypes for the Plain People of Ireland, would really possess, but their geographical location, until now so clearly that of Ireland, is no longer bound by spatial realism. The limits of knowledge, botany, time and place dissolve, and during that night they cross an unspecified folkloric country. Realistic knowledge, spatiality or vegetation is irrelevant before lyricism and the narrator's desire to exhibit erudition. While realist Trellis might believe that it is art to conceal art, for the modernist narrator, art is the structure, art is the form, art is non-realism and non-concealment of device.

Inasmuch as the discrete fragments comprising *At Swim-Two-Birds* cannot be reconciled into a systematic form, the disparate and contradictory fragments of Irish literature and identity cannot be conveniently or satisfactorily structured. Paradoxes and contradictions cannot be erased, as the fragments comprising the text, and the fragments comprising Ireland, operate to radically different rules, ethics, histories and understandings. As Kim McCullen writes: 'O'Brien's text releases a collective and at times subversive interrogation of the discursive construction of Irish culture without invoking a "norm" or a "real", by initiating an interanimated dialogue among the various discourses vying for ascendancy'.[45] The non-hierarchical, paratactic intermingling of discourses is the result of fragmentation: as fragments each vignette, be it plot point, character study, digressive aside, summary or exegesis, is presented without privilege or particular status. The reader, indeed the writer, may make value judgements regarding their relative worth, but fragments are radically other to comparative weighting. The Ireland of the dreamscape is as valid as the Ireland of the Furriskey's sitting-room, as real and legitimate as the Ireland of the narrator's uncle or the narrator's friends. While the inanity and foolish complacency of Lamont, Furriskey and Shanahan is mocked, the self-conscious erudition of the narrator is also subjected to wry, authorial scorn: 'Witticisms were canvassed, depending for their utility on a knowledge of the French language spoken in the medieval times. Psycho-analysis was mentioned – with, however, a somewhat light touch' (AS 25). When we read fragments, we treat them with the openness the narrator's manifesto argues should be afforded to characters: 'It was undemocratic to compel characters to be uniformly good or bad or poor or rich. Each should be allowed a private life, self-determination and a decent standard of living. This would make for self-respect, contentment and better service' (AS 25). Characters are not automatons, but creatures of independent will and desire who can be instructed, manipulated and forced, but not wholly controlled. Authorial intentionality cannot reign free. But we should not presume that this means that the narrator is an exemplary author: the openness and democracy that the narrator purports to support is in fact based on an undisguised elitism: 'A wealth of references to existing works would . . . effectively preclude mountebanks, upstarts, thimbleriggers and persons of inferior education from an understanding of contemporary literature' (AS 25).[46]

While there is undeniable openness to this instability, it is difficult not to infer a sense of O'Nolan's frustration at Ireland's fragmentary state. Nonetheless, it is clear that far worse than a state of acknowledged fragmentation is a nation priding itself on a false and created purity. In a subversive parody of the obsessive pre-occupations of the Gaelic League, members of the uncle's committee peevishly fret about the inclusion of the 'old-time waltz' in their planned *céilidhe*, as it is deemed to be insufficiently Irish: 'We have plenty of our own dances without crossing the road to borrow what we can't wear. . . . It's all right but it's not for us. Leave the waltz to the jazz-boys' (AS 133). In a mode of 'Irishness' created by the Abbey Theatre, the Gaelic League and the works of Yeats, Synge and Gregory, what counts as pure, legitimate and authentic comes from a past either created or anachronistically understood. What is deemed 'Irish' is contrived from a folkloric fabrication of the past, and what has been adopted and naturalized – the waltz – suddenly becomes destructively alien. Further ridiculing this neurotic mania with normative Irish life is the fact that the same committee members, concerned that a red carpet might be too reminiscent of English royalty, are able to plan for no more than 'A few words in Irish' (AS 135) before the real speeches in English get underway. Purity is adhered to in theory and while convenient: one demotes a dance to the category of imperial imposition and yet bothers to learn no more than a *cúpla focail as Gaelige* [a few words in Irish].

As is repeatedly the case in *At Swim-Two-Birds*, the fragments of fiction and the fragments of reality merge. The issues raised by the uncle and his friends mirror a similar issue that occurred in UCD in 1934. The L&H representative on the S. R. C. – Liam Delaney – voted for a dance as oppose to a *céilidhe* to be held on St Patrick's night, and as a result of outrage in the L&H, wrote a vitriolic piece in *Comhthrom Féinne*. In this he argues that the university 'was not founded to . . . develop our racial mistakes. It was instituted to drag our countrymen from their barbarous and unchristian practices, and reveal to them International civilisation'.[47] *Céilidhes*, as folk dance events, are, he claims, demeaning to students, as they are only 'suited to our quaintly-garbed peasantry', being 'barbaric', and 'little removed from the cat's purr or the monkey's tom-tom'.[48] Delaney sees the *céilidhe* as antiquated, countrified and of the peasantry. The uncle's committee see the waltz as dangerously modern, urban and of a foreign counterculture. Both are equally prejudiced, one creating a new Ireland by moving away from its supposed past, one creating a new Ireland by moving back towards its supposed past. But while Delaney's article is noteworthy for a direct, aggressive arrogance, the committee's conversation is riddled with ellipses, euphemisms, insinuations and ambiguities. They never wholly clarify their positions but hint and allude.

This is most noticeable when Mr Connors asserts that Mr Hickey danced the waltz twenty-three years ago at the Rotunda Gardens. As Declan Kiberd notes, twenty-three years before 1939 was 1916, and the Rotunda Gardens was where the British held republican rebels before taking them to prison.[49] But why Mr Hickey would waltz at that place and at that time isn't specified. Out of choice, or under coercion? As an apolitical pastime or a pointed positioning? As a gesture of defiance or a gesture of compliance? As a fighter or a bystander? All we are told is that he admits his actions, is silent, and when later once again addressed, 'bestirred himself with reluctance' (AS 135).

While we should blindly sympathize with neither Delaney nor the committee, in fictionally representing the opposing side of Delaney's views, O'Brien reveals a deeper, more nuanced, more fragmented picture of the problems of Irish identity than Delaney's superciliousness and obvious class chauvinism can explain. For O'Nolan, well-versed in Irish and European literature, identity is *a priori* contaminated and fragmented – always already in a state of flux. The concept of a pure (Irish) identity is a fiction; Ireland is as much the place of Joycean perambulations as it is Western cattle rustling, as much the site of home-grown high art as it is the site of imported popular fiction. The uncle, opposed to the waltz, is a member of an opera society performing Gilbert and Sullivan. Shanahan reddens with anger when he feels that the myths recounted by Finn are insufficiently appreciated – 'stuff that brought scholars to our shore when your men on the other side were on the flat of their bellies before the calf of gold . . . I'd have the tongue out of my head by the bloody roots before I'd be heard saying a word against it' (AS 75). And yet, having paid lip service to his glorious heritage, he claims it's too much for the 'man in the street' and that 'you can get too much of the stuff' (AS 75). Dermot Trellis has an Irish first name and an English surname, and lives in a pub bearing the extremely Anglo-Saxon name of 'Red Swan', but situated in Croppies Acre, a name which recalls the Irish revolutionaries. His mother hailed from the North of Ireland, while his father was from the south. If noble warriors did run and jump and play like Finn, they no longer do, as all glorious activities are now long jump competitions and handball. There is no purity, there are no dominant narratives and, as is ever the case in O'Nolan, there are no heroes.

Autobiographies

The romantic work was not simply a becoming of itself, but the becoming of the author: an autobiography, 'quintessence'[50] or 'encyclopaedia'[51] of the subject. In a burst of inspiration, instinct and intention the author produces the work, and in that act produces herself, so that the work is thus both the 'portrayed' and the 'portrayer',[52] the 'producer' and the 'product'.[53] The work (re)presents the author at the moment of creation; once the work has been written and is capable of being analysed, the self that created it is no more. The finitude of the subject has been destroyed; the subject is now a work which is always in excess of itself and therefore infinite. However, in opening herself up to this infinity, the subject also loses herself in the symphilosophy and infinite complexities of language. We cannot speak of a fragment, but rather of fragments, an unending, non-totalized plurality, and in the same way we do not speak of a subject, but subjects, the fragments dissolving the ego to create a universal symphilosophy. The fragment is an absolute close-up of a subject at a single moment in time, a microscopic concentration on a cell of thought to the extent that it reads as an anonymous particle, rather than the singular thought of a named and known subject. The fragment is thus absolutely individual and a collective, symphilosophic writing, identity through non-identity.

At Swim-Two-Birds is an autobiographical text on a number of levels. The narrator writes his life into his texts – Trellis as his uncle, Orlick as himself – and Flann O'Brien/Brian O'Nolan writes his into his – Brinsley is Niall Sheridan, Kerrigan is Niall Montgomery. As O'Nolan showed fragments to Sheridan so the narrator shows extracts to Brinsley, and Sheridan found himself, as do the characters, leading a double life outside and inside the work of fiction.[54] Many of the narrator's 'biographical reminiscences' have been noted to be actual events from O'Nolan's time as a student.[55] Each storyteller tells his or her own story in every work, narrating him or herself, and thus becoming both progenitor and progeny. But while the text is a writing of the self, the modernist fragments of *At Swim-Two-Birds* create the self not just from 'original' writings, but from quotations. The subject is thus posited and understood through an *a priori* act of fragmentation; the self comprises not (just) vignettes of the self, but vignettes of the self constituted through vignettes of others. The self, and the text, is thus composed through alterity, through fragments of other writings chosen to express or reflect the emotions and identity of the author. There can be no ontological essence removed from these external influences, no immediate and independent fashioning of the self. The symphilosophy of the German Romantic fragment was as a result of the fact that the self must write itself through a universal language; in the modernist fragments of *At Swim-Two-Birds,* the self is constructed not simply through a limited and recycled raw material, but through a limited and recycled raw material still in a composite form. Thus, the narrator creates his characters and writes himself through extracts from the *Conspectus,* the back of copybooks, and tracts by the Christian Brothers. When he shaves he does so in a mirror superimposed with the name of a brand of ale, attempting to see parts of his face through the cracks in the letters. It is not merely that the image of his face is fragmented, as the words prevent him from seeing more than a section at a time, but that his (fragmented) face and identity are constructed through and between the fragments of this lettered mirror. If the 'modern novel should be largely a work of reference' (AS 25), then so too is the modernist subject.

As part of the symphilosophy, the subject is individual and of a multiplicity, operating as 'a plurality of minds and a whole system of persons'.[56] As a symphilosophic endeavour, the *Athenäum,* the journal produced by the German Romantics, included series of unattributed fragments written by Friedrich Schlegel, August Schlegel, Friedrich Schleiermacher and Novalis. This mode of collective authorship, where individual but anonymous fragments were collated into a non-totalized whole, is echoed, albeit to markedly less philosophical ends, in O'Nolan's early work for *Blather. Blather* was written by a group of collaborators including Ciarán O'Nolan, Niall Sheridan, Niall Montgomery and Donagh MacDonagh. The majority of the texts were written anonymously or pseudonymously, and in keeping with the tradition of the *Athenäum,* it is difficult to distinguish the authorship of the pieces. This concealment of identity was continued into O'Nolan's work for the *Irish Times,* when he, Niall Montgomery and Niall Sheridan wrote pieces for the *Cruiskeen Lawn* under the name Myles na gCopaleen. The principle of authorial collusion on a text of fragments was also to be exercised in book length in the melodramatically entitled *Children of Destiny.* O'Nolan 'proposed that he, Devlin, MacDonagh and

555

5255255555

I [Sheridan] should write the book in sections and then stick the pieces together in committee'.[57] *Children of Destiny* was to be the great Irish novel, a book 'made, not written' according to 'the principles of the Industrial Revolution' and the assembly line, and therefore with a 'better chance of becoming a bestseller'.[58] While *Children of Destiny* was never written, the principles of collective authorship are taken up in the torture of Trellis, where Orlick, Shanahan, Furriskey and Lamont pen the persecution together, and on the manuscript of *At Swim-Two-Birds*, O'Brien refers to himself not as author but as 'chief controller'.[59]

Finally, and perhaps most importantly, Schlegel writes that 'as yet no genre exists that is fragmentary both in form and in content, simultaneously completely subjective and individual, and completely objective and like a necessary part in a system of all the sciences'.[60] Thus, Schlegel's fragments are not fragments, but failed and interrupted fragments, the projects of fragments, the becoming of fragmentation. They do not exist and are thus non-works or unworkings. As failures, they cannot be wholly totalized but remain open. As Critchley notes, 'the "Athenäum Fragments" are *not* themselves fragments, they *should* not be fragments, they are merely indications or forewords for future fragments, promissory notes for an infinite work yet to be written'.[61] Centred and centreless, singular and plural, unique and highly stylized, the fragmentary form is a highly self-conscious form that is yet invisible, insubstantial compared to the process that it allows to take place. Thus, Blanchot names it the 'work of the absence of (the) work'.[62] In writing a book in fragments, one is writing a failed and impossible project of *almost* fragments, fragments that are not yet quite all their theory promises them to be. This sense of failing to achieve quite what has been promised, as what is promised can (perhaps) never physically exist, is precisely the right mode in which to represent Ireland of the 1930s.

Literary reproductions

If one cannot copy – hire – a character, one must create one.[63] For the narrator, the act of literary creation becomes a mode of reproduction termed 'aestho-autogamy' (AS 40), that is, the production of 'a living mammal from an operation involving neither

fertilization nor conception' (AS 40).[64] Inverting – parodying – the
case of a pregnancy caused by an unknown father,[65] the narrator
proposes procreation in which the mother is absent, and the process
of conception and pregnancy reduced 'to the same mysterious
abstraction as that of the paternal factor in the commonplace case
of unexplained maternity' (AS 40).[66] Thus, the character is brought
into being in an ejaculatory burst of literary inspiration. But what
appears to be a sexless birth, and also potentially an immaculate
conception[67] – it seems unlikely that the narrator shares Stephen
Dedalus' early sexual experiences with women, and Trellis's
ignorance means that, significantly, he is 'reduced . . . to utilising
disguised males as a substitute for females' (AS 199) – is not the act
lauded by the Catholic Church, but an act of masturbation, which
the narrator elevates to a mode of God-like solo creativity.[68] The
sublimation that is literary creation is re-cathected to lone sexual
desire, and the novel is once more likened to masturbation, as both
reading and writing become bedroom activities 'self-administered
in private' (AS 25).[69] Hence Trellis' obsession with remaining in
bed, Byrne's devotion to his bed and the narrator's determination
to be alone in his room, despite the accusations of his uncle. The
formula of aestho-autogamy is in actuality an extended shaggy-dog
story leading to an implied pun on (mental) masturbation, but, as
shown below, it also betrays a rather more disturbing engagement
with women, the Church and sexual engagement of all forms.

The traditional argument against autoeroticism is that it fails
to be productive of life; in *At Swim-Two-Birds* we have the
redemption of solo sexuality as Trellis creates a life born of man
alone, as the *male* writer – the possibility of a female author seems
wholly ignored by the narrator – creates new life from his body
and pen. While Tracy uses his wife as a conduit for the creation of
'a middle-aged Spaniard who lived for only six weeks' (AS 41), Trellis
surpasses him and creates Furriskey without female involvement.
The creative pen/penis is hyperbolically physically realized, as the
author is able to create not simply literary characters, but literary
characters who exist both in his books and on the same plane of
reality as him. So much so that he is able to rape one, and cause
her to give birth to a son: 'Trellis creates Miss Lamont in his own
bedroom and is so blinded by her beauty (which is naturally the
type of beauty nearest to his heart), that he so far forgets himself
as to assault her himself' (AS 61).[70] Thus, Orlick is created in a

very different way to his mother. Aestho-autogamy is the concept of male fecundity, in which man can produce life without female involvement and characters are created not *ab ovo*, but *ab sperma*. The creation of Orlick, however, involved a (forced) sexual act between the author and the product of his masturbatory creation/ fantasy. Neither a character, existent on the same plane of reality as his creator without being wholly human, nor anthropoid of equal ontological status, the quasi-illusionary Orlick is produced when Trellis is transfixed by the woman he has created and is swayed by sexual desire rather than a sexualized desire for literary creativity.

As such, aesthetic reproduction reveals a troubling relation to purity and control. The nascency of Sheila Lamont is an act of pure creativity, without the impure involvement of the female body. Having created her alone, Trellis possesses her; she is of his body, an extension of him. Assaulting her is thus the incestuous rape of a confused, newly created woman, an attack which leads to childbirth and death: 'She was violently assaulted by the accused about an hour after she was born and died indirectly from the effects of the assault some time later. The proximate cause of her death was puerperal sepsis' (AS 206). But it is also – and this should not diminish the abhorrence of the attack – (displaced) masturbation, a narcissistic obsession with (a newly produced) part of the self. In this case, the female character becomes no more than an object within a self-involved and self-obsessed autoerotic fantasy, as the male author becomes sexually aroused by his literary creativity. For the narrator and his friends, the assault of Sheila Lamont is thus a source of amusement, as the rape is ignored before the implicit support given to creativity as male, literary masturbation. Through this privileging of male prolificacy, the traditional, Catholic relation between 'good' sex as the production of life and 'bad' sex as pleasure-driven bodily involvement becomes inverted: masturbation becomes a pure act of creation that produces literary life, while heterosexual sex is an act of base desire and control.

The 1929 Censorship of Publications Act stated that any text deemed 'indecent or obscene', or which 'advocate[d] the unnatural prevention of conception or the procurement of abortion or miscarriage or the use of any method, treatment or appliance for the purpose of such prevention or such procurement' could be brought before the Board.[71] In other words, the only sexual act which could be legitimately alluded to, but not described, was reproductive sex

conducted by a married couple. Aping compliancy with this act
O'Brien loudly and overtly condemns contraception, and so when
the Athenian Oracle is asked about abortion – 'Whether it be lawful
to ufe Means to put a ftop to this growing mifchief, and kill it in
the Embryo' (AS 102) – the answer given is a resounding no: 'fuch
practices are murder' (AS 103). This apparent obsequious obedience
receives a lighter touch when the narrator alludes to contraception
by virtuously refusing to employ a euphemism for it: in college
'some were devoted to English letters, some to Irish letters and some
to the study and advancement of the French language' (AS 48).
The epistrophic pattern of the sentence demands the phrase 'French
letters', but as this was a slang term for 'condom', the narrator
primly avoids it while loudly evoking it.

More overtly addressing contraception while still employing an
ostensibly conservative touch, Tracy writes that if the principles of
creating offspring born as educated adults could be applied outside
of literature, then 'those mortifying stratagems collectively known
as birth-control would become a mere memory if parents and
married couples could be assured that their legitimate diversion
would straightaway result in finished breadwinners or marriageable
daughters' (AS 41). When marriage is wedded to this mode of
literary creativity, it ceases to be a 'sordid struggle' and becomes
instead 'an adventurous business enterprise of limitless possibilities'
(AS 41). Thus, O'Brien radically parodies the demands of Censorship
Act and produces a mode of reproduction in which the pleasure
principle is located in the pecuniary. Contraception becomes
irrelevant before the orgasmic delights of financial reward, and thus
the Catholic Church and the Censorship board may be sure that the
horrors of birth control are no longer a cause for concern, because
heterosexual sex will always bring financial reward and none will
attempt to avoid engendering life. But concealed beneath this overt,
if flippant, support of the Church's war against contraception is the
proposed eradication of heterosexual sex. In other words, implicit
to this manner of parturition is the replacement of heterosexual sex
with the masturbatory creativity of the male author, and under the
guise of condemning birth control and non-reproductive sex the
narrator smuggles in the highly contraband topic of masturbation.
Straight sex is replaced by the controlled creative eugenics of
(literary) masturbation, and literary merit and family values located
in the literary/onanistic process of the male author.

Literary nascency produces valuable life in the form of a necessary character, while heterosexual sex produces offspring serving no narrative purpose. When the narrator's friends, showing little concern for the excessive patriarchal power lauded in the rape, ask why Trellis does not force Sheila to commit suicide, and thereby solve the problem of the extraneous character, their question is worded with a flippancy and insensitivity that is no doubt intended playfully, but is nonetheless disturbing: 'It was asked why Trellis did not require the expectant mother to make a violent end of herself and the trouble she was causing by the means of drinking a bottle of disinfectant fluid usually to be found in bathrooms' (AS 145). Such is the privileging of the male, authorial perspective that when the narrator's friends reflect on the 'the general chaos which would result if all authors were disposed to seduce their female characters and bring into being, as it were, offspring of the quasi-illusory type' (AS 144) the situation is not viewed in terms of clear abuses of the ethics of power or control, but only as lamentable narrative complications. Of course, while proposing the death of the mother is abominable, it only *indirectly* causes the death of the child, and does not, therefore, technically count as the promotion of abortion. Under the censorship laws, maternal suicide is a perfectly reasonable option.

Similarly, in Trellis's trial Tracy testifies that Trellis impregnated a female character he had lent him, and subsequently Tracy was obliged to explain and accommodate two redundant characters: 'I created an otherwise unnecessary person to whom I married her and found honest if unremunerative employment for her son with a professional friend who was engaged in a work dealing with unknown aspects of the cotton-milling industry' (AS 199). This 'impaired the artistic integrity of [Tracy's] story', involved the addition of an explanatory footnote and 'added considerably to [his] labours' (AS 200). Thus, the male author's creative masturbation is portrayed as a laudable literary act, while heterosexual sex, with its lamentable involvement of the female, is the result of common, base desire condemned for its lack of literary purity.[72] That heterosexual sex is predominantly described in terms of forced acts the narrator deems unworthy of comment.

Even more problematic, however, than basic heterosexual sex is heterosexual sex with a created character, as in an act of secondary or displaced masturbation it becomes a focusing of the libido not on a 'healthy' sexualized process of literary creation, nor even an unfortunate act of base sexual gratification, but an unhealthy, non-literary act of self-obsessed pleasure, the by-product of which is a son with an overdeveloped Oedipus complex. In other words, masturbation for art is a noble, transcendental thing, while masturbatory sex with an extension of the self is a base, self-involved act. Masturbation in order to produce offspring is revered, while masturbation for pleasure is reviled. Thus, while the societal condemnation of masturbation is overturned and mocked, the Catholic insistence that sex be reproductive is retained. Masturbation is, therefore, both redeemed and condemned, and the shackles of the Catholic Church both overthrown and tightened. The text's indeterminate relation to the Catholic Church and God can perhaps be best expressed through the pronouncement made by Orlick's wise Shanahan: 'God is the root of minus one . . . too great a profundity to be compassed by human cerebration' (AS 190). God is an irrational number, outside of computation, beyond human systems, and in excess of numerical logic. But since the root of a minus number is also referred to as an imaginary number, there is also the subtle implication that God does not exist. Or, since the imaginary number is usually represented by a lower case i, that each individual/character, inasmuch as he or she can write, is God, irrational creator and controller.

Despite O'Nolan's later rejection of *At Swim-Two-Birds* as juvenile rubbish, the association between gender, literature and sex is repeated in his last completed novel. In the manuscript of *The Dalkey Archive*, O'Nolan included a passage about Joyce's wife, Nora Barnacle, in which Joyce says that while she was good to him she was of no help with his writing:[73]

> "she didn't give me any help with my scrilling. As a matter of fact she thought I was wasting my time, and couldn't read my stuff."
> "Well, a wife's duties are multitudinous but co-authorship with her husband is scarcely one of them. Somebody would be sure to denounce such union as literary incest."[74]

Precisely which works Nora was incapable of assisting him with is ambiguous, although it is potentially both the two-penny religious tracts and the works normally attributed to Joyce. But it is interesting to see that while Joyce complains that his wife wouldn't help him, he at least was interested involving her in his writing. Mick, on the other hand, makes the strange comparison between incest and a husband and wife writing team. This correlation can be read in two ways. The first implies simply that while a sexual union is correct and appropriate, a literary involvement becomes excessively close, claustrophobic and taboo. It is a crossing of boundaries and a wholly inappropriate mode of engagement – husband and wife should never come together to create literature, as writing is a solo, masculine mode of propagation. The second, leading from this, would be to argue that as writing is a solitary act which creates life, the involvement of another party will not aid the initial production, but interfere, so to speak, with the created 'offspring'. Thus, the incest involved is in the immorality of involvement with a spouse's literary child. Regardless, we find repeated here not simply a representation of Nora as useless and suffocating, but also the insinuation that a woman's involvement in writing is a miscarriage of morality. Interestingly, while this section on the immorality of conjugal production is dropped from the published version, an offspring from the physical union is saved: in the manuscript, all of Joyce's family dies, but in the published version O'Nolan seems to spare a thought for the lonely old man and spares his son. Not his daughter or wife, but his son.

Gender and eugenics

Gender relations within O'Nolan's works are generally problematic. In *At Swim-Two-Birds* the narrator, surrounded by male friends and family, very rarely makes mention of women in his biographical reminiscences, and his descriptions of university life allude to them so infrequently that one would be forgiven for thinking that the college remained a male preserve. In general women are depicted as alien creatures occupying a wholly different category to the vivacious male students, being either 'Modest girls bearing books [who] filed in and out of the channels formed by the groups of boys' (AS 33) or 'Young postulants or nuns . . . their eyes upon the floor and their fresh young faces dimmed in the twilight of their hoods, passing to a private cloakroom where they would spend the intervals between their lectures in meditation and pious practices' (AS 45). That their bodies might function in the same way as men seems a startling notion to the student, so much so that the act of passing some women on their way to the bathroom stands out in his mind as an event worthy of recall: 'I recall that I surmised that they were preceding to an underground cloakroom or lavatory for the purpose of handwash or other private act' (AS 50). In direct opposition to these studious, virginal wraiths, whose semi-presence occasionally haunts the corridors, are the male students, whose energy, enthusiasm and vibrancy makes the university very much the place of, as Hopper establishes, homoerotic 'ball-games' (AS 48).[75] The debating society is presented as an all-male assembly, and the crowd's reaction when a package containing Kelly's landlady's underwear is opened is utterly masculine.[76]

Inasmuch as the female students are tolerated within the male preserve, so too are the four female characters within the narrator's writing suffered. But these women are not untouchable, virginal students, but women as possessed objects, owned through employment, marriage or rape. While the narrator may fail in his half-hearted night-time pursuit of women – '*Purpose of walk*: Discovery and embracing of virgins. We attained nothing on our walk that was relevant to the purpose thereof but we filled up the loneliness of our souls with the music of our two voices' (AS 48) – women in his literary activities are far easier to possess, although equally two dimensional. As the classic victim who conveniently dies in childbirth, we know nothing of Sheila Lamont apart from her beauty. As the mindless servant whose carelessness accidentally saves her master, we know nothing of Teresa apart from her ugliness. Peggy is a dull, vapid wife, average to the point of being imbecilic, who shows even less learning than her husband and his friends, and the Pooka's spouse is repeatedly referred to with distaste: 'I would not be in the least surprised to learn that my wife is a kangaroo, for any hypothesis would be more tenable than the assumption that she is a woman' (AS 106). The only other women to figure in the narrator's texts are the maids stolen in a cattle raid. Here the *Táin Bó Cúailnge* or Cattle Raid of Cooley is rewritten as/reduced to a Western, where sexism and racism combine to equate the black women with cattle, but with none of the respected, if objectified, position that cattle would have had.

Female characters are isolated to the domestic sphere; Peggy's involvement in the rebellion against Trellis is based solely on her wish to marry Furriskey. Once that end has been accomplished, she is no longer involved. She plays no part in the torture or trial of Trellis; the sole female courtroom participant is not even a human, but a cow. Her one deviation from the role of respectable, passive wife is a conventional act of marital infidelity, resulting in her marriage being blessed with the 'advent of a little stranger' (AS 164). While the male characters not only revolt against the acts Trellis forces upon them, but also refuse to conform to the personalities imposed upon them, no such active resistance is afforded the female characters. They remain as they are created/hired by Trellis, as the narrator is incapable of imagining women outside the categories of virgin/ whore/mother/hag. Thus, while Finn MacCool may have been hired as a paternal guardian, when not supervised by Trellis he attempts to rape Peggy. While Furriskey is created as an evil rogue, he falls in love and vows to be virtuous and faithful. While Shanahan and Lamont are intended to be minor characters they become major players. Alterity and self-determination is found in the men, but while the female characters are technically afforded the same freedom, under the narrator's pen they are incapable of realizing it.[77] As the male characters are never restricted to the roles that Trellis conceived them to play, the careful literary eugenics of masturbation aren't as successful as Trellis might hope. One can create a human being with every literary care, imbuing him or her with a painstakingly designed cultural memory – '[Furriskey] entered the world with a memory but without a personal experience to account for it' (AS 9) – but neither this identity or designed history may be accepted. The Gaelic League may not have attempted the horrors associated with eugenics, nor did they try to tamper with physical breeding, but, as performed in the textual/sexual creativity of Trellis, they attempted to bring into being adults with a national memory of a glorious past, but no personal experience or evidence to support it.

The 'psycho-eugenics' (AS 41) of aestho-autogamy calls attention to an interest in population control held by intellectuals of the right and the left at the end of the nineteenth and start of the twentieth centuries, but which was swiftly abandoned and suppressed once the atrocities of the second world war were made public. The term 'eugenics' was coined by Francis Galton and comes from the Greek *eugenes* meaning 'good in stock'. The term thus describes the

> science of improving stock, which is by no means confined to
> questions of judicious mating, but which, especially in the case

of man, takes cognisance of all influences that tend in however remote a degree to give to the more suitable races or strains of blood a better chance of prevailing speedily over the less suitable.[78]

Eugenics was divided between the positive and the negative, wherein the former promoted breeding designed to create a stronger, smarter, healthier society, while the latter worked to prevent those judged unfit from 'polluting' the population. While the concept of 'more suitable races' and better 'strains of blood' should undoubtedly be recognized as heinous, eugenics was supported by 'Virginia Woolf, T. S. Eliot, W. B. Yeats, George Bernard Shaw, D. H. Lawrence, H. G. Wells, Rebecca West, Arnold Bennett, J. M. Synge, Aldous Huxley, F. Scott Fitzgerald'.[79] For *At Swim-Two-Birds*, published in 1939, eugenics was a topic of legitimate debate, and the narrator's interest in creating a mode of reproduction in line with the principles of selective breeding is an indicator of a level of erudition rather than extremism. This is mirrored in the 1934 short story 'Scenes in a Novel', which O'Nolan wrote under the pseudonym Brother Barnabas. The narrator, whom we may assume is Brother Barnabas, writes (probably) posthumously about his novel and the murderous rebellion his characters undertake. Barnabas writes that in giving his villain Carruthers McDaid 'a good but worn-out mother and an industrious father' but making him 'a worthless scoundrel, a betrayer of women and a secret drinker' he 'coolly negativ[ises] fifty years of eugenics'.[80]

Lamont gives a typically mangled version of eugenics during the tea-party scene at the Furriskey's, in which he blames 'bad blood' for acne: 'When the quality of the blood isn't first class, out with our friends the pimples' (AS 157). As he continues, 'There would be less consumption in this country . . . if the people paid more attention to their blood. Do you know what it is, the nation's blood is getting worse, any doctor will tell you. The half of it is poison' (AS 157). The Irish, he implies, are managing to breed themselves to death, breeding in so 'unsuitable' a way as to slowly pollute their own blood. Against this poisonous inbreeding, which produces unfit people/characters, is the narrator's psycho-eugenics, which creates useful adults, perfectly bred to purpose. In Joyce's *Portrait*, Stephen Dedalus argues against the presumption that attraction between the sexes is based on an unconscious sense of their suitability as breeding partners, as it leads to a 'new gaudy lectureroom' where the lecturer, 'with one hand on *The Origin of Species* and the other on the new testament, tells you that you admired the great flanks of Venus because you felt that she would bear you burly offspring'.[81] In other words, Stephen rejects this because it 'leads to eugenics rather than to esthetic'.[82] But in *At Swim-Two-Birds*, the narrator has married aesthetics with eugenics and created a mode of breeding dedicated to the production of the perfect character. Importantly, for O'Brien this mode of production does not produce a super-race of physical and intellectual perfection, but a race that is wholly appropriate for the task at hand. In other words, the author breeds that which is apposite for the required role in the work of literature, not that which is independently or abstractly 'perfect'. Life is created for a purpose dictated by the author; the independence of the life generated is an unfortunate by-product rather than artistic aim, and the character autonomy detailed in the narrator's manifesto belied.

The problematic ethics behind the notion of breeding the perfect puppet is clarified when the corresponding 'real-life' situation is expounded: when aestho-autogamy is applied outside of literature, the perfect result is simply one who earns. The ideal character is expressly designed for a specific literary situation; the model offspring is one who offers financial reward without the expense of education and nurturing. Thus, breeding through psycho-eugenics will produce 'finished breadwinners and marriageable daughters' (AS 41). Similarly, the mixing of bloodlines between angels and humans could produce 'a houseful of adult and imperceptible angels', which would be an attractive

> alternative to the commonplace family . . . because the saving in clothes and doctors' bills would be unconscionable and the science of shop-lifting could be practised with such earnestness as would be compatible with the attainment and maintenance of a life of comfort and culture. (AS 106)

The aesthetics behind the production of *apposite* life is based on a capitalist reverence of commodity and financial reward. It is also a very Catholic notion, as it is proposed in order to prevent the need for birth control. In this brave new world one instantly produces drones perfectly tailored to the capitalist system and thereby eradicates the need for the horrors of contraception. However, underlying this is the knowledge that Trellis's eugenics does not

work, and the perfect characters that he attempts to breed rise up
against him. The creation of a race – be they characters, or the Irish
– designed to conform to a certain type and think and act as they
are bid is impossible.

The creation of proles stamped with 'the ineluctable badge of
mass-production' (AS 32) leads to the type of slave(y) represented
by Teresa, a character expressly designed as contrived *deus ex
machina*. Teresa is portrayed as an ugly but serviceable (literary)
tool: 'a stout girl of high colour, attired in grey and divided at the
centre by the terminal ridge of a corset of inferior design' (AS 32).
The nondescript uniformity of Teresa's clothes and the mundane
prominence of a garment designed to invisibly create an attractive
female form make her a figure of banal unsightliness. Not only
does her corset fail, it obviously fails, and serves no purpose other
than to reveal itself in its failure. But dull, unsubtle transparency
is precisely what Teresa embodies; the rushed artificiality of her
'rescue' of Trellis is highlighted by the narrator, who writes 'By a
curious coincidence as a matter of fact strange to say it happened
that . . .' (AS 215). She is visible only through her homogenous
invariability, as one of 'the Ford cars of humanity; . . . created to
a standard pattern by the hundred thousand' (AS 32). She is one
of the nondescript lumpenproletariat, the disempowered, alienated
products of modern Irish capitalism, who do not even have the
crass inquisitiveness of the Plain People of Ireland. While she saves
Trellis, she does so mindlessly and accidentally. She rescues through
an act of book-burning, creating an accidental holocaust through
a blatant disregard for the literary. Her response to the sight of
her employer, locked outside the house, barefoot and dressed in
no more than his nightshirt, is the inane 'You could easily get your
death, Sir' (AS 216), while her 'soft, sullen face' (AS 216) betrays
no engagement or interest beyond rote response. Thus, while the
realist novel was first popularized by the swelling readership of the
middle classes, in *At Swim-Two-Birds* the selfish, dictatorial author
is saved by the working classes. *Saved by the act of not reading,
but employing*, of understanding writing as no more than useless
words on a page valuable only as tinder. The type of knowledge
respected and possessed by the class that creates the Plain People
of Ireland is mocked by O'Brien, and their relation to Ireland and
self-identity repeatedly problematized. Similarly, the corduroys or
'gombeen bourgeoise' of *Cruiskeen Lawn* are despicable, but far

more threatening than both is the horror of a class that is wholly removed from any form of identity, that is adrift in global, capitalist modernism, that has neither interest nor awareness of history or position or literature. It is no accident that within O'Brien's text this sub-class is presented through the figure of a woman.

With a few minor exceptions – the Pooka, for example, whose club foot and tail do not prevent him from meticulous attention to his appearance – the physical in *At Swim-Two-Birds* is depicted as pimple-strewn, noisome and repugnant. The students are repeatedly attacked with bouts of copious vomiting, and those of the uncle's generation are beset with phlegm: Mr Corcoran sneezed, 'spattering his clothing with a mucous discharge from his nostrils. . . . I retched slightly' (AS 95). The narrator has styes in his eyes, a bed and body infested with lice, and 'a queer smell' (AS 23) both in his room and on his person, smelling, according to his friends, like a room in which 'there had been a hooley the night before, with cigars and whisky and food and crackers and women's scent. . . . A stale spent smell' (AS 46). In person Trellis is 'flabby and unattractive . . . and was accustomed to trace the seasonal changes of the year by inactivity or virulence of his pimples. His legs were puffed and affected with a prickly heat' (AS 26), while his son fairs little better, as his

> dark well-cut clothing was in sharp contrast to the healthless-rubiness of his face; there were pimples on his forehead to the size of sixpences and his languorous heavy eyelids hung uneasily midway over the orbs of his eyes; an air of slowness and weariness and infinite sleep hung about him like a cloak. (AS 145)

But while the male body is portrayed as disgusting, it is generally done so with geniality or fraternal mockery. It is 'natural' for the male body to be noisome, and while the natural may be lamented, to portray it is merely to subscribe to honest reality.[83] The female body, however, should 'naturally' be a place of beauty and modesty; when it is not so it becomes unnatural and aberrant. The Pooka's bed is 'bad country' (AS 105) because of his wife's presence, her body is a 'hard and joyless country' (AS 112), and in response to a question regarding her potential animality, her husband replies: 'I cannot say whether there is fur on my wife's legs for I have never seen them nor do I intend to commit myself to the folly of looking at them' (AS 107). While the natural ugliness of the masculine form may be described in detail, and with some relish – 'He was addicted to unclean expressions in ordinary conversation and spat continually, always fouling the flowerbeds on his way through the Green with a mucous deposit dislodged with a low grunting from the interior of his windpipe' (AS 20) – the abnormal unattractiveness of the feminine physique remains hidden, both from the eyes of her husband and from the eyes of the reader. It is euphemistically referred to, and its abhorrence insinuated by the refusal to see it. As such the female body is censored, and the male reaction to it similar to that parodied in the Cruiskeen Court of Voluntary Jurisdiction. When what appears to be *Madame Bovary*, a 'filthy' work of 'immoral literature' is brought to the attention of the court, the judge asks the negligent lawyer, Mr Lax, if he had read the text, to which the reply is simply: 'Certainly not, my lord. I would not soil my eyes with such nefarious trash'.[84] The female body is so shocking that one does not read its horrors; one is warned of its outlines by the censoring bedclothes, and one does not look. While describing the birth of Orlick might be acknowledged to be 'fraught with obstacles and difficulties of a technical, constructional, or literary character' (AS 144), not least as a result of the narrator's presumed ignorance regarding the specific details of birth, the narrator's decision to avoid this section is somewhat excusable. But his failure to engage with the external physicality of the female characters is less so. The Pooka's wife is kept conveniently hidden beneath the bedclothes; Gorgon-like, she is shrouded, so as not to offend the (male) gaze, reduced to no more than a 'black evil wrinkle in the black sackcloth quilts, a shadow' (AS 103–4). Despite the extended conversation raging regarding her humanity – or lack thereof – she is granted no more than two lines, or rather, one line, repeated. Once to the Good Fairy she says 'Your granny' (AS 106), and marks her husband's departure with 'Your granny, Fergus' (AS 113). Never seen, and allowed utter no more than the same line twice, she is isolated from the twisting dialectic of the Good Fairy and the Pooka, whose colloquy is positioned literally above her head.

Even the Good Fairy, who is without physical form – 'I have no body' (AS 124) – has a greater corporeal presence than the Pooka's wife. The Good Fairy perfectly embodies, or rather, disembodies, the paradoxical formlessness of the fragment. Without form, 'like a point in Euclid . . . position but no magnitude' (AS 146), he is nothing and everything, locatable only through speech. His formlessness enables him to be all forms, and as a result he is located undecidably between the masculine and the feminine, the embodied and the disembodied, the good and the evil. Technically androgynous, the Good Fairy is given the power of a masculine pronoun – 'I felt him nodding his head against my hip' (AS 124) – and yet called a woman by Mr Justice Lamphall (AS 201) and described as possessing a voice 'sweeter by far than the tinkle and clap of a waterfall and brighter than the first shaft of day' (AS 104). The queerness of the fairy – both terms used to refer to the homosexual male – is repeatedly established, but rather than the fairy ever possessing a definite identity, he (in)visibly hovers between possible (gender) identities, refusing to let his form take form.[85] Thus, while technically without body, the Good Fairy is continually referred to as sitting, pointing, holding cards and threatening to vomit. And while christened 'Good Fairy', the angel is bigoted, petty and a cheat. He is all-seeing and all pervasive, and yet without front or face. The transparency that the moral or ethical might be expected to possess is stretched to the point of invisibility, and the Good Fairy becomes impossible to read in a univocal fashion. As a result, he provokes confusion and anger among the Plain People – as Shanahan says, 'talk about face value, that fellow has no face. By God it's a poor man who doesn't have that much' (AS 140) – and his mercurial, temperamental instability can be manipulated by the steady forces of evil. The Good Fairy is the truth of an 'odd number', a third, ambiguous position between the masculine and the feminine, the substantial and the intangible, the ethical and the unethical. Within *At Swim-Two-Birds,* no identity or position is wholly fixed, and 'queerness' isn't isolated to the Good Fairy. Should we understand the word 'queer' to be specifically sexually loaded beyond its colloquial Irish use – 'odd', 'unusual', or simply as an intensifier – then the shrouding of the Pooka's wife might indicate not the concealment of the ugly female, but the dissemblance of a homosexual relationship. Despite the fact that the Good Fairy, who has been under the bedclothes to investigate, continually speaks of not just of kangaroos, but of female kangaroos, and the female personal pronoun is repeatedly used, the Pooka's wife is described as bidding goodbye to her husband in a 'queer muffled voice' (AS 113). Is the Pooka's wife male or female, or somewhere between the two? Is 'queer' used to signify a non-heteronormative individual or relationship? Since the Pooka deems it necessary to inquire as to 'the sex of Miss Lamont' (AS 111), there can be no security in pronouns, gender-specific terms or titles. All become deictic marks that even context will not allow to unambiguously signify.

Joyce once wrote that 'modern man has an epidermis rather than a soul'.[86] For O'Brien, modern man is a palimpsestic series of shallow, pimple-strewn layers that contrive, and fail, to form a definite identity. While modern woman barely exists for him, modern man is a shifting structure rather than deep content, and as a result the narrator finds it next to impossible to create rounded characters. Brinsley complains that Lamont, Furriskey and Shanahan are no more than three proper names signifying a single basic identity, and so in an attempt to present them as independent entities the narrator writes a '*Memorandum of the respective diacritical traits or qualities of Messers Furriskey, Lamont and Shanahan*' (AS 161). The differential qualities that the narrator bestows upon them are of a wholly superficial quality, being distinctions between the shapes of their heads, configuration of their noses, pedal and volar traits, 'unimportant physical afflictions' (AS 161), mannerisms, attire, and favourite foods and flowers. The privileging of the material in this way both reflects the narrator's disregard for character development and performs the inability of Lamont, Furriskey and Shanahan to understand the theoretical, ephemeral or recondite. They represent the antithesis of formlessness, and instead champion the manifest, the obvious, the traditional and the univocal. During Trellis's torture, they are obsessed with the infliction of physical damage whose effect is immediately visible. While Orlick wishes to impose a subtle torment formed linguistically – 'I will pierce him with a pluperfect' (AS 168) – Lamont, Furriskey, and Shanahan desire 'A nice simple story with plenty of the razor' (AS 169). In conversation they appreciate the factual, and yet the particulars they present are wholly inaccurate – Socrates' death from hemlock is bestowed upon Homer, who is also accused of persecuting Christians, Pegasus is deemed to be a fiddle player and 'Onward Christian Soldier' is misquoted (AS 153–6). Thus, when Orlick writes them into his tale he makes them wise according to their understanding of wisdom: the possession of facts. A critical engagement with the facts themselves is unnecessary. Hence, in direct opposition to the narrator's modernism – 'One book, one opening, was a principle with which I did not find it possible to concur' (AS 13) – is the traditionalist or realist Lamont's 'I like to know where I am, do you know. Everything has a beginning and an end' (AS 63).

In literary realism, style and form are rendered invisible before the characters and actors produced: effectively one does not read the words but see the events. While Orlick wishes to produce a (modernist) torture of style *as* substance, where the literary is balanced with the physical and the words of hurt both lyrically thrill and physically rend, Shanahan, Furriskey and Lamont ignore style and structure, and wish for a transparent mode of writing such that the words become invisible before the imagery produced. They wish for a writing that produces immediate, visible effect, and one whose basic realism will appeal to – and torture – the senses. But Orlick does not wish (simply) to damage the body of Trellis, but his soul, and thereby inflict not just hurt in the present tense, hurt that sustains while the pain remains, but a hurt not restricted by time or place. A formless hurt, a wound that will cause eternal suffering. While Trellis exerts a God-like control over his characters, inflicting them 'with certain physical afflictions, most of which were degrading and involved social stigma' (AS 202) when they complained about their treatment, Orlick plays the role of vengeful God with greater force. Caught in the grips of an excessive Oedipal conflict, Orlick does not wish to call a plague of lice or boils upon his father, but wishes to rend him at the very soul, and condemn him to the everlasting bonfire. The cycles of hell to which he consigns him are evident in his use of the Sweeny saga as a structure; the torture of Trellis will repeat old tortures, and thus the torture will have always taken place in each old tale, and will take place in every retelling. But it is not only the use of old myths and a high literary style that discomfort Orlick's fellow torturers; they are unsure of his use of the Church. Ignorant of the fact that the Sweeny story ends with eventual victory of Christianity against mad, barbaric paganism, they listen only to the beginning, and are immediately discomforted. Fearful of any implications of blasphemy or anti-Catholic sentiment, Furriskey says, 'You won't get far by attacking the church' (AS 172). And so, having rejected a story involving odd truths, Orlick writes them one full of even lies: instead of Sweeny and Christianity, they get the Pooka, and they write themselves into yet another association with the devil. But it is not just the involvement of the Pooka that causes the torture scene to become increasingly violent. It is the fact of being involved in the act of writing itself. While the perfect author should not be dictatorial, once in possession of the pen all characters become controlling despots and patriarchs. What begins as a revolution based on freedom and the self-determination becomes a new terror of control and cruelty. Once independence had been achieved in Ireland, revolutionary fervour turns towards inculcating a new form of oppression and censorship. When the judges, who are also the jury, sit at the bar, justice is revealed to be the kangaroo court of a public house, and the newly appointed magistrates of the peace play cards, cheat, steal, fail to listen and collapse from inebriation. All that has changed is that they now wear robes and drink their pints of plain from long-stemmed glasses. As Engels once wrote of Ireland: 'The worst about the Irish is that they become corruptible as soon as they stop being peasants and turn bourgeois. True, this is the case with most peasant nations. But in Ireland it is particularly bad. This is also why the press is so terribly lousy'.[87]

Notes

1 Keith M. Booker, *Flann O'Brien, Bakhtin, and Menippean Satire* (New York: Syracuse University Press, 1995), 29.

2 David Cohen, 'An Atomy of the Novel: Flann O'Brien's *At Swim-Two-Birds*'. *Twentieth Century Literature* 39.2 (1993): 208.

3 Joshua D. Esty, 'Flann O'Brien and the Post-Post Debate'. *ARIEL: A Review of International English Literature* 26.4 (1995): 37.

4 Joseph Brooker, 'Children of Destiny: Brian O'Nolan and the Irish Ready-Made School', *http://eprints.bbk.ac.uk/172/1/brooker4.pdf*, 15.

5 Dennell Downum, 'Citation and Spectrality in Flann O'Brien's *At Swim-Two-Birds*'. *Irish University Review* 36.2 (2006): 305.

6 Peter Childs, *Modernism* (London: Routledge, 2000), 207.

7 Cronin, 49.

8 Friedrich Schlegel, '*Athenäum* fragments'. *Lucinde and the Fragments*, trans. Peter Firchow (Minneapolis: The University of Minnesota Press, 1971), F53. NOTE: Schlegel's fragments are referenced by the number of the fragment rather than the page.

9 Friedrich Schlegel 'On Incomprehensibility'. In *Classical and Romantic German Aesthetics*, ed. J. M. Bernstein, trans. Peter Firchow (Cambridge: Cambridge University Press, 2003), 305.

10 Schlegel, '*Athenäum*', F238.

11 Philippe Lacoue-Labarthe and Jean-Luc Nancy, *The Literary Absolute: The Theory of Literature in German Romanticism*, trans. Philip Barnard and Cheryl Lester (Albany: State University of New York Press, 1988), 40.

12 Maurice Blanchot, *The Infinite Conversation*, trans. Susan Hanson (Minneapolis: University of Minnesota Press, 1993), 353.

13 Blanchot, *Infinite Conversation*, 8.

14 Anne Clissman, *Flann O'Brien: A Critical Introduction to his Writings* (Dublin: Gill and MacMillan, 1975), 86.

15 Cronin, 124.

16 Cohen 'Anatomy', 224, Foster 'Introduction', 5, Gallagher 'Frontier Instability', 11, Giebus 'At Swim-Two-Birds', 73, Taaffe 'Reader', 247, Comer 'Mortal Agency', 105 (he refers to Trellis' 'novel-in-progress'), to name but a few.

17 Lacoue-Labarthe and Nancy, 48.

18 The words on the page are at the same time the foundation of life: when the pages describing the created characters are burned, the torture of Trellis ends and they cease to exist.

19 Schlegel, '*Athenäum*', F206.

20 Schlegel, '*Athenäum*', F297.

21 Schlegel, '*Athenäum*', F22.

22 Blanchot, *Infinite Conversation*, 359.

23 Friedrich Schlegel, 'Critical Fragments', *Lucinde and the Fragments*, trans. Peter Firchow (Minneapolis: The University of Minnesota Press, 1971), F14.

24 Jacques Derrida, 'Aphorism Countertime', trans. Nicholas Royle. In *Psyche: Inventions of the Other II* (Stanford: Stanford University Press, 2008), 128.

25 Derrida, 'Aphorism', 131.

26 The problems Derrida had with Schlegel's fragments, and his decision to use 'aphorism' rather than 'fragment', were based on their representation in Lacoue-Labarthe and Nancy's *Literary Absolute*, which over-emphasized their isolation and self-containment. Derrida's aphorisms are closer to Schlegel's fragments – independent and yet connected – than he realized.

27 For example, 'fraxinella' is a 'species of garden dittany' while for 'dittany' we are told to 'see fraxinella above' (AS 192).

28 Maurice Blanchot, *The Writing of the Disaster*, trans. Ann Smock (Lincoln: University of Nebraska Press, 1995), 58.

29 Ibid., 5.

30 Peter Brooks, *Reading for the Plot: Design and Intention in Narrative* (Cambridge, MA: Harvard University Press, 1992), 12.

31 Niall Sheridan, 'Brian, Flann and Myles'. In *Myles: Portraits of Brian O'Nolan*, ed. Timothy O'Keeffe (London: Martin, Brian and O'Keeffe, 1973), 44.

32 Jacques Derrida, 'Ellipsis'. In *Writing and Difference,* trans. Alan Bass (London: Routledge, 2001), 378.

33 Friedrich Nietzsche, 'Aphorism 260'. In *The Gay Science,* trans. Josefine Nauckhoff (Cambridge: Cambridge University Press, 2001), 150.

34 Although the Pooka does admit to anthropophagy, with a possible side of homosexuality, having eaten the loins of a man the night before (AS 105).

35 Eva Wäppling, *Four Irish Legendary Figures in* At Swim-Two-Birds (Uppsala: Almqvist and Wiksell, 1984), 82–98.

36 Blanchot, *Writing of the Disaster,* 36.

37 The word *fadó* is the Irish for a 'long time ago', and '*Fadó, fadó*' was the phrase with which the famous Irish *seanachaí* (storyteller) Peig Sayers began her stories.

38 Ciaran Ua Nuallain, 'The Return of Finn'. *Comhthrom Féinne* 11.1 (April 1935): 8.

39 Todd A. Comer, 'A Mortal Agency: Flann O'Brien's *At Swim-Two-Birds. Journal of Modern Literature* 31.2 (2008): 109. This is as a result of Comer's mistakenly hearing the watch and the bells sounding 'simultaneously' (109) and presuming that the 'narrator's subjection is complete' (109).

40 Cohen, 223.

41 The names of these characters, who tried to lure Lamont and Shanahan into slavery, come from the phrase in Virgil's *Aeneid* '*timeo danaos et dona ferentes*', meaning 'I fear the Greeks even if they bring gifts' . . .

42 It is unclear if O'Nolan realized this. In *Portraits* John Garvin quotes him as saying 'They all go out [reference to the epigraph] . . . when the skivvy burns the MS. that sustains their existence' (*Portraits* 58).

43 Jean-François Lyotard, *The Differend: Phrases in Dispute,* trans. Georges Van Den Abbeele (Minneapolis: University of Minnesota Press, 1988), xi.

44 Blanchot, *Infinite Conversation*, 153–4.

45 Kim McMullen, 'Culture as Colloquy: Flann O'Brien's Postmodern Dialogue with Irish Tradition'. *Novel: A Forum on Fiction* 27.1 (1993): 71.

46 Sheridan echoes this sentiment in relation to the *Children of Destiny* project (or O'Brien quotes their original conversation) when he says that 'Compulsory education had produced millions of semi-literates, who were partial to 'a good read'. . . . We must give them length without depth, splendour without style' (*Portraits* 42).

47 Liam Delaney, 'Dance v. Céilidhe'. *Comhthrom Féinne* 7.2 (February 1934): 42.

48 Ibid.

49 Declan Kiberd, 'Gaelic Absurdism: *At Swim-Two-Birds*'. *Irish Classics* (London: Granta Books, 2000), 515.

50 Friedrich Schlegel, 'Dialogue on Poetry'. In *Dialogue on Poetry and Literary Aphorisms*, trans. Ernst Behler and Roman Struc (University Park: The Pennsylvania State University Press, 1968), 103.

51 Schlegel, 'Critical', F78.

52 Schlegel, '*Athenäum*', F116.

53 Ibid., F238.

54 Sheridan, 44.

55 See, for example, Anne Clissman, *Flann O'Brien: A Critical Introduction to his Writings* (Dublin: Gill and MacMillan, 1975), 104–5.

56 Schlegel, '*Athenäum*', F121.

57 Sheridan, 42.

58 Sheridan, 40. Sheridan describes the process of writing the book: 'Existing works would be plundered wholesale for material' (*Portraits* 42).

59 Carol Taaffe, *Ireland Through the Looking Glass: Flann O'Brien, Myles na gCopaleen and Irish Cultural Debate* (Cork: Cork University Press, 2008), 38.

60 Schlegel, '*Athenäum*', F77.

61 Simon Critchley, *Very Little . . . Almost Nothing* (London: Routledge, 1997), 110.

62 Blanchot, *Infinite Conversation*, 353.

63 The idea of hiring characters is loosely repeated in a Cruiskeen Lawn article, in which Myles writes, referring to drama, that 'The best characters have already been established by the masters, so why try

to better them? New *activities* may, of course, be ascribed to them'
(CL 25 February 1955).

64 A slight problem in terminology should be noted here, as while the
narrator says that the process does not involve fertilization, the term
'aestho-autogamy' means aesthetic self-fertilization.

65 This is further satirized in an 'extract' from *The Athenian Oracle*, an
anthology of questions and answers taken from a late seventeenth
century text, in which the question is asked: 'Whether it be poſſible
for a woman ſo carnally to know a Man in her ſleep as to conceive,
for I am ſure that this and no way other was I got with Child' (AS
102). The answer given is a resounding 'no'.

66 This is also described as a 'successful act of procreation involving two
unknown quantities' (AS 41). The 'unknown' in this case refers to
the fact that no physical pregnancy can be seen, not that the birth is
a self-engendering by the character. The press announcement of the
birth attributes the act of creation to Trellis, as does the rest of the
passage.

67 According to Taaffe, this phrase appears four times in the original
(*Looking Glass* 55).

68 In a further mockery of this, the offspring of the sexless, virgin
birth may not be a virgin: 'He [Furriskey] is apparently not a virgin,
although it is admittedly difficult to establish this attribute with
certainty in the male' (AS 40).

69 In opposition to the play, which is 'consumed in wholesome fashion
by large masses in places of public resort' (AS 25).

70 Ostensibly Trellis's aims are to write a moral tract, and thereby take
arms against the 'spate of sexual and other crimes recorded in recent
times in the newspapers – particularly in those published on Saturday
night' (AS 35). But this ethical act, so fuelled by Saturday night
reading, is performed through the graphic presentation of sexual
assault: 'he is putting plenty of smut into his book. There will be no
less than seven indecent assaults on young girls and plenty of bad
language' (AS 35). Under the guise of appealing to the masses, Trellis
is thus able to supplement or extend the pleasure of reading about
sexual attack through the voyeuristic pleasure of writing rape. This
act of inscription takes physical form when Trellis physically rapes of
his characters. The masturbatory fantasy of writing thereby becomes
an act of bondage, and the master/slave dialectic is transposed into
the realm of the literary through the hierarchy of author/character as
dominant/submissive.

71 Censorship of Publications Act, 1929, Irish Statute Book *http://www.
irishstatutebook.ie/1929/en/act/pub/0021/sec0006.html#sec6.*

72 Tracy, however, seems to be convinced that the techniques of aestho-autogamy can be applied to heterosexual sex, as couples could collectively give birth to mature, work-ready offspring. This, he argues, would mean that couples would not be tempted by the 'mortifying stratagems collectively known as birth control' as their 'legitimate diversions would straightaway result in finished breadwinners or marriageable daughters' (AS 41). Mixing aestho-autogamy with heterosexual sex would therefore produce good Catholics, engaging in sensible, productive sex.

73 He also makes a rather bad joke about her name, writing than 'Barnacle' was not her surname, just a name Joyce made up, and which lasted due to 'Stupid American commentators' (Dalkey Archive Manuscript 147, BC. Hereafter referred to as DA MS). As Joyce says, 'When we were all younger, I said to her 'Nora, you cling so closely to me that I'll call you my barnacle' (DA MS 147). He then gives an etymology of 'barnacle'.

74 DA MS 148, BC.

75 Keith Hopper, *Flann O'Brien: A Portrait of the Artist as a Young Post-Modernist* (Cork: Cork University Press, 2009), 69.

76 In a wry inversion of O'Nolan's position in the L&H, the narrator is described as remaining superiorly aloof: 'When I attended these meetings I maintained a position where I was not personally identified, standing quietly without a word in the darkness' (AS 49).

77 That said, there is, as ever, an exception. While male characters rebel, the only character that actively rebels to the point of rejecting the proper name that Trellis bestows on her is female. Although not a human female, but a cow (AS 204).

78 Francis Galton, *Inquiries into Human Faculty and its Development* (New York: Macmillan, 1883), 25.

79 Childs, Donald A., *Modernism and Eugenics: Woolf, Eliot, Yeats and the Culture of Degeneration* (Cambridge: Cambridge University Press, 2001), 13.

80 Brother Barnabas, 'Scenes in a Novel'. *The Journal of Irish Literature* 3.1 (January 1974): 15. Also mention of potential rape – 'Dammit, you can't call me squeamish. Think of that bedroom business in Chapter Two, you old dog' (16).

81 James Joyce, *A Portrait of the Artist as a Young Man* (Oxford: Oxford University Press, 2008), 175.

82 Joyce, *Portrait*, 175.

83 The obsession with the body is taken to more extreme degrees during the torture of Trellis, where the minutiae of torment is lovingly described. In a sadistic move away from Sweeny, who is able to comfort himself with poetry and a love for the landscape, Trellis is forced to endure the psychological persecution of praising not the country but his abusers.

84 CL 11 December 1942. When the judge retires to the privacy of his room to read the book and ascertain for himself the depths of its depravity, it transpires that the work hidden behind the cover of Flaubert's work is in fact *An Outline of Irish Grammar* by the Irish Christian Brothers. As suggested by Brooker, the shopkeeper is so embarrassed by the pornographic excesses of the Gaelic League and the language revivalists that he hides his book on Irish grammar behind the less obscene but officially banned book of French infidelity (Brooker, '"Estopped by Grand Playsaunce": Flann O'Brien's Postcolonial Lore'. *Journal of Law and Society* 31.1 (2004): 30).

85 Keith Hopper's 'The Dismemberment of Orpheus: Flann O'Brien and the Censorship Code' (*Barcelona English Language and Literature Studies* 11 (2000): 119–31) and his *Portrait* give a reading of the use of the term 'queer' in *At Swim-Two-Birds*.

86 James Joyce, *James Joyce in Padua*, trans. and ed. Louis Berrone (New York: Random House, 1977). As quoted in Steven Connor, *The Book of Skin* (Cornell: Cornell University Press, 2004), 9.

87 Frederick Engels to Karl Marx, 27 September, 1869, in *Ireland and the Irish Question: A Collection of Writings by Karl Marx and Frederick Engels*, ed. R. Dixon, trans. Angela Clifford et al (New York: International Publishers, 1975), 274.

2

Driven to repeat

In *The Third Policeman*, O'Brien describes the endless cycles of the same to which the narrator is condemned as hell:

> it was again the beginning of the unfinished, the re-discovery of the familiar, the re-experience of the already suffered, the fresh-forgetting of the unremembered. Hell goes round and round. In shape it is nearly circular and by nature it is interminable, repetitive and very nearly unbearable. (TP 207)

The narrator's hell is not a hell that punishes through violent physical torture, nor through constant, annihilating mental anguish. The cycles of this hell are not those of Dante, the repetitions are not those of Tartarus, the similarities not those of Hades, the patterns neither Celtic nor Christian. O'Brien's inferno is a modernist hell of nauseous uncertainty, alienation and defamiliarization, where identity, agency and control are eroded but not destroyed, as narrator may never dissolve into the peace of utter oblivion. The narrator's hell is a hell of the everyday askew; a timeless, alienating construct that traps him within an eternity of repeated, uncanny bewilderment. It's a hell otherwise, a 'sort of hell',[1] an afterlife as continued, confusing life. Not quite a hell on earth, although Myles has equated them – 'I want to upset once for all this luciferian aberration and state boldly that we are all in hell, or in something so near it as makes no matter'.[2] The hell of *The Third Policeman* is not a hell in the sense of a place of punishment designed by an omniscient deity. It is, rather, a *hellish* space of uncanny, undead survival. The narrator dies, but he lives on after his death, surviving the explosion that killed him to enter a strange, uncanny space of reanimated corpses, automatons, split subjects, doubles, surreal landscapes, anthropomorphic bicycles, wooden legs, mechanical eyes, daemonic houses, unsettled time and infinite revolutions and repetitions.[3] The narrator persists after his demise, continuing mechanically but resolutely the task that killed him – the search for the black box, and all the box implies. The narrator's hell is not a hell created by a divine power, but a demonic, eternal survival powered by desire and drive.

That desire would lead to an infinite recurrence is not new. For the inhabitants of the Greek hell Tartarus, desire leads to endless, punishing repetitions: Sisyphus' major crime was deeming his powers of creativity to be equal to those of the gods, and so his sentence – to repeatedly push a rock towards the summit of a hill, only to have it roll back before it reaches the apex – enacts an infinite repetition of cycles of aspiration and frustration. Similarly, Tantalus, who stole ambrosia from the gods and told people their secrets, was punished for this desire for equality by being sentenced to stand in a lake underneath a fruit tree with low branches, the water receding when he tried to drink and the branches moving when he tried to eat. He was thus condemned to eternal desire – a hunger and thirst that can never be satisfied. Ixion's lust for Hera was punished by being tied, for all eternity, to a flaming wheel of desire. The Danaides were punished for the murder of their husbands by being made to carry water to a bath where they could wash away their sins. However, their only implement to transport the water was a sieve. Tityos was, like Prometheus, condemned to have his constantly regenerating liver eaten by an eagle for the attempted rape of Leto. The five perpetual sufferers are all punished by the infinite repetition of a penalty, with Ixion's, Sisyphus' and Tantalus' punishments all being explicitly tied to desire. The immortality of drive is represented in Ixion's flaming wheel of desire and Sisyphus' repetitive labour, while Tantalus' punishment is eternal desire itself – to be always taunted by a tantalizing object of desire which is only out of reach when one tries to acquire it. Desire and drive are infinite, and the sufferers of Tartarus have hells of immortal want. Desire and drive mean infinite hunger, infinite pain, infinite labour.

This chapter argues that while the narrator dies, the drive does not, and so, powered by internal helical gears, the narrator exists, he insists, he survives, he lives on, as a ghost, as a fantasy, as a trace, as a phantasm within himself. As O'Brien 'quotes' de Selby in the text's epigraph: 'Human existence being an hallucination containing in itself the secondary hallucinations of day and night . . . it ill becomes any man of sense to be concerned at the illusory approach of the supreme hallucination known as death' (TP epigraph). The narrator dies, but caught in the cycles of the drive he survives and lives on in an undead hallucination which apes (the hallucination of) life. The narrator's landscape is a constructed, undead space, and the narrator walks or cycles in a site of rotary survival that weaves between unconscious and consciousness.

For Lacan, the subject is a split, barred subject suffering from a constant desire caused by a primal absence or loss. The barred subject embarks on what is ostensibly a path of desire, curving around objects that never fill the lack felt. As Sean Homer writes, 'the Lacanian subject of the unconscious is essentially *no-thing*; it is a lacking subject who has lost his or her being'[4]: once dead the narrator of *The Third Policeman* becomes a no-thing, doubly so, as he is both unnamed, and without a bicycle.[5] Being a no-name, no-thing and having a no-bicycle, he is constituted by absence and lack, and caught in the repetitive, curved space of desire. The narrator is trapped in an undead, impossible oneiric space beset with temporal, logical and structural contradictions because the unconscious does not know time or contradiction, reality or grammar, but is a place of repressed desires.[6] The narrator is lost and confused within it, because, as Lacan writes, 'our position in the dream is profoundly that of someone who does not see. The subject does not see where it is leading, he follows'[7]: the reason for the subject's confusion and doubt is that he does not control his unconscious, because his unconscious is outside himself.[8] In the final dying seconds of his life, the narrator creates a hell of infinitely short and infinitely long duration, and what remains of him will eternally trace a repetitive path between law and desire. This chapter traces the path of the narrator's drive and desire, from the black box to Divney to de Selby. O'Nolan wasn't ignorant of psychoanalysis; in a Keats and Chapman anecdote, an old man who leaves all his money to a cat's home is described as having an 'aid-to-puss complex',[9] Myles claims to have written *Is Mise Mé Féin*, 'An inquiry, conducted in Irish, into Freud's attempts to dissect the ego; notable for my heroic exploits in the sphere of technical terms',[10] and Niall Sheridan speaks of him describing Proust and Kafka as 'layabouts from the slums of Europe poking around in their sickly little psyches'.[11] O'Nolan's personal library also contains a 1905 edition of William James's *Psychology*. But regardless of O'Nolan's knowledge or ignorance of psychoanalysis, this chapter makes no claims regarding O'Nolan's intentions; it simply reads the structures of *The Third Policeman* through the structures of the drive.

Desire and drive

Lacan once remarked that 'There is nothing so dreadful as dreaming that we are condemned to live repeatedly [*à répétition*]. Whence the idea of the death drive'.[12] In *Beyond the Pleasure Principle*, Freud investigates repetition which does not serve pleasurable ends, but repeats a forgotten trauma: the 'patient cannot remember the whole of what is repressed in him, and . . . is obliged to *repeat* the repressed material as a contemporary experience instead of . . . *remembering* it as something belonging to the past'.[13] This 'compulsion to repeat',[14] 'perpetual recurrence of the same thing',[15] or what Žižek describes as a 'blind automatism of repetition'[16] to which the physic apparatus is subordinated, is the death drive [*Todestrieb*], usually understood as a regressive or conservative movement towards the reinstatement of an earlier state, that is, non-being. A drive is a constant force that comes from within the subject, existing between the psychic and the somatic, and which constantly, untiringly aims for satisfaction. Freud distinguishes between two basic groups of drives: the sex/life drive – Eros – which 'aims at complicating life and at the same time, of course, preserving it',[17] and the death drive – Thanatos – 'the task of which is to lead organic life back into the inanimate state'.[18] Thus,

> the life of the organism moved with a vacillating rhythm. One group of instincts rushes forward so as to reach the final aim of life as swiftly as possible; but when a particular stage in the advance has been reached, the other group jerks back to a certain point to make a fresh start and so prolong the journey.[19]

However, Freud stresses that despite the oppositional nature of the drives, both are 'conservative in the strictest sense of the word, since both would be endeavouring to re-establish a state of things that was disturbed by the emergence of life'.[20] Freud thus acknowledges that 'the distinction between the two classes of instincts does not seem sufficiently assured'[21]: as such, the libidinal contains elements of the thanatic, and the deathly contains elements of the erotic.

In *New Introductory Lectures*, Freud emphasizes the indefati-
gability of the drive by formulating its repetitive impetus in terms
of a daemonic possession:

> There are people in whose lives the same reactions are perpetually
> being repeated uncorrected, to their own detriment, or others
> who seem to be pursued by a relentless fate, though closer
> investigation teaches us that they are unwittingly bringing this
> fate on themselves. In such cases we attribute a "daemonic"
> character to the compulsion to repeat.[22]

In 'Beyond' he employs Mephistopheles's lines from Goethe's
Faust – '*ungebändigt immer vorwärts dringt*' (unrestrain'd still
presses on for ever)[23] – to allegorize the death drive's destructive,
unrelenting force. The drive has no care for survival, just its own
satisfaction. It pushes on like one possessed, and it possesses
the subject through a tireless impulse to repeat: performing,
forgetting and performing again. Certain fears of psychoanalysis
are based, Freud argues, on precisely this sense of possession; as if
analysis might disturb something 'better left sleeping – what they
are afraid of at bottom is the emergence of this compulsion [to
repeat] with its hint at possession by some "daemonic" power'.[24]
Thus, while the death drive names '*an urge inherent in organic
life to restore an earlier state of things*',[25] that is, non-existence,
the drive's demonic ability to press on forever means that rather
than formulating the drive in terms of a nirvana principle turned
towards the quietude of death, we should read it as Žižek does,
as 'the very opposite of dying – a name for the "undead" eternal
life itself, for the horrible feeling of being caught in the endless
repetitive cycle of wandering around in guilt and pain'.[26] Thus
the death drive is an 'uncanny *excess* of life . . . an "undead"
urge which persists beyond the (biological) cycle of life and
death', as 'humans are not simply alive', but driven towards a
surplus or 'beyond' of life.[27] The death drive is not a movement
towards death, but a fixation that causes a repetitive circling
around something: 'This rotary movement, in which the linear
progress of time is suspended in a repetitive loop, is *drive* at its
most elementary'.[28] It is the 'eternal-undead',[29] animation beyond
death, represented by an undead living on.

In *Looking Awry*, Žižek compares the operation of the drives to
the labours of Sisyphus and to Zeno's paradoxes. Sisyphus' pushing

of the stone up the hill is infinite labour because once the peak is reached, the stone descends. But, paradoxically, it is also infinite labour because reaching the top of the hill is, according to the third of Zeno's paradoxes, impossible, given that distance is infinite: there is always a further half of a distance that must be crossed, and as such the goal, while getting closer, also infinitely retreats. Žižek likens this to the drive, whose goal is reaching the peak for the last time, that is, attaining full satisfaction. But not only is satisfaction not to be gained in the object of desire itself – 'By snatching at its object, the drive learns in a sense that this is precisely not the way it will be satisfied'[30] – the real *purpose* of a drive is not the goal, but the aim, and the ultimate aim of the drive is simply the infinite repetition of the drive itself: the drive can attain satisfaction without attaining its aim, as the drive 'contains' its own margin of dissatisfaction. The pleasure/displeasure of the drive is the repetition of the closed circuit; as the reality principle and the fact that the true object of the drive is an impossible, ideal object prevent the drive from ever fully achieving satisfaction, the object cathected is the repetition of the drive itself: 'the weird movement called "drive" is not driven by the "impossible" quest for the lost object; it is *a push to enact "loss" – the gap, cut, distance – itself directly*'.[31]

The narrator's infinite failure is brought about by the unending cycles of the death drive – it's always about a (bi)cycle – but it's also about desire. While the drive is not itself simply or solely motivated by an impossible quest for a lost object, the desire for a replacement object is not separate from the oscillation of the drive. And so we look at the object cause of desire – the *objet petit a*. The *objet a* is 'the object around which the drive turns',[32] or, as Žižek puts it, 'the chimerical object of fantasy, the object causing our desire and at the same time – this is its paradox – posed retroactively by this desire; in "going through the fantasy" we experience how this fantasy-object . . . only materializes the void of our desire'.[33] Ostensibly, desire has no object, as we desire something that was never attainable – possession of the mOther, the imaginary whole self, being wholly desired by the Other – and which, as such, was lost before it was possessed. We desire based on this sense of absence or loss, and our desire will always exceed each specific object of desire, as it is always marked by an insufficiency or lack. We thus move in a series of metonymic displacements or slippages from one object to the next; each object arouses our desire, attempts to fill our desire but cannot, as each object is 'necessarily lacking, unsatisfied, impossible, misconstrued'.[34] The *objet a* thus operates as an avatar or heuristic for the difference – the loss – between the 'original' object cathexis and the object that the drive/desire can currently attain. The *objet a* is the paradigmatic lost object of the drive, which, as Lacan terms it, 'tricks' the drive into infinitely circling around the limits of an already absent point of cathexis.[35] Thus, as Fink writes, we understand 'the object [of the drive] as *cause* of desire, not as something which could somehow *satisfy* desire'.[36] The object of the drive is an ideal object, and the desire for this object is displaced onto material objects. In tracing the path of drive and desire in *The Third Policeman*, we see different objects being desired; we cannot presume that as we move from the black box to Divney to de Selby that we reach the truly desired object, as 'the object of desire, in the usual sense, is either a phantasy that is in reality the support of desire, or a lure'.[37] The subject sustains itself by desiring, but what it desires relates not to objects but to the Other.

Objet a interrupts the totality or closure of the pleasure principle as it is a lack within desire that causes desire to circle on itself without the closure of satisfaction. Thus, as Žižek writes, '*objet a* prevents the circle of pleasure from closing, it introduces an irreducible displeasure, but the psychic apparatus finds a sort of perverse pleasure in this displeasure itself, in the neverending, repeated circulation around the unattainable, always missed object'.[38] This is *jouissance*, pleasure in pain, and the circular motion is the drive itself, which keeps us curving around the object of desire without connecting it with. The *objet petit a* is the manifestation or embodying of the circling of desire – it is our desire (falsely) realized in a shifting object. It is not an avatar of the object we desire, but of the structure, the cogs, the wheels of desire turning through a frame of repeatability. In other words, while desire shifts from one object to another there is a consistency to the objects that are cathected. The *objet petit a* is the frame of this consistency.[39] In the oneiric space of *The Third Policeman*, the turning of desire can be traced through the position of the black box, and the way that the box relates to a desire for Divney and for de Selby. The black box is twice so desired as to result in murder – the narrator and Divney kill Mathers, and Divney then kills the narrator.[40] But it, of course, is not desired in and of itself – it is not a fetishized cathected object – but is desired at a step removed, as it is desired for what it contains, and what those contents can permit. Full of money, it can enable Divney to marry Pegeen Meers, the narrator to publish his book on de Selby, and both to be rid of the other. The black box is, then, representative of desire itself, and the alterations and transformations it undergoes after the narrator's death map out the circling of desire within the undead space. It is desired, but never for itself, and it is impossible to attain, always disappearing in the distance under the dark coats of murderers or wheeled off through official channels by equally mysterious policemen. The black box constantly eludes: 'the *objet petit a* . . . exists (or, rather, insists) in a kind of curved space in which, the more you approach it, the more it eludes your grasp'.[41]

The metamorphosis that the black box undergoes in the afterlife is preceded by its first deathly alteration – desire kills, as the black box becomes a bomb. But the narrator survives his death and finds himself in an afterlife animated by the wheels of desire. The immortality of the drive is manifested through the impossibility of stasis, and so as revenants drive and desire circle on – his last action before death and his first action after it continue the cycle of driving desire: 'the fingers of my right hand, thrust into the opening in the floor, had closed mechanically, found nothing at all and came up again empty. The box was gone!' (TP 24). The refusal of the drive to cease drags the narrator into an undead survival that traces the looping pattern of the drive as it rotates around the morphing, present/absent *objet petit a*. Before death, the black box lead to the *jouissance* of the 'queer' inseparability of Divney and narrator, but after death its importance swells until the narrator 'began to think [he] would never be happy until [he] had that box again in [his] grip' (TP 37). Its contents increase from 'three thousand pounds' (TP 15) to 'ten thousand pounds' worth of negotiable securities [as] a conservative estimate' (TP 39), and eventually explode into omnium – the energy of everything. But before the object of desire swells to be the force enabling – and granting – desire, it changes, and within the timeless place of the narrator's undead unconscious becomes a watch. And here it becomes not simply the object of frustrated desire – wanted but never attained – but exemplifies the lost object that was never originally possessed, as the watch never existed. Hearing of a magical police station from the reanimated Mathers, the narrator decides to enlist official assistance in finding the box, but resolves to report the loss not of the stolen box but of 'my American gold watch. . . . I had no American gold watch' (TP 38). As the narrator stays in the company of the police, the black box begins to recede from his mind, and the fake gold watch begins to become increasingly real. Although Joe repeatedly reminds him that the watch doesn't exist and was never lost (TP 115, 167), in its absence he begins to lament the loss of a treasured possession. By the time he is to be hanged it has become, in its absence, valuable enough to be bestowed on a much-loved companion (TP 167). Supplementing this metamorphosis are the 'replacement' boxes which fill the jurisdiction – MacCruiskeen's chests, his boxes that make light and music, the boxes in eternity, the coffin the narrator dreams he is in, the elevator box. In searching for the black box, the narrator remains in a box – in his head, and in a coffin.[42]

Tricking 'death' once again, the author escapes from the barracks and cycles to Mathers' house, where the object cathected morphs back into the black box. But, when the narrator gets to the house where the box last was, he finds that it is, as always, elsewhere. Fox sent the black box back to the narrator's home, and it is there the narrator must return to set the wheel of the drive spinning again. But before he returns home, the import of the box grows even larger. The monstrous policeman tells him that the black box contains 4.12 ounces of omnium. As MacCruiskeen previously explained to the narrator, 'Some people . . . call it energy but the right name is omnium because there is far more than energy in the inside of it, whatever it is. *Omnium is the essential inherent interior essence which is hidden inside the roots of the kernel of everything and it is always the same*' [emphasis added] (TP 113). Omnium means everything, the whole of an investment, and also, vitally, a cycling race. It is an 'inutterable substance' which could 'mak[e] ribbons of the natural order, invent intricate and unheard of machinery . . . interfer[e] drastically with time' (TP 195). It is everything ever desired and can give everything ever desired, and if you had 'even the half-full of a small match-box of it you could do anything and even do what could not be described by that name' (TP 114). While some 'might call it God' (TP 114), the shifting, chimerical focus of libidinal investment is the power of the libido itself in all its fullness and lack – as Shelly Brivic mentions briefly, focussing on its deficiency rather than power: 'Omnium is described as having no particular form, colour, or any other quality. It is the infinite regress concretized as a substance, the unsatisfiable margin that drives all desire'.[43] Realizing the power of omnium, the narrator begins to wish to change the very structure of desire, that is, the Symbolic Order itself:

> Formless speculations crowded in on me, fascinating fears and hopes, inexpressible fancies, intoxicating foreshadowing of creations, changes, annihilations and god-like interferences. . . . *I could do anything, see anything and know anything with no limit to my powers save that of my imagination. Perhaps I could use it even to extend my imagination.* I could destroy, alter and improve the universe at will. [Emphasis added] (TP 195)

That which eludes the narrator is the very force of desire, and thus his survival is powered by the pleasure/displeasure experienced by the drive in failing to attain the object of its desire. If the black box contains everything, in losing it the narrator has lost everything: the absence of the black box becomes the absence of everything. He is kept alive by the absence of life, driven by the cycles of drive/desire.

Žižek formulates a distinction between the drive and desire, arguing that 'Desire is a metonymic sliding propelled by a lack, striving to capture the elusive lure: it is always, by definition, "unsatisfied"'.[44] Drive, on the other hand, is always-already satisfied in its pursuit of the impossible lost object. Thus, we see that desire is frustrated by its failure to attain the object it wants, while the drive finds satisfaction in the failure. The drive wants jouissance, even if it drives the subject to death – in the case of *The Third Policeman*, beyond death – and jouissance is located in the driving – cycling – itself. Žižek places 'the eternity of drive against the finitude of desire',[45] thereby contrasting the atemporal inexhaustibility of the revolutions of the drive with the temporally grounded limitations of desire. Desire may wane, but the drive cycles on, infinitely. Thus, the repetitiveness of the *Todestrieb* is not a link to morality and finitude, but *'immortality* – . . . a "thrust", which persists beyond the (biological) cycle of generation and corruption, beyond the *"way of all flesh"* [emphasis added].[46] It is precisely the failure of the drive to achieve satisfaction that gives it immortality: 'drive relies on a fundamental, constitutive *failure* . . . [and yet, the] drive's self-affection is never fully self-enclosed, it relies on some radically inaccessible X that forever eludes its grasp – the drive's repetition is the repetition of a failure'.[47] What we experience in *The Third*

Policeman is the perpetuation of the psyche – in death the drive continues to animate the body of the narrator. The narrator becomes lost in his own phantasmagoria and perpetuates as a phantom within the fantastical parish. *The narrator is eternally animated by the pleasure/displeasure of perpetual failure.*

Time and space

The narrator moves through his space of afterlife in a state of constant defamiliarized unease caused by the improper, illogical and destabilizing functioning of a familiar system. Throughout his undead survival, the fact of his death is constantly repeated and constantly repressed. He dreams of his own funeral: 'Lying in my dark blanket-padded coffin I could hear the sharp blows of a hammer nailing down the lid' (TP 124). He is sentenced to death and nearly hanged. His journey to eternity is marked by feelings of imminent demise. When forced by Fox to directly confront the possibility of his death, he suffers a near physical collapse, yet quickly represses the terror:

> "I do not understand your unexpected corporality after the morning on the scaffold."
> "I escaped," I stammered.
> He gave me long searching glances.
> "Are you sure?" he asked.
> Was I sure? Suddenly I felt horribly ill. . . . My limbs weakened and hung about me helplessly. Each eye fluttered . . . and my head throbbed. . . . I knew that I would be dead if I lost consciousness for one second. I knew that I could never awaken again or hope to understand afresh the terrible way in which I was if I lost the chain of the bitter day I had had. (TP 189–90)

The fact of the narrator's death is forced upon him, and it nearly brings about the collapse of his animation. But again, this fact is repressed and the cycles continue. As Freud writes in 'Thoughts for the Times on War and Death',

> What we call our "unconscious" – the deepest strata of our minds, made up of instinctual impulses – knows nothing that is

negative, and no negation; in it contradictories coincide. For that reason it does not know its own death, for to that we can give only a negative content. Thus there is nothing instinctual in us which responds to a belief in death.[48]

The psychoanalytic subject of desire cannot envision its own death and sees itself as living on in immortal survival. Animated by the unconsciousness's refusal to recognize its mortality, and by the immortality of the drive, the narrator continues to tread the circular path of desire, suspecting but repressing the fact of his death, impossibly living beyond it and yet incapable of bearing witness to it.

It is precisely the narrator's awareness and repression of his death that shapes the calming, if uncanny, rural scenes of his place of undead survival. The rustic idyll offsets the deep confusion and unease that the policemen bring to the narrator, and is employed to enable him to constantly and determinedly ignore his death. Hence, his afterlife is marked by signs of healthy country life and industry: 'The air was keen, clear, abundant and intoxicating. Its powerful presence could be discerned everywhere . . . breathing life into the world' (TP 40). He is constantly surrounded by hyperbolically soothing pastoral scenes of growth and abundance, and the sound of birds and humans continually reassure him that he is part of a live, harmonious, organic whole. They also bolster him when the policemen insist on imparting complex and impossible information – 'The scene was real and incontrovertible and at variance with the talk of the Sergeant' (TP 89). While the narrator recognizes that this safe, non-threatening pastoral is, like everything else in the district, a construct – 'Everything seemed almost too pleasant, too perfect, too finely made' (TP 41) – he is still invigorated by the bucolic scene and feels 'full of an appetite for going about my business and finding the hiding place of the black box' (TP 41).

When the narrator speculates on death and the events that follow it, neither heaven nor hell is mentioned as a final resting place. Instead, the afterlife is repeatedly formulated in terms of energy disseminated and perpetuated in another form. Thus, the narrator thinks that he will become part of the wind, a river or a mountain, while Joe speculates about becoming a wave, the spirit of a beautiful place or the smell of a flower (TP 164–7). This movement away from a Catholic heaven/hell of eternal stasis to an afterlife as disseminated life demonstrates an expectation in the narrator of a life which lives on, in various forms, and whose energy is repeated. Thus, against the hellish undead afterlife of the drive the narrator posits a heavenly union between his life force and that of the world, a unity found in MacCruiskeen's mixing of sound and light waves which becomes contamination in the atomic theory. Rather than being perpetuated within the drive – albeit one responding to and playing with his desires – he imagines a perpetuation 'in some healthy way, free and innocent of all human perplexity' (TP 164), that is, free from drive and desire.

Inasmuch as the unconscious refuses the laws of non-contradiction – the narrator is dead and alive – it rejects *chronos*, that is, sequential time. When the narrator dies, his demise is marked by a sudden metamorphosis in time and space, manifested by changes in temperature, light and air. When, after life and beyond time, the first sound that he hears is evidence of human life/death, time shudders and begins the jagged, irregular cessations and commencements that mark the loops of his animated death: 'the universe [was held] standstill for an instant, suspending the planets in their courses, halting the sun and holding in mid-air any falling thing the earth was pulling towards it' (TP 25). Later, noticing darkness outside, he feels that the sun did not traverse the sky but fell back upon itself: 'had risen a bit, stopped, and then gone back' (TP 37). He thus becomes 'a sempiternal man' (TP 68) in the constant irregularity that is death – 'This is not today, this is yesterday' (TP 63) – and, in a space where the distinction between what was, what is, and what will be is meaningless, resolves 'not try to tell of the space of time which followed' (TP 26). Faced with evident temporal collapse, the narrator realizes that measurement and memory become meaningless. The advent of a repetitive time has placed time and space beyond signification; to quote Adrian Johnston, 'One could succinctly encapsulate repetition as an intratemporal resistance to time itself, a negation of time transpiring within time'.[49] Repetition prevents a progressive, linear temporality, causing time to stagnate and dissolve in cycles of the same. But these repetitions and temporal confusions do not (simply) stem from divine punishment, but can be seen as manifesting from the timelessness of the unconscious, and the repetitions of the death drive.

In *The Interpretation of Dreams*, Freud argued that 'a prominent feature of the unconscious processes [is] that they are indestructible.

In the unconscious nothing can be brought to an end, nothing is past or forgotten'.[50] This is re-emphasized in 'The Unconscious':

> The processes of the system Ucs. are *timeless*; i.e. they are not ordered temporally, are not altered by the passage of time; they have no reference to time at all. Reference to time is bound up, once again, with the work of the system Cs.[51]

Thus, for Freud, the unconscious and the drives abide, existing outside of time as a systematic, progressive succession of units of equal distance from each other. This is not to hyperbolically claim that the unconscious is wholly antithetical to all notions of temporality, for, as Derrida clarifies, 'the unconscious is no doubt timeless only from the standpoint of a certain vulgar conception of time'.[52] Time for the psyche is a time(lessness) of interruptions, hesitations, repetitions and leaps, as events from the past are 'experienced' in the future, and the future rewrites events from the past. Events are repeated in loops that return, indifferent to their distance from the 'original' event. The *Todestrieb* curves towards the non-existence of the past/future, that is, towards the state of inertia that was and is to come, and which is, despite the temporal nature of these terms, outside time. Hence, we can argue that trapped in a phantasmagorical space where the unconscious holds sway, the narrator exists in a place indifferent to a measured movement of time. Despite the fact that O'Brien describes the narrator's days in hell as three, even this is not certain, so much does time unravel. The narrator dies in the morning, talks to Mathers for an unspecific amount of time and goes to bed with the sun setting. But this day exists in a border place, framing the narrative, and so we set this day aside as the passage to repetition. On the first morning of his death, the narrator gets up and leaves Mathers' house. En route he has a nap, meets Finnucane and arrives at the barracks. That night he sleeps, but is awoken by a dream of death. On the second day, he goes to eternity, and on his return goes to bed. On the third day, he awakes to the sound of the scaffold, asks the one-legged builder to find Finnucane and goes back to bed. He awakens to the sensation that 'it was not the same day at all but a different one and maybe not even the next day' (TP 156). He narrowly escapes hanging and falls asleep once more. He is awakened by MacCruiskeen, they speak, and he falls asleep again. When he awakes, he escapes on the bicycle, meets Fox and then Divney, and the cycles begin again. Thus, his days are not only split and multiplied by sleep; the time spent asleep causes the passage of time to be elusive. This place of woken death is punctuated by sleep and is thus an undead waking marked by recurring sinking into deathly sleep.

Contained within the erratic time of the narrator's repetitions is an interlude in the timeless eternity of a 'heaven full of doors and ovens' (TP 157). Reached after an orphic journey in which the narrator feels himself once again close to death, O'Brien's underworld heaven is entered through a humble church door. But the comfort and familiarity that such an ingress might offer is belied by the coldness of the iron interior, the functionality of the door-lined corridors, the artificiality of the tangles of wires and pipes overhead, and the utter absence of anything overtly religious or 'heavenly'. The narrator's eternity is a place of wish fulfilment, but like the rest of his undead existence, the 'down below – over there – beyant' (TP 157) of the next life lies very much beyond the pleasure principle. This is a place wholly outside of time and change, as while inside its pig-iron walls one does not age, beards do not grow, cigarettes do not burn out, whiskey doesn't inebriate and hunger never arrives. This is an eternity of the bodily or the corporeal, rather than an eternity of the soul. It is a place outside of difference and, therefore, of utter, unchanging stasis: 'It has no size at all . . . because *there is no difference anywhere in it* and we have no conception of the extent of its unchanging coequality' [emphasis added] (TP 138). This elimination of difference is echoed in the magnifying glass found inside eternity, the glass which magnifies to invisibility as 'It makes everything so big that there is room in the glass for only the smallest particle of it – *not enough of it to make it different from any other thing that is dissimilar*' [emphasis added] (TP 141). At the heart of the narrator's cycles of repetition is an iron core of the static: the second day of the (approximately) three-day cycles is spent in a place outside time. In the middle of repetition is timelessness, as repetition undoes time. And thus eternity is marked by the constant sound of grinding cogwheels – the turning of a (bi)cycle's helical gears (TP 143) – that measure out not progressive time but time in a loop and the changelessness of infinite repetitions. As the time of eternity is the dead time of repetition, so too is the space the repeated same. Eternal space loops in on itself, as exiting one hall leads into the same hall: the coiling iron passageways are the loops of the narrator's repetitive drive.

While eternity is itself beyond time and change, it contains within it everything imaginable and unimaginable. Within eternity the narrator is shown objects which '*lacked the essential property of all known objects*' (TP 139) – their shape was not a shape. Within eternal space is the possibility of witnessing that which is not only outside of language, but outside perception and the Symbolic Order: 'their appearance, if even that word is not inadmissible, was not understood by the eye and was in any event indescribable' (TP 140). Containing everything possible and impossible, and able to present it upon request, eternity is a place of wish fulfilment, and the narrator, greedy as always, is quickly driven by 'the commercial possibilities of eternity' (TP 140). He asks for gold, whiskey, gems, bananas, a fountain pen, paper, a suit, underwear, shoes, banknotes, matches, a bag and a murderous weapon which instantly turns people into powder (TP 141–2). But when he tries to leave eternity with his new wealth, he is stopped by the sergeant, who tells him that the stasis of eternity disallows any bodily change between the time of entry and exit. Inasmuch as one cannot take possessions to the next world, one cannot bring them back. The place of wish fulfilment is the wrong place/time to have wishes fulfilled, as in a place outside time, difference and the big Other, that is, outside society, the objects of desire are revealed to be not desired for themselves. In themselves they are useless, as without time they are merely embodied lack, and the wish fulfilment of this Fritz Lang-like eternity is meaningless. When the narrator realizes that the 'beyant' of eternity is beyond the pleasure principle, he gives vent to his frustration with regressive tears: 'I turned to the wall and gave loud choking sobs and broke down completely and cried loudly like a baby' (TP 145). To interrupt his crying, MacCruiskeen gives him a sweet, and so he 'rammed the lot into [his] mouth and stood there sobbing and sucking and snuffling' (TP 146).

The boxes that line the walls of eternity refer to the desired black box itself, and we learn that the contents of the black box, no longer money but omnium, is the driving force or power behind eternity. The smaller eternity within the narrator's repetitive infinity thus metonymically represents his own fate: as the smaller eternity is without time and space and change, the entirety of his place of oneiric survival is without time and space and change. As the smaller eternity is powered by omnium (the force of drive and desire), the entirety of the narrator's undead existence is powered by (omnium) the force of drive and desire. Drive and desire perpetuates the narrator's eternity – all of it – and it is fuelled by *jouissance*. When Fox explains to the narrator the real power of the box the narrator quickly turns to obscene thoughts of punishment and darkness, as he visualizes the cold, mechanical wish-fulfilling 'heaven' of eternity as a hell of 'unbeholdable corruptions containing tangles of gleaming slimy vipers each of them deadly and foul of breath, millions of diseased and decayed monsters . . . rats with horns walking upside down . . . trailing their leprous tails on the policemen's heads' (TP 197). As he continues,

> nothing I could do could restrain the profusion of half-thought extravagances which came spilling forth across my mind like a horde of swallows – extravagances of eating, drinking, inventing, destroying, changing, improving, awarding, punishing and even loving. I know only that some of these undefined wisps of thought were celestial, some horrible, some pleasant and benign; all of them were momentous. (TP 200)

Faced with the power of the libido, everything becomes excessive and dark, and tries to break free of the Symbolic Order. Eternity, omnium and the policemen-as-law – forces of desire – all pertain to the Real.

In a letter to O'Keeffe O'Nolan refers to J. W. Dunne's *An Experiment with Time* (1929) and *The Serial Universe* (1934) as inspiration for *The Dalkey Archive*, that is, for *The Third Policeman*.[53] Dunne's *Experiment with Time* stems from a series of dreams whose subject matter were events experienced *after* the dream. Dismissing, with beautifully measured care, the occult and the prophetic, he explains temporal inconsistencies or confusions like déjà vu and predictive dreams as '*normal* . . . *images of past experience and images of future experience blended together*'.[54] Our view of a time that follows a linear path marked by units of equal magnitude and distance is, he argues, habitual rather than accurate, as time does not ceaselessly progress towards a future cut off from a growing past by a travelling present,[55] but is *simultaneously occurring*. Time is serial, but not in a progressive sense. Rather, 'it is akin to the "Chinese boxes" type – the type where every term is contained in a similar but larger (in this case *dimensionally* larger) term'.[56] Thus, each 'unit' of time is *'contained within a field one dimension larger, travelling in another dimension of Time, the larger field covering events which are 'past' and 'future', as well as 'present' to the smaller field'.*[57] An individual observes a particular event positioned, as she would view it, in relation to a past that has taken place and a future to come. The individual then observes this observation, but the point at which she does so is not successive to the first, but occurs, so to speak, in the larger box. Thus, each unit of time is contained within another unit of time, and all take place simultaneously. One is privy to future events in dreams because one's ability to impose a linear progressivity to time is relaxed. From this Dunne concludes that serialism reveals a form of soul – like Joe, a 'superlative observer'[58] – whose immortality in relation to absolute time, that is, non-subjective time, the time in which all time occurs simultaneously, outlasts the existence of the individual who lives and dies within a given temporal space.[59] The way O'Nolan later recounts Dunne's theories is less than rigorous, writing in 1957 that 'High up in an aeroplane on a clear day you can see the entire road between Dublin and Naas, [and] be simultaneously aware of two places widely separated. If you leave Dublin by car, Naas is in the future',[60] and in 1962, 'the idea is that time is as a great flat motionless sea. Time does not pass; it is we who pass'.[61] Nonetheless, the Chinese boxes motif found in the structure of *At Swim-Two-Birds* and the content of *The Third Policeman* does link time to an infinite regression: MacCruiskeen's 37 chests are all identical, and each fits exactly into the preceding chest. The narrator wonders, in an echo of Preformationism, if he is 'a body with another body inside it in turn, thousands of such bodies within each other like the skins of an onion, receding to some unimaginable ultimum' (TP 123). In a regressive mise-en-abyme structure, eternity is contained within eternity, death within death and repetition within repetition.[62]

The infinite regression of Dunne's temporal structure and MacCruiskeen's chests can be likened to Zeno's first two paradoxes – the infinite regression of endless movement-as-stasis across increasingly microscopic distances. As Johnston writes, this represents

desire in its relationship to *objet petit a*, since desire is perpetually impelled towards an object that infinitely distances itself. Desire is sustained through the impossibility of ever reaching the forever receding object *a*. Desire exists strictly within the space of Zeno's paradox: An unending series of Imaginary substitutes and Symbolic interdictions guarantees that the finish line qua Real Thing will never actually be crossed.[63]

The regressive elements of the undead space and the repetitions of the hellish drive go on infinitely and contain a form of mechanized, wish-fulfilling eternity, but they are what Hegel would call a 'bad infinity' – an infinity comprising no more than a series of the finite. This can be thought in terms of infinite regression – 'the vain effort to attain the infinite through the endlessly repeated act/process of adding always one more particular element to a finite series of preceding elements. . . . Object *a* is a crystallised manifestation of the bad infinity of *Trieb* [drive]'.[64]

The bad infinity of finite points is comparable to the third of Zeno's paradoxes, which de Selby employs to prove not the impossibility of travel but the senselessness of buying train tickets. This paradox understands motion as impossible as one is constantly at rest, or as Aristotle writes, the idea that 'a flying arrow is stationary. The results by granting that time is composed of moments'.[65] In other words, as 'that which is travelling exists always in a moment, the flying arrow is motionless'.[66] For de Selby 'a journey is an hallucination' as life is simply 'a succession of static experiences each infinitely brief' (TP 52), and movement comprises 'resting for infinitely brief intervals in innumerable intermediate places' (TP 52) between two points. But, while for Zeno the point is the impossibility of motion, de Selby draws the conclusion that relocation is not: one may not move, but one still can arrive at a new place. In other words, the paradox simply becomes a way of avoiding a train fare: in order to travel from Bath to Folkstone, de Selby locks himself in his room with a series of postcards depicting sites between the two towns and thereby employs the impossibility of moving to cheaply traverse the country.

As we will see below, de Selbian logic provides a structure to the narrator's undead existence – here it is in order to point to the 'reality' of the narrator's situation. While the narrator follows the de Selby anecdote with the lines 'Of my own journey to the police-barracks I need only say that it was no hallucination' (TP 54), the reader – when repeating the text – is aware that it is a fantastical creation of the narrator. Furthermore, the paradox points to the

breakdown of a concept of progression or succession into a series
of static images – the stills from a reel – that each show microscopic
difference, and are, as such, repetitions of the almost-identical. We
see that the repetitions in *The Third Policeman* are never simply
repetitions of the same, but repetitions with difference. Thus, not
only are there slight changes in the description of the narrator's
'first' sighting of the barracks, his journey there is markedly
different. When the narrator is alone his way to the barracks is
warmed by the sun and presents a gentle pastoral scene. After he
appears to Divney his journey is troubled by darkness: 'the sky was
livid and burdened with ill omen. Black angry clouds were piling in
the west, bulging and glutted, ready to vomit down their corruption
and drown the dreary world in it' (TP 204).

In the first cycle to which we are privy the narrator began alone,
but is now accompanied, and all events must accommodate two
people rather than one. But as this time the narrator doesn't meet
Mathers or Martin Finnucane important 'plot' points are altered –
will Mathers still be killed by Finnucane in the undead space? Will
the narrator *and* Divney be charged with the murder? Will Finnucane
come for Divney, who does not have a wooden leg? Will the bicycle
scene become a threesome, or will another willing ride appear? And
most importantly, while in the 'first' repetition the narrator seeks
out the barracks, in this instant he comes 'accidentally' upon it.
Does the black box retain its importance now he's accompanied by
the one who possessed it? The cycles are exemplified in the way in
which the narrator repeats his questions about the black box: 'In the
weeks which followed I asked him where the box was a hundred
times in a thousand different ways. *He never answered in the same
way but the answer was always the same*' [emphasis added] (TP 18–
19). Blanchot describes ambiguity as 'the difference of the identical,
the non-identity of the same',[67] that is, confusion and uncertainty
is caused by a minimal difference between repetitions. The *space
of the undead drive is ambiguous* – its sameness is not identical,
its repetitions obliged to follow no living logic of identity. What
matters is the drive that pushes the narrator onwards, and how
that drive alters to fixate on different, unobtainable objects. There
is no sound reason to presume that the story of hellish survival
contained in *The Third Policeman* is the story of the narrator's first
traversing – the 'first' time he nears the barracks is accompanied
by a shock of import or recognition (TP 54), and he narrates with

some foreknowledge: 'Perhaps it was this lie which was responsible for the bad things that happened to me afterwards' (TP 38) – nor to assume that the cycles follow each other in a successive, linear, countable order. This is an eternity of the narrator's construction, and each cycle is a different same of desire and prohibition. Divney is not included in 'hell' due to a divine punishment – why would the ring-leader and murderer of two occupy the same cycle of hell as the lackey he led into the crime, and who only killed once? – but is included in the undead space at the narrator's wish, in an act of repetitive jouissance. The pleasure/pain of the narrator's and Divney's proximity becomes dragged into the afterlife, so that the narrator is able to kill the man who killed him and take him on a queer journey in death. If everything is a construct of the narrator's desire, so too is his ghostly trip to haunt his own house, and so too is his murder of Divney.

The repetitions, of course, also point to a greater complexity in the structure of the novel. At the end of each cycle, the narrator forgets what has gone before, and thus each time enters the barracks as if for the first time. This forgetting, however, is arguably not a failure to recall, or even a repression, but the erasure of the previous cycle. Inasmuch as the narrator has not forgotten his name, but no longer has one, the previous cycles of the drive have ceased to be. They are erased in the impossible act of the narrator's transcription. *The Third Policeman* is a cryptography – a writing from the tomb – and a thanatography in a double sense. Thanatography means a writing of death, but it is also a writing of Thanatos, that is, a writing of the death drive. The death drive writes itself and interrupts itself, erasing itself as it loops on itself. In a writing that refuses to present itself as an oral tale – the footnotes radically repudiate it – the reading becomes a séance operating as if through a Ouija board: the undead narrator writes but retains no script to guide him through his next cycle. In *At Swim-Two-Birds* we saw how writing produced events rather than just script – in *The Third Policeman* writing tells the story but produces no script that the narrator can retain. Furthermore, the narrator tells his story in the past tense, and therefore from a point of knowledge somewhere in the future. The narrator does not remember each cycle, and so on each occasion he enters the barracks as if for the first time. But each time he tells his story, in the past tense, from a point in the future. The narrator, therefore, must write his story at a point just in advance of the experience, caught in an eternal loop of repetition, but out of synchronization with the events that occur to him. The narrator has himself become a mystic writing pad – he writes on himself, but the part that writes/experiences may not read, and at the end of each (doubled) loop he forgets. Repetition is thus repeated – the experiencing and the narration – and the narrator is once again split.

Desire and the law

The narrator's desire/drive is an *arrêt de mort*, that is, a death sentence and a reprieve from death, as it is the cause of his death, but also that which enables him to survive after his murder. And while his undead living on is powered by the drive, the drive is fuelled by dissatisfaction and prohibition: by a 'no' that continually animates desire. As Žižek writes in *The Plague of Fantasies*:

> Desire emerges when drive gets caught in the cobweb of Law/prohibition, in the vicious cycle in which "*jouissance* must be refused, so that it can be reached on the inverted ladder of the Law of desire" (Lacan's definition of castration) – and fantasy is the narrative of this primordial loss, since it stages the process of this renunciation, the emergence of the Law.[68]

A repeated 'no!' of prohibition and negation resounds throughout the narrator's undead space of drive/desire, a 'no' that interrupts and perpetuates the drive: 'The father, the Name-of-the-father, sustains the structure of desire with the structure of the law'.[69] After his death and the disappearance of the black box, the first person who confronts the narrator is the man he killed, still visibly wounded from the blow, but reanimated as a robotic figure of negation whose answers are as automatic as his movements. Murder negates, and so Mathers speaks as one who is 'rejected, reneged, disagreed, refused and denied' (TP 31). The constant negation of the murder victim is both a vehement condemnation of the narrator's act and a foreshadowing of the punishing and proscribing 'no' of the policemen. But inasmuch as the law of the policemen is a twisted, corrupt law, so the negation of the victim is inconsistent in its consistency – Mathers matches a negation in the question with a negation in his answer, and thus negation is wheeled around into an affirmative. The 'no' even of the murder victim is a contaminated, corrupted and compromising negative.

When the narrator asks Mathers for the black box Mathers sharply asks him 'What is your name?' (TP 32). Shocked, the narrator realizes that he has no name: '"I have no name", I replied' (TP 33). The narrator does not simply articulate his namelessness in terms of a forgetting, he emphasizes its absence – he is now unnameable and cannot be renamed. The man he killed establishes his namelessness, and thereby the man he kills is the first to tell the narrator of his death. The narrator's lack of a name – and later of a bicycle – metonymically represent his death; he is nameless and has no bicycle because he is not an ontological essence. Mathers tells him that this namelessness, that is, the fact that he is dead, will mean that he can never possess the black box: 'Then how could I tell you where the box was if you could not sign a receipt? That would be most irregular. I might as well give it to the west wind or to the smoke from a pipe. How could you execute an important Bank document?' (TP 33). From the very beginning the narrator is told by the man he killed that he will never possess the object of his desire, but caught in the repetitions of drive and prohibition he persists and endures.

It is unsurprising that the narrator's namelessness would be supported by a de Selbian theory of naming. Arguing that the earliest names were 'crude onomatopoeic associations with the appearance of the person or object named' (TP 42, footnote), de Selby extends this to a universal theory of names, which purports to be able to categorize people into groups indexed through race, colour and temperament based on a study of the letters of his or her name. Certain groups, he argued, could not be matched with other groups. Without a name, the narrator cannot be placed into de Selby's categories and thereby has none. This further supports the fact that the narrator does not exist: not only does he not have a name, but also he has no group. And as a result, he is to be punished: '*You are going to be hung for murdering a man you did not murder and now you will be shot for not finding a tiny thing that probably does not exist at all and which in any event you did not lose*. I deserve it all, I answered, for not being here at all' (TP 117).

When the narrator meets the policemen, his namelessness not only means that his quest for the box will be infinite, but it also places him outside the law: 'If you have no name you possess nothing and you do not exist and even your trousers are not on you although they look as if they were from where I am sitting. On the other separate hand you can do what you like and the law cannot touch you' (TTP 64). But when he is about to be hanged for a murder he did and did not commit, and he protests that he is outside the law, the sergeant responds:

> "For that reason alone [the narrator's namelessness] . . . we can take you and hang the life out of you and you are not hanged at all and there is no entry to be made in the death papers. The particular death you die is not even a death (which is an inferior phenomenon at the best) only an insanitary abstraction in the backyard, a piece of negative nullity neutralized and rendered void by asphyxiation and the fracture of the spinal string. If it is not a lie to say that you have been given the final hammer behind the barrack, equally it is true to say that nothing has happened to you."
> "You mean because I have no name I cannot die and that you cannot be held answerable for death even if you kill me?"
> "That is about the size of it," said the Sergeant. (TP 105–6)

Being nameless, bicycleless and undead, the narrator is outside the law. But, as we will see with Bónapárt in the next chapter, in O'Nolan's texts being outside the law means being outside its *shelter*, not its force. He is caught within the cogs of the law as punishment and prohibition – it is there to penalize, not protect. In his undead space of wheeling drive, he is caught in the forbidding, bewildering web of an incomprehensible law. It is important to note that, unlike Trellis, the narrator never meets judges – he never enters courts of justice, corrupt or otherwise. A trial pre-supposes a concluding judgement; the narrator will never be tried, just continually restrained by the oppressive proscription of a corrupt, inexorable law. While the narrator may appear to escape – he is not hanged for the murder of Mathers – this is no more than a momentary reprieve in the midst of unending legal cycles. The decision to hang the narrator is an unlawful implementation of the law rather than a miscarriage of justice: there is neither judgement nor trial, just the punishment of an arbitrarily chosen victim in order to prove the successful operation of the law. That is, ostensibly the narrator is to be hanged simply because he is present/absent – there in 'body' if not in name. Of course, the very fact of his presence also makes him guilty: he is trapped in the law's domain because of his murderous desire for the black box. Within the space of the narrator's drive, the law is represented as an incomprehensible, false and unreasonable institution, and the narrator as an innocent party caught in its mindless exercise of its powers. But while the policemen are stereotypes of a corrupt and corpulent rural constabulary, they also possess unfathomable and indescribable knowledge whose esotericism bewilders and distresses the narrator. Despite the narrator's refusal to listen, the policemen repeatedly allude to the narrator's death, the Sergeant names him as Mathers' murderer without hesitation, they are the guardians of eternity and infinity, and they possess knowledge of shapes, colours, sounds, textures and music which defy both perception and description. When he meets Fox, the third policeman looks him in the eye, and the narrator is 'as dazzled as if [he] had accidentally glanced at the sun' (TP 192). The narrator may wish to deny it, but the law is the light that sees. It is a voice both condemning his act and preventing the cycles of the drive from ever closing, and it is a source of pained confusion for the narrator. The Sergeant and McCruiskeen steal bicycles, and money that might purchase more bicycles, in order to prevent the vicissitudes of the atomic theory from overwhelming the population. They break the law – they steal – in order to prevent the public from becoming embodiments of the drive, and yet are the personification of the denial that perpetuates the drive.

The barracks which the policemen inhabit is a flat, two-dimensional, 'completely false and unconvincing' (TP 55) construct that gains depth and aspect only as the narrator approaches. Thus, the law takes shape in and through the undead presence of the narrator, that is, the barracks is an instrument of law animated by him and for him alone: 'It was momentous and frightening; the whole morning and the whole world seemed to have no purpose at all save to frame it and give it some magnitude and position so that I could find it with my simple senses and pretend to myself that I understood it' (TP 56). His undead space is driven by the force of the desire and the force of the abjuration of that desire – all is there to frame the eternal search for the black box and the search's eternal interruption. The policemen that the narrator meets figure as motorized instruments of law and punishment; Sergeant Pluck describes MacCruiskeen as 'a walking emporium, you'd think he was on wires and worked with steam' (TP 78), while Pluck himself is even more horrifically mechanized: 'The Sergeant shook his head and tapped his forehead three times with his finger. . . . It was a booming hollow sound, slightly tinny, as if he had tapped an empty watering-can with his nail' (TP 159). But while the law is enforced by mechanical automatons, the victim is equally a construct. When the narrator first saw Mathers, he felt that his eyes 'were not genuine eyes at all but mechanical dummies animated by electricity or the like, with a tiny pinhole in the centre of the "pupil" through which the real eye gazed out secretively and with great coldness' (TP 26). Both the law and the victim are animated by the narrator himself, and when he finally meets the dread third policeman he meets a hyperbolic, obscene amalgamation of the two. Fox is neither the personification of Truth,[70] nor the 'author' of the narrator's hell,[71] nor 'the last observer in the series'[72] nor God, the devil or 'the chief agent in the punishment of the narrator'.[73] The third policeman comprises policeman and victim, requiring that the narrator face both before the cycles spin around again.

> The great fat body in the uniform did not remind me of anybody that I knew *but the face at the top of it belonged to old Mathers.* It was not as I recalled seeing it last whether in my sleep or otherwise, deathly and unchanging; it was now red and gross as if gallons of hot thick blood have been pumped into it. The cheeks were bulging out like two ruddy globes marked here and there with straggles of purple discolouration. The eyes had been charged with unnatural life and glistened like beads in the lamplight. When he answered me it was the voice of old Mathers. (TP 189)

While the narrator recognizes Mathers immediately, he doesn't recognize the large, overweight body. But it is, of course, the equally obese bodies of Pluck, MacCruiskeen and Inspector O'Corky. The first time he saw the Sergeant he is struck not only by his weight, but by an inexplicable sense of disharmony: 'a very disquieting impression of unnaturalness, amounting almost to what was horrible and monstrous' (TP 56). The third policeman comprises the gross, unnatural body of the law and the swollen face of the victim. This overdetermined form is an uncanny admixture of his crime: the victim of the offence and the punisher of the offence in one engorged, hideous form. Thus, in the house of the man he killed the narrator is forced to confront a law not merely biased towards the victim, but the law embodied in the victim. The body of the law speaks through the mouth of the victim, and the law itself dwells within the walls of the victim's house. Thus, the prohibiting law/ victim speak in unison to tell him that the black box is his, but that it has once again been moved out of reach.

In the house where Mathers' eyes seemed to gaze unnaturally at him, and Fox will later lock him in a terrifying regard, the narrator sees an uncanny, elusive light, a light that belongs nowhere in the house proper and is 'wrong, mysterious, alarming' (TP 181). The more he tries unsuccessfully to locate the source of the light, the more convinced he becomes that it is controlled by something 'unspeakably inhuman and diabolical' which is trying to lure him 'on to something still more horrible' (TP 184). This light comes from a place inside the house, and yet other to the house, as it fits in the cracks or fissures in the house's structure. In each place where it should be it is not; it is always somewhere other. It remains constantly hidden and yet visible – its light can be seen but its source cannot be found. As such, both the dark, portentous house and the shifting, elusive light can be seen to represent what Lacan refers to as the 'gaze'. Lacan writes that 'I see only from one point, but in my existence I am looked at from all sides'[74]: the subject may look at an object, but the object is already gazing at the subject, and from a point the subject cannot see. The gaze is thus 'not a seen gaze, but a gaze imagined by me in the field of the Other'.[75] The subject is always already gazed at by the Other through the object, and this constant gaze is a source of anxiety, as it reveals the lack within the Symbolic Order. As the narrator stands, staring at the dark house and the light which seems to come from nowhere, he feels gazed on by a malevolent force as the law, the victim, the big Other all focus their accusing gaze upon him. Lacan argues that '*The objet a in the field of the visible is the gaze*'[76] – the gaze threatens to undo desire through the eruption of the Real and reveal that at the heart of our desire is nothing but lack. Thus, the gaze calls attention to the lack which both causes desire and interrupts it. The shifting light represents both the inability to locate desire within the Symbolic Order and the lack/excess in desire itself; as Lacan wrote, in love and desire the object is never in the right place: '*You never look at me from the place from which I see you*'.[77] The narrator knows he is looked upon by the house of the black box, but he cannot find the gaze itself until, in desperation, he throws a stone, breaking a window – the veil masking the Other – and forcing a confrontation. And so the anonymous, uncanny gaze of the house is interrupted by the shadow of something coming to the window and 'gazing out into the night to see who had thrown the stone. Then it disappeared, making me realise for the first time what had happened and sending a new and deeper horror down upon me' (TP 186). The gaze of the Other materializes into an immediate threat, and the narrator thus meets the third policeman. Who is, like the narrator, driven mad by a box (TP 159), sleeps in the same room as the narrator – beside him as the narrator sleeps beside his soul – and interferes with eternity. The law is within the narrator, and it carries with it certain characteristics of the narrator. And as such, it is impossible to escape. Thus, the borders of the jurisdiction – the outskirts of the cycle – are protected by Fox (TP 102) who is 'always on his beat and never off it and he signs the book in the middle of the night when even a badger is asleep' (TP 67). That is, within the space of the drive/desire, the law cannot be eluded.

In *The Third Policeman*, the law's primary pre-occupation is, famously, bicycles, that is, the revolutions of the drive, and the Sergeant's atomic theory. Pluck's atomic theory, ostensibly a theory of contamination, argues that repetitive movement causes an exchange of atoms between objects.[78] An excess of cycling causes the people of the parish to become part-bicycle, and there are bicycles 'half-partaking of humanity' (TP 88). Too much walking gives you feet of clay, and the Sergeant's grandfather died being a horse in everything but 'extraneous externalities' (TP 93). Thus, the law – and the other inhabitants of the jurisdiction – is part machine, a hybrid of the wheel and the human. However, the Sergeant's atomic theory doesn't simply point to the mechanical functioning of the law, but reflects a deep sense of contamination within the narrator himself. After the narrator hears of the atomic theory, he begins to feel the wood atoms in his prosthetic limb infest his body, slowly turning him into dead lumber: 'I thought that . . . its woodeness was slowly extending throughout my whole body, a dry timber poison killing me inch by inch. Soon my brain would be changed to wood completely and I would be dead' (TP 119). Atomic theory names a contamination, as atoms of wood or metal permeate living flesh and change them. Everyone in the parish suffers from some form of impurity – they are all infected by foreign atoms, and all a composite of human and bicycle or horse or road or wood. All possess the prosthetic or the synthetic, and all are artificial constructs. Everyone, therefore, takes on a hyperbolic form of the narrator's own affliction – being part human and part other.

In Martin Finnucane we do not simply see a representation of the narrator's own feebleness but meet his powerful double. Finnucane, whose eyes the narrator cannot meet (TP 45), has the narrator's disability but none of his weakness; like the narrator he is a murderer, but a successful one, who kills to steal not money, but life itself: 'If I kill enough men there will be more life to go round and maybe then I will be able to live till I am a thousand' (TP 48). Finnuncane is 'captain of all the one-leggèd men in the country' (TP 49), who commits the same murder as the narrator, but in a bolder, braver way – with a shiny, purposeful knife rather than a simple farmer's spade – and for nothing – he does not need a black box – and everything – life itself. When the narrator is to be hanged for the murder he/Finnucane committed the narrator sends for his double to save him, and the one-leggèd men prove enough of a threat for Fox to get involved and the other policemen to take emergency action. They use their disability to trick the policeman by taking off their prosthetic limbs and tying themselves together, thereby making two men seem like one. But the one-leggèd men are defeated – we infer – by MacCruiskeen's unthinkable and unknowable coloured paint, that is, by the law wielding powers beyond the Symbolic Order. But even before the one-leggèd men are defeated the law permeates – defeats – all, as the narrator's murderous double speaks like the policemen: 'What way will you bring it about or mature its mutandum and bring it ultimately to passable factivity?' (TP 50). Not only does the law merge with the victim, but it also merges with the perpetrator. Everything in the oneiric space of the parish is touched by the voice of the law. When the powerful leader Finnucane dispenses largess to the narrator in the form of a sovereign, it is no more than a shiny penny (TP 50): all desire is produced, prevented and faked by the law.

Desire and knowledge

The narrator's namelessness is offset by his sudden acquaintance with his soul, whom he names Joe. The narrator thus becomes split in two, into a nameless physical presence and an internal soul he deems 'friendly, . . . my senior in years and . . . solely concerned with my own welfare' (TP 26). This internal voice thus acts as an older, wiser voice of conscience, whose views are regressive, conservative, parochial and sexist, and yet astute, supportive and comforting. Joe oscillates between the usefully observant – he notices that Mathers replies only in the negative, he suggests that the narrator's namelessness might save him from prosecution, offers advice for dealing with Finnucane, and observes the scaffold builder's wooden leg – and the banally repetitive – his responses to Mathers are dull and clichéd: 'This is very wholesome stuff, every word a sermon in itself. Listen very carefully. Ask him to continue' (TP 31). He is the voice of prim prudishness, not wanting to hear Mathers' sins in any detail, and deeming sexual relations in women positive only when they are dull mechanical acts: '*Of course the teacher was blameless, she did not take pleasure and did not know*' (TP 92).[79] He does, however, occasionally call attention to the narrator's murderous act – '*I suppose a smash under the chin with a heavy spade could be called a "lift"*' (TP 130) – and to the lies the narrator tells himself – 'You have no watch' (TP 115). Joe's meditations on the personal histories associated with various names show a certain dreamy inventiveness at odds with his thoughtless reactions to sin and women, but are also somewhat sarcastic condemnations of the narrator's arrogance: '*A bit overdone, perhaps, but it is only a hint of the pretensions and vanity that you inwardly permit yourself*' (TP 44).

When the narrator begins to dream that his soul is one of a series of regressive homunculi, Joe threatens to leave and makes a speech in which he argues that humanity is caught in cycles of birth and death that cause humankind to progress. Describing life through Dunne's theory of simultaneous 'presents', Joe argues that each person contains all life within him or her, that each is a part of a multitude, and that when he leaves the narrator the narrator will be nothing, as all his humanity – significance, dignity, knowledge, and appetite – will be lost. Without Joe – the contradictory voice of humanity in its strength and weaknesses, with its accumulated wisdom and prejudices – the narrator is no more than an empty husk. Without the voice of human reason – flawed, illogical and judgmental, but also intuitive, insightful and perceptive – the narrator is nothing and has nothing to leave behind. He will die and leave no legacy, as it will be as if he never existed. Inasmuch as the policemen tell him that he must have inherited his namelessness from his father – 'I was once acquainted with a tall man . . . that had no name either and you are certain to be his son and the heir to his nullity and all his nothings' (TP 59) – Joe tells the narrator that he in turn will pass on this emptiness. Both the policemen and Joe speak of a legacy of nothingness or lack, and this is precisely what the narrator fears. This is what drove him to pursue the black box, because the narrator does not desire money, but knowledge. In the hyperbolic undead space, this knowledge is represented through the omnium that the box eventually contains, but in life de Selby was the avatar of this knowledge. The narrator desired to publish the definitive book on de Selby, a magnum opus of a detailed study on a single author. In other words, the narrator desired to know all there was to know about an admittedly insane thinker. He desired to fully inhabit a field of knowledge, and be secure, finally. His parents died early, and a worker usurps his farm: for the narrator de Selby represents an intellectual home, a place he can own and control. Hence the philosopher-scientist's name de Selby: in German, which O'Nolan studied for his BA, the phrase *sich selber* means 'oneself', and *ein und dieselbe* means 'one and the same'. The master's name signifies the desire to internalize, and thereby wholly possess, knowledge. It is not simply a quest for self-knowledge, but a wish to transcend the self.

The narrator's interest in de Selby began with a theft – he got his first de Selby text by stealing it – and so begins the cycles of desire and transgression: 'perhaps it is important in the story I am going to tell to remember that it was for de Selby I committed my first serious sin. It was for him that I committed my greatest sin' (TP 9). De Selby, as the avatar of the impossible desire to wholly possess knowledge – who better than an insane philosopher and scientist to show the folly of this goal? – reveals *The Third Policeman* to be a corrupted Faust myth, in which the narrator is a debased Faust, and Divney a debauched Mephistopheles. While Faust sought knowledge, the narrator seeks knowledge *and* fame: he doesn't kill for money to research de Selby, he kills for money to publish his *de Selby Index* and be respected by the world as the definitive commentator. As Lacan puts it, *man's desire is the desire of the Other* – we desire what we think the Other desires (in us), and we desire to be recognized within the social system of the

Other. Of course, the texts he would write on de Selby would be, as everything is in the afterlife, excessive: 'I could write the most *unbelievable* commentaries on de Selby ever written and publish them in bindings *unheard* of for their luxury and durability' [emphasis added] (TP 195). While the narrator refers to de Selby throughout his afterlife and is driven by a desire to assume the follower's mantel, his commentary on de Selby contains many comments that show little respect for the thinker. Nonetheless, when the narrator finds out the power of omnium, he decides to bring 'de Selby himself back to life to converse with me at night and advise me in my sublime undertakings' (TP 196). The only thing listed after this pinnacle of desire is to make himself invisible, that is, to write himself out of the entire Symbolic Order. As is exhibited throughout *The Third Policeman*, desire is always tainted by distaste, and the narrator's wish to possess de Selby is stained by ambivalent feelings towards the man and the work. That withstanding, the infinite nature of the task of commenting on de Selby can be seen to perfectly inhabit the infinite repetitions of the narrator's afterlife. If each repetition of the drive is different, then each repetition will enable the narrator to provide different footnotes explicating different aspects of de Selby's life and work. As such, *the narrator's infinite repetitions enable him to 'live' his magnum opu*s – the differences between each repetition enable him to explicate different areas of his critical engagement. Thus, the *de Selby Index* is given through the repetitions of his undead survival – his drive infinitely (re)writes an infinite version of his book.

However, in typical O'Nolan style, the sphere of knowledge that the narrator wishes to possess is infinite, as not only is de Selby's corpus as crazed and confused as de Selby himself, much of it is missing or hotly disputed, and the secondary material forms an even more demented web. The discipline that the narrator has chosen is as infinitely regressive and expansive as MacCruiskeen's chests, and operates according to a similar, transgressive logic. And so, murdered in his attempt to publically possess de Selby via the black box, the narrator finds himself in an afterlife constructed according to de Selbian logic, that is, with little or no logic, and in which his search for knowledge is permanently interrupted by bewildering encounters with objects, places and situations that defy comprehension or explanation – that is, impossible objects of the Real.[80] So defiant of understanding is the space of the narrator's afterlife that M. Keith Booker has referred to *The Third Policeman* as a 'highly carnivalesque deflation of epistemological pretensions'.[81] Questioning never leads to clear answers – Mathers always relies in the negative, and, as the Sergeant says, 'The first beginnings of wisdom . . . is to ask questions but never to answer any' (TP 62). Both Booker and Roy Hunt understand the black box as representative of the quest for forbidden knowledge, and Hunt formulates it in terms of desire and the post-lapsarian: 'as in the traditional story of the Fall, the narrator's overwhelming desire for that which is forbidden him by law leads to his downfall'.[82] But while both understand this desire in terms of a divine punishment, Hunt in particular reads the hellish absence of an attainable or recognizable Truth as the failure of religion, rather than the breakdown of epistemology in the inferno.[83] When the narrator speculates that he is a body in an infinite series of bodies, he asks what would finally end the series: 'Who or what was the core and what monster in what world was the final uncontained colossus? God? Nothing?' (TP 123) Incapable of deciding whether these thoughts came from 'Lower Down' or 'Higher Up' (TP 123) we must, along with the narrator, remove God and judgement from the equation – as Thomas Shea writes, 'I doubt that O'Brien is even mildly interested in moral themes of crime and punishment'.[84] Hence, Hugh Kenner refers to the hell of *The Third Policeman* as 'a *comic* hell, devilless and Godless',[85] while Francis Doherty writes that the narrator's 'new world is one in which he now invents himself as well as finds himself, everything being generated from himself, from dreams, fantasies, memories, fictions'.[86] While omnium is linked to God (TP 114), *The Third Policeman* recognizes it as a force, not a divine, paternal presence.

Of course, inasmuch as the death drive involves the repetition of the same mistake and an inability to recognize and learn from repetition, the narrator's inability – refusal – to identify the repetitions of his undeath mean that while he is driven by the desire to possess knowledge – or to be known to possess knowledge – he is not in a position to learn. His lack of memory prevents him from acquiring new knowledge – he simply regurgitates the scholarship acquired in life. The narrator may be living on through the immortality of the drive, but the hellish space of the drive prevents new learning, foils familiarity and thwarts acceptance of his fate: his desire for knowledge is rift by a cyclical structure rejecting all new understanding. As such, the immortality of his drive is punishing, and like the perpetual sufferers in Tartarus, his desire is penalized by an infinite frustration of desire. But O'Brien's hellish internal space differs from Tartarus in terms of memory. The fabled offenders against the gods did not have their memories erased by Hades' waters of Lethe; they are chained by a desire stronger than frustration. They know that each time they have failed, but bound by a drive they continue to labour. However, as with the case of the narrator, memory always fails in the face of the drive – the knowledge of previous failures will never be sufficient to break the power of the drive, and they are, as such, forgotten. They are *as if forgotten*, such is the power of the drive.

Memory cannot be trusted in *The Third Policeman* as what consciousness can recall is incomplete and lacking, and the narrator 'remembers' through hints and traces: 'it reminded me forcibly, strange and foolish as it may seem, of something I did not understand and had never even seen' (TP 166). While he decides that 'the best thing to do was to be believe what [his] eyes were looking at rather than to place [his] trust in memory' (TP 27), this becomes a great strain, as what is presented to him is impossible to believe (TP 84). The absence of a memory of the repetitions of an event prevents the narrator from becoming inured to it, or even deriving pleasure from it. Camus proposes that it is the knowledge of the repetition, or, more accurately, the knowledge of the hopelessness of the task that elevates the actions of Sisyphus to tragedy:

> I see that man going back down with a heavy yet measured step toward the torment of which he will never know the end. That hour like a breathing-space which returns as surely as his suffering, that is the hour of consciousness. At each of those moments when he leaves the heights and gradually sinks toward the lairs of the gods, he is superior to his fate. He is stronger than his rock. *If this myth is tragic, that is because its hero is conscious.* [emphasis added][87]

There is no tragedy in O'Nolan's works – his heroes are both too blind and too self-involved. The narrator is no hero of perseverance and determination, and is caught not in a hell of divine punishment but in the hellishness of the death drive.

Desire and sexuality

Should we understand the narrator's infinite cycles as cycles of the drives – death drive and life drive – then the sexualized language of his afterlife can be of no surprise. In a space of Eros and Thanatos, it is inevitable that rooms are penetrated (TP 84), that men walk 'finely from the hips . . . through the afternoon, impregnating it with the smoke of [their] cigarettes' (TP 84) and that the man the narrator killed would be found in the 'crotch of a ditch' (TP 99). A bicycle is 'born' from beneath a tree as a result of Gilhaney 'feeling promiscuously' and 'inquiring into its private parts with strong hands and grunting from the efforts of his exertions' (TP 81–2). But while sex might be in the air, it should not penetrate the female: it is always masturbatory, homosexual or queer. As the narrator says, in what must be a play on 'fiddle' and onanism: '"Women I have no interest in at all", I said smiling. "A fiddle is a better thing for diversion"' (TP 50). Woman are portrayed as impediments to comfort: 'a skinny wife in the craw of a cold bed in springtime' (TP 78), and even what seems soft in them is hard, as when the feel of a woman's back is broken down into its parts 'Half of the inside of the smoothness is as rough as a bullock's hips (TP 144). Sexual encounters are considered impure: MacCruiskeen fears to ruin the purity of the chests by putting letters from Bridie in them, as not only are they written by a woman, they had 'hot bits in them' (TP 73). Rape is mentioned casually: we are told that de Selby's nephew raped a Swedish maid and that de Selby had to pay a large settlement to avoid a court case. No moral judgement is given, merely the fact that based on de Selby's theory of names the nephew should have never touched the woman (TP 42, note).

The narrator's mother in particular is described with violence and pointed implication. While the narrator claims to know nothing of his father other than the fact that he was a 'strong man' who talked about Parnell – a man ruined by his relationship with a woman, Katherine O'Shea[88] – his perfect remembrance (TP 7) of his mother leads to little more information. She is described as no more than a woman with a face which 'was always red and sore-looking from bending at the fire' (TP 7) who made tea, sang songs, had a cat she ignored and owned a public house. But behind this insubstantiality there is a hint of something sordid in his mother's dealings with the pub's customers: 'it is possible that things happened differently with my mother and with the customers late at night' (TP 7). When his parents leave – die – the men from the funeral home describe him as a 'poor misfortunate little bastard' (TP 8), perhaps merely through a tendency to swear, perhaps to indicate promiscuity in his mother. Either way, their relationship is described in the same way as his relationship with Divney: queer. The term 'queer' is a complicated one in O'Nolan – while queer can imply homosexuality, in Ireland the term tends to more generally refer to someone odd, peculiar, who doesn't respond well to social situations – the narrator, with his bookish withdrawal and wooden leg, would have been 'queer', regardless of his apparent sexuality. In fact, in Michael O'Sullivan's biography of Brendan Behan, who did claim to have homosexual encounters, he defines 'queer' as 'a man who prefers women to drink'![89] While homosexuality does play a part in *The Third Policeman*, it is important to note that the term 'queer' does not directly or unequivocally signify non-'normative' sexual relationships.

The bicycle in *The Third Policeman* can be understood as the manifestation of the drive, of a libidinal energy and force, and as such is a highly sexualized object. Even before the narrator's famous bicycle sex scene, atomic theory causes inanimate objects to become filled with libidinal energy, and in the case of the bicycles, this is manifested in lasciviousness in the male bicycle and the unspeakable in the female bicycle: 'there are other things connected with ladies and ladies' bicycles that I will mention to you separately some time. But the man-charged bicycle is a phenomenon of great charm and intensity and a very dangerous article' (TP 90). As a result of their driving libidos, the bicycles must be locked up: 'I always keep it [the Sergeant's bicycle] in solitary confinement when I am not riding it to make sure it is not leading a personal life inimical to my own inimitability' (TP 101). There is also a hint that the sexual activity that the Sergeant engages in is itself somewhat Sadean: the cell where the bicycle is kept contains 'a mass of peculiar brass and leather articles not unlike ornamental horse harness but clearly intended for some wholly different office' (TP 173).[90] Riding a bicycle becomes not a masturbatory action – autoeroticism is rarely condemned in O'Nolan's texts – but a sexual one involving two partners of greater or lesser degrees of humanity. The sexual act of riding a bicycle becomes problematic only when bicycles are shared between genders, and unspeakably depraved only in the case of the woman. Thus, when Gilhaney takes the new female schoolteacher's bicycle out to the 'lonely countryside' (TP 92) his action is casually dismissed as immoral. But when the schoolteacher then has to take Gilhaney's Joe says '*I have never heard of anything so shameless and abandoned. Of course the teacher was blameless, she did not take pleasure and did not know*' (TP 92). Male coupling with a female bicycle cannot be condoned, but female coupling with a male bicycle is horrifying, excusable only as long as the woman was not aroused. In the case of the female, the drive must be outside the pleasure principle.

De Selby was, we are told, unable to distinguish between men and women, that is, he presumed that all women were men and that women, therefore, simply did not exist. This is used by one of his commentators to suggest 'dark' sexual proclivities, presumably, homosexuality:

Du Garbandier . . . has seized on this pathetic shortcoming to outstep, not the prudent limits of scientific commentary but all known horizons of human decency. Taking advantage of the laxity of French law in dealing with doubtful or obscene matter, he produced a pamphlet masquerading as a scientific treatise on sexual idiosyncrasy in which de Selby is arraigned by name as the most abandoned of all human monsters. (TP 174 note)

Similarly, his narcolepsy was also used by the fiendish du Gardandier to create sly insinuations about sexual activities in public toilets: when de Selby fell asleep in a lavatory a court case ensued, and his commentators used the incident to assail 'the savant's moral character in terms which, however intemperate, admit of no ambiguity' (TP 173 note). Homosexuality takes an ambiguous position in O'Nolan's texts – when overtly referred to it becomes problematic, immoral and illegal, but when smuggled in it becomes a viable – indeed, preferable – replacement for women. This can be seen in the position of women in relation to atomic transfer in bicycles. Barbery and his wife share what is knowingly referred to as a criss-cross bicycle, which, possessing male and female human atoms, becomes 'a very confused bicycle' (TP 161). But, pointedly, the bicycle's confusion stems not from its composite gender, but the fact that not even its male particles can desire Mrs Barbery: 'if you ever laid your eye on big Mrs Barbary I would not require to explain this thing privately to you at all' (TP 161). Mixed atoms are problematic only when (unattractive) female atoms contaminate the graft – same sex mixing causes no comment. O'Feersa, we are told, is only twenty-three per cent bicycle, as he shares his bicycle with his brothers, which means that the bicycle absorbs atoms from all three brothers, and that each ride taken on the bike has an incestuous quality. It also means that the atoms that the brothers absorb must contain parts of each brother. Incest and homosexuality is quietly inserted without condemnation, while sex with an overweight woman loudly proclaimed to be obscene.

The infamous bicycle sex scene begins when the narrator is wooed by the Sergeant's bicycle, and determinedly ignoring 'the sturdy cross-bar' (TP 177) describes her as 'ineffably female and fastidious' (TP 177). The longer the narrator stares at the bicycle, the more transfixed he becomes, running his hands 'sensuously' (TP 177) over the saddle and giving her human body parts – a 'rear thigh' (TP 178). He formulates her femininity in terms of passivity and submission; she crouches 'submissively' (TP 177), beckoning him to lend his 'mastery' (TP 177), and reflects his emotions: 'Both of us were afraid of the same Sergeant, both were awaiting .... both were thinking ... and both knew ...' (TP 178). When they move off into the night he feels her 'agile sympathy' (TP 179) beneath him as she accommodates 'her left pedal patiently to the awkward working of [his] wooden leg' (TP 179). With his genitals on her face – 'inexplicably it [the saddle] reminded me of a face' (TP 177) – and his phallic prosthesis on her pedal she finally 'shuddered beneath me awkwardly. . . . Feeling I had been inconsiderate I jumped quickly from the saddle to relieve her' (TP 180). The ride ends with the bicycle shuddering in orgasm, or, perhaps more in keeping with O'Nolan's apparent attitudes to women's pleasure, shuddering bearing his.

As Andrea Bobotis establishes, this ride is complicated by the fact that the narrator refuses to recognize the masculinity of the bicycle and the fact that it contains the Sergeant's atoms – it is, after all, the Sergeant's bike. Thus, the act is neither a heterosexual act, nor a straightforward homosexual one. The act that marks the end of the cycle is a queer one, that is, it moves between genders as the male is forced to ostensibly cross-dress in order to assuage the narrator's fears regarding his desire. As Bobotis argues, in dressing the bicycle up as a stereotypically submissive female, misogyny is used to traffic the feminine between the narrator and the Sergeant as a 'mere placeholder for their own desire'.[91] However, Bobotis also contends that the suppression of the masculinity of the bicycle enacts a positive transgression of stable gender categories in an 'erotic cross-dressing, in which both 'actual' and 'imagined' genders are both (in)significant'.[92] As redeeming as this reading may be, it is difficult not to read the narrator's designation of the bicycle's gender as anything but the suppression of a homosexual encounter – the narrator does not move beyond stable identity politics, but attempts to disguise the identities involved. The narrator is not aroused by a man dressed as a woman, but is aroused by a man whom he feels obliged to hide behind a feminine guise.

In 1955, Myles combined the themes of bicycles and cross-dressing in a *Cruiskeen Lawn* article entitled 'Bicyclicism'.[93] Proposing that a bicycle has a 'personality and a private life', he notes that the gender of a bicycle is important, as female bicycles possess an 'ineffable otherness'. Men trying to ride female bicycles become 'self-conscious and . . . engaged in obscure manoeuvres', and one man who took a female bicycle into 'the country for a spin . . . came back intoxicated'. Bicycles also possess the ability, we learn, to change gender, as when a man finds a female bicycle left in the place of his male one, it is not, Myles argues, a case of theft, but of 'dread gynandromorphism' – the 'horrifying' act of becoming female. This shift of gender is performed in Hugh Leonard's stage version of *The Dalkey Archive*, which closes not only with the end of the world, but with the complete physical transformation of Sgt. Fottrell into a bicycle. O'Nolan initially disagreed with the idea, as it was 'contrary to the theory and theology of bicogenesis',[94] as the Sergeant only rides his bicycle once in the play and a sufficient transfer of atoms could not occur. But he eventually acknowledged that it was 'truly very funny',[95] based on the fact that Sgt. Fottrell's transmogrification involved a gender change, as he comes out as a bicycle from behind a door marked MNÁ, that is, the women's toilets. Given that Leonard can't have read *The Third Policeman*, this addition is remarkably prescient, especially as the Sergeant's bicycle in *The Dalkey Archive* is possessed of a study high crossbar to slap for emphasis (DA 47).

Cross-dressing and gender confusion abound in the letters that O'Nolan wrote to the *Irish Times* while he was writing *The Third*

Policeman. In one pseudonymic series, it is proposed that all the leading modernist authors were Irish, and that Joseph Conrad was female, as her real name was Josephine Cumisky from Galway:

> Cool, slim and unhurried, this lissom slip of a girl had the sea in her blood . . . Little by little she acquired proficiency in the argot of the sea, and soon she was as foul-mouthed as the lowest stevedore that ever battened a hatch. . . . A strong growth of superfluous hair beneath her lower lip . . . helped to make the deception possible.[96]

As Conrad she sailed the world and met Georges [sic] Sand. Sand, the pseudonym of Amantine Lucile Dupin, is famous not only for her novels and affairs with various musicians, authors and intellectuals, but for her forays into men's clothing. Thus, O'Nolan, writing as Lir O'Connor, has Conrad, whom he refers to as female, marry George Sand, whom he designates male. Lir's sister, Luna, enters the fray and claims that O'Nolan – Flann O'Brien – is a woman. She writes that she was not deceived

> by Miss O'Brien's delicious fooling when she alluded to herself as a stuffy old gentleman. Call it intuition, if you will, but from the very outset I detected in F.O.B's letters the sentiments and emotions of a woman like myself, weak, foolish and human. I often wonder what she is like. Is she a middle-aged lady novelist, with the usual military moustache, or is she a "bright young thing" with shingled skirts and all the trappings of Miss 1940?[97]

While O'Nolan's interest in cross-dressing and gender confusion may consider itself 'naïve' humour which simply reinforces normative gender boundaries – aping the other gender is considered 'innocently' funny because the transgressing of a category boundary produces a humorous incongruence – the proliferation of instances of gender ambiguity speaks more to a pre-occupation in O'Nolan regarding the meaning of orientation and identity. The fundamental reason for this interest is only speculatively available, and linked to a potentially complex weave of desire and repression; suffice to say that the attention paid by O'Nolan should not be dismissed.

The narrator's use of gender-specific pronouns relating to the bicycle almost occludes the fact that the sexual scene takes place between the narrator and an object, regardless of its gender. We can presume from the fact that the Sergeant has been able to stand still in the novel that he has not surpassed the 50th percentile in human-bicycle atomic exchange, and so when the narrator rides the bicycle he engages in a sexual act with an object that is part-man and part-machine. An uncanny admixture of the male, the female and the machine, the narrator's final ride ends with a shudder and a quick dismount. If we see the bicycle in general as representing the drive, this bicycle represents the confusion of the drives, and the undecidability between Eros and Thanatos. The bicycle is male and female, human and machine, sex and death. It represents eroticism and the libido, but also the death drive, as it is cyclical and repetitive – it *is* always about a bicycle – and an instrument of death, as a bicycle pump was used in the Mathers' murder. This excess of gender identity and sexual desire is symptomatic of the death drive, as it refuses identity, and is, Lee Edelman writes, queer.[98]

We end the cycle of the policemen's beat – policemen/law obsessed with bicycles/drive – with a shuddering orgasm, that is, a *petite mort*, or little death. The cycle of the death drive – Thanatos – ends with an act of coupling – Eros – with the avatar of the drive(s) itself – the bicycle. If we treat the barracks as the main body of the drive, on this repetition Mather's and the narrator's houses are the point of the join between the loops. On the cycle narrated in *The Third Policeman,* the narrator's entrance to the barracks is marked by waking up with his double, and his exit by a consummation with a polyvalent bicycle. The bicycle accompanies him to his house, but is gone when he leaves it. It belongs to a completed cycle, and while it was able to cross the frame of Mather's house, it cannot enter the new cycle. Importantly, as he gets off the bike at his old house he feels 'happy and fulfilled' (TP 201) – the black box is full of omnium and has been sent to his house by 'express bicycle' (TP 194), and he has consummated a union – *temporary* closure – of the drives with another bicycle. This loop draws to a close, and we approach a new beginning.

While the narrator kills in order to publish his book, Divney kills for love, that is, in order to marry Pegeen Meers. But in O'Nolan's texts, love is usually presented as a euphemism for lust, and Divney's desire is deemed the base actions of a man incapable of sublimating

sexual energy into a nobler end. When the narrator sees Divney
again he sees that both he and Pegeen Meers have suffered from
desire – she has 'grown old, very fat and very grey. Looking at her
sideways I could see she was with child' (TP 201). The narrator's
initial description of Pegeen as obese receives no amendment when
he sees she is pregnant: whether Pegeen is pregnant, or fat and
pregnant, for the narrator she is still an embodiment of the obscenity
of female fecundity, a fertility which has an equally deteriorating
effect on Divney: 'He had grown enormously fat and his brown hair
was gone, leaving him quite bald. His strong face had collapsed to
jowls of hanging fat' (TP 201).

Much has been made of the narrator's relationship with Divney –
their 'queer' inseparability, and sharing of a bed: 'I slept with him
always after that. We were friendly and smiled at each other but
the situation was a queer one and neither of us liked it' (TP 13).
The queer – strange, peculiar, odd or of non-'normative' gender/
sexuality – *jouissance* that the narrator gets from his association
with Divney led him to bring Divney into the next cycle of the
drive, and Divney's dissolution into an old, fat, bald, drunk,
harassed husband is the narrator's revenge for Divney's sexual
betrayal – his relationship with Pegeen – and murderous act. If we
presume that the cycles of repetition are infinite loops of the drive,
then we must presume that all events remain within the cycles. The
narrator's visit to his old home is not a haunting, but the illusion
of a haunting, and no more 'real' than anything else. When Divney
tells the narrator that he has been dead for sixteen years, and that
Divney killed him, the narrator is told no more than what the
narrator is, on some level, already aware. The narrator leaves in
a dramatic storm – 'Black angry clouds were piling in the west,
bulging and glutted, ready to vomit down their corruption and
drown the dreary world in it' (TP 203–4) – in which he feels empty,
erased of memory and concern. Then he comes to the barracks,
stops, waits for Divney, and then enters with him to once again
meet the Sergeant for the first time. On this cycle he brings Divney
into the barracks with him because he desires the pleasure/pain of
Divney's company. Because he desires Divney, the man who killed
him, and yet the man whose 'strong face' he would give 'everything
[he] had in the world and every cashbox in it' to see (TP 190).
Because, after all, 'even if I [the narrator] did own everything, he
owned me' (TP 11).

The narrator's feelings for Divney are complex, and as multi-layered as the bicycle with whom he has the novel's only obviously erotic scene. Having replaced the constant companionship of Divney in life with the constant companionship of Joe in the afterlife, the narrator never invests a queer element in his relationship with Joe until he dreams that Joe becomes embodied and lies beside him. In a dream in which the narrator feels that he dissolves until he is broken down into the 'strange uncounted essences of terrestrial and spiritual existence', that is, 'a flux of colour, smell, recollection, *desire*' [emphasis added] (TP 121), Joe begins to take shape. Joe becomes external to him, and lies beside him as Divney would have done. And suddenly, given a physical, external form, Joe becomes monstrous and untouchable: 'I kept my hands carefully at my sides in case I should accidentally touch him. I felt, for no reason, that his diminutive body would be horrible to the human touch – scaly or slimy like an eel or with a repelling roughness like a cat's tongue' (TP 121). The pleasure of human contact becomes obscene and mirrors the description of eternity when the narrator speculates on using the omnium to torture the policemen. While women are throughout maligned as dangerous, their danger is a common one. The queer relationships that the narrator has with the men in his life are better but also worse – their jouissance is stronger. The narrator may know what he desires, but that desire also scares him. When the physical 'reality' of his sexual preference is made clear, it very quickly becomes dark.

Two years after *The Third Policeman* was written Heath Edwards of the Gate Theatre asked O'Nolan if he would write an Irish version of Karel and Josef Čapec's *The Insect Play*. O'Nolan sets the Čapecs' drama of Czech post-war disillusionment in contemporary, Emergency Ireland, and renames it *Rhapsody in Stephen's Green* (1943). The first act is noteworthy for O'Nolan's alteration from Čapec's heterosexual, promiscuous, precocious butterflies – 'None of my lovers was the first'[99] – to homoerotic, discontented bees; thereby, with the exception of the brief appearance of the Queen, writing women out of the act. Cyril and Cecil are bees disillusioned and alienated by a life of constant drudgery that offers only the 'choice between the sensuous delight of stinging with the rather charming death that follows, or keeping oneself . . . you know . . . chaste and alive in the hope of meeting the Queen' (RS 30–1). While this act contains one of O'Nolan's few instances of clearly expressed heterosexual desire, it is clear that the longing for orgasmic death throes is far greater than the simple orgasm involved in sexual union with the Queen. But the pleasure of stinging is not simply the release of death, but the thanatic/erotic jouissance of homosexual penetration – in each instance the suicidal sting is embedded in a male. The lure of this sex/death is far greater than the hope of meeting the Queen: 'When a bee is young and healthy and bulging with honey, he simply can't help himself. Stinging may be immoral but really I am sure it must be very nice. Matter of fact, I think I'll soon do a spot of stinging myself' (RS 30).

The first instance occurs when a *very young and agile bee rushes in, beside himself with hysteria and delight* and dies screaming 'I've done it! I've done it! Oooooooooh! . . . I stung a man, I stung a man! I stung him, I tell you! Oooooooooooooh!' (RS 31). The fatal act is seen as inappropriate for one so young – 'I say, he is rather a rotter to be doing that at his age' (RS 31) – not because it is suicidal but because it partakes of 'Unnatural deeds' (RS 31). Overcome with the frustration of saving themselves for the queen and the vulgarity of work, Cyril and Cecil decide to forgo chastity and die with 'just one glorious . . . marvellous . . . sting' (RS 33). To ensure that they die together, they decide not simply to sting a man but each other, and thus they stab each other in a parody of anal penetration: *'They turn back to back suddenly and bump their bums together'* (RS 34). They die in a *'frenzied prancing'* (RS 34) of delight/agony. Left with no companion other than an old, somnolent drone whose only contributions have been barren quotations from Shakespeare, the Queen realizes that her aloofness has destroyed the hive, and she commits suicide by stinging a man, although her act, heterosexual instead of homosexual, offers her no erotic relief. The stage notes for her death are a simple *'she dies after a brief and noisy paroxysm'* (RS 37). O'Brien took the insincere love affairs of heterosexual butterflies and replaced them with genuine desire whose homosexual focus leads to death. A homosexuality whose contamination of Eros and Thanatos brings about death is presented as clearly preferable to heterosexual sex.

Notes

1   BON to William Saroyan 14 February 1940.
2   CL 22 December 1950.

3 So much so that the introduction to Nicholas Royle's *The Uncanny* ((Manchester: Manchester University Press, 2003), 1–2) reads like a description of *The Third Policeman*.

4 Sean Homer, Jacques Lacan (London: Routledge, 2005), 71.

5 That is, without a way to control drives. And when he does find a bicycle, that control is lost in a sexualized, libidinal space.

6 See, for example, Sigmund Freud, 'The Unconscious'. In *The Standard Edition of the Complete Psychological Works of Sigmund Freud* XIV. Ed. and trans James Strachey (London: Vintage, 2001), 186–7.

7 Lacan, *The Four Fundamental Concepts of Psychoanalysis: The Seminars of Jacques Lacan Book XI*, trans. Alan Sheridan (New York: W. W. Norton, 1998), 75.

8 Lacan, *Fundamental Concepts*, 131.

9 CL 19 April 1961.

10 CL 29 August 1949.

11 Sheridan, 40.

12 Jacques Lacan, 'Aristotle's Dream', trans. Lorenzo Chiesa. *Angelaki: Journal of the Theoretical Humanities* 11.3 (2006): 83.

13 Sigmund Freud, 'Beyond the Pleasure Principle'. In *The Standard Edition of the Complete Psychological Works of Sigmund Freud* XVIII. Ed. and trans. James Strachey, in collaboration with Anna Freud, assisted by Alix Strachey and Alan Tyson. (London: Vintage, 2001), 18.

14 Freud, Beyond, 19.

15 Ibid., 22.

16 Slavoj Žižek, *The Sublime Object of Ideology* (London: Verso, 1989), xxvii.

17 Sigmund Freud, 'The Ego and the Id'. In *The Standard Edition of the Complete Psychological Works of Sigmund Freud XIX*. Ed. and trans. James Strachey (London: Vintage, 2001), 40.

18 Freud, Ego & Id, 40.

19 Freud, Beyond, 40–1.

20 Freud, Ego & Id, 40.

21 Ibid., 42.

22 Sigmund Freud 'New Introductory Lectures on Psychoanalysis'. In *The Standard Edition of the Complete Psychological Works of Sigmund Freud XXII,* trans by James Strachey (London: Vintage, 2001), 106–7.

23 Freud, Beyond, 42.

24 Ibid., 36.

25 Ibid.

26 Slavoj Žižek, *The Parallax View* (Cambridge MA: The MIT Press, 2006), 62.

27 Žižek, *Parallax*, 62.

28 Ibid., 63.

29 Slavoj Žižek, *The Plague of Fantasies* (London: Verso, 2008), 41.

30 Lacan, Fundamental, 167.

31 Žižek, *Parallax*, 62.

32 Lacan, *Fundamental*, 243.

33 Žižek, *Sublime*, 69.

34 Lacan, *Fundamental*, 154.

35 Ibid., 168.

36 Bruce Fink, *The Lacanian Subject: Between Language and Jouissance* (Princeton: Princeton University Press, 1995), xiii.

37 Lacan, Fundamental Concepts, 186.

38 Slavoj Žižek, *Enjoy Your Symptom!: Jacques Lacan in Hollywood and Out* (London: Routledge, 2008), 56.

39 Žižek, Plague, 53.

40 In Francis Doherty's 'Flann O'Brien's Existential Hell', Doherty notes that Mathers's name is a combination of mother and father, and that in killing his neighbour he has killed a representative of his parents (*The Canadian Journal of Irish Studies* 15.2: (1989) 57). As tempting as a reading of Oedipal murders and phallic symbols (bicycle pumps) might be, this essay does not attempt to psychoanalyse either the narrator nor O'Nolan nor the text itself, but reads *The Third Policeman* through the structures of drive and desire posited by Freud and Lacan.

41 Slavoj Žižek, 'Surplus-Enjoyment Between the Sublime and the Trash.' *Lacanian Ink* 15 (1999): 100.

42 For more on boxes and their danger in *The Third Policeman* see Robert W. Maslen, 'Flann O'Brien's Bombshells: *At Swim-Two-Birds* and *The Third Policeman*'. *New Hibernia Review* 10.4 (2006): 99–101

43 Shelly Brivic, '*The Third Policeman* as Lacanian Deity: O'Brien's Critique of Language and Subjectivity'. New Hibernia Review/Iris Éireannach Nua 16:2 (2012): 123.

44 Slavoj Žižek, 'In His Bold Gaze My Ruin Is Writ Large'. In *Everything You Always Wanted to Know About Lacan (But Were Afraid to Ask Hitchcock)*. Ed. Slavoj Žižek (London: Verso, 1992), 228.

45 Žižek, *Plague*, 40.

46 Slavoj Žižek, *The Ticklish Subject: The Absent Centre of Political Ontology* (London: Verso, 2000), 294.

47 Žižek, *Ticklish*, 304.

48 Sigmund Freud, 'Thoughts for the Times on War and Death'. In *The Standard Edition of the Complete Psychological Works of Sigmund Freud* XIV. Ed. and trans. James Strachey (London: Vintage, 2001), 296.

49 Adrian Johnston, 'Life Terminable and Interminable: The Undead and the Afterlife of the Afterlife – A Friendly Disagreement with Martin Hägglund'. *CR: The New Centennial Review* 9.1 (2009): 175.

50 Sigmund Freud, 'The Interpretation of Dreams, Part 2'. In *The Standard Edition of the Complete Psychological Works of Sigmund Freud* V. Ed. and trans. James Strachey (London: Vintage, 2001), 577.

51 Freud, 'Unconscious', 187.

52 Jacques Derrida, 'Freud and the Scene of Writing'. In *Writing and Difference*, trans. Alan Bass (London: Routledge, 2001), 269–70.

53 21 September 1962. Dunne's 1929 text is also used in a terrible Keats and Chapman pun. Keats meets Dunne, a man who likes his food, and invites him for dinner. Dunne is horrified to be served a mess of green herbs and asks Keats what is going on. '"An experiment with thyme", Keats said.' (CL 21 May 1943).

54 J. W. Dunne, *An Experiment with Time* (London: A. & C. Black, 1929), 54.

55 Dunne, 54.

56 Ibid., 151.

57 Ibid.

58 Ibid., 208.

59 Dunne 207. This directly relates to the narrator's dream.

60 CL 11 March 1957.

61 BON to TOK, 21 September 1962, SIUC.

62 Mary O'Toole's essay, 'The Theory of Serialism in *The Third Policeman*' (Irish University Review 18.2 (1988): 215–25) offers a good exegesis of Dunne and makes useful connections between Dunne's and de Selby's theories.

63 Adrian Johnston, *Time Driven: Metapsychology and the Splitting of the Drive* (Evanston, IL: Northwestern University Press, 2005), 296–7.

64 Johnston, *Time Driven*, 326–7.

65 Aristotle, *Physics*, ed. and trans. Hippocrates G. Apostle (London: Indiana University Press, 1969) 239b30–1.

66 Ibid., *Physics*, 239b6–7.

67 Blanchot, *Infinite Conversation*, 395.

68 Žižek, *Plague*, 43.

69 Lacan, *Fundamental Concepts*, 34.

70 Booker, *Menippean Satire*, 48.

71 Hopper, *Portrait*, 114.

72 O'Toole, 219.

73 Clissmann, 178.

74 Lacan, *Fundamental Concepts*, 72.

75 Ibid., 84.

76 Ibid., 105.

77 Ibid., 103.

78 Much has been written on atomic theory in *The Third Policeman*, and it has been understood primarily in terms of O'Brien's engagement with Einstein's theories on the interchangeability of mass and energy (Booker, *Flann*, 56, Doherty, 61). For an extended reading of *The Third Policeman* in relation to relativity see Charles Kemnitz, 'Beyond the Zone of Middle Dimensions: A Relativistic Reading of *The Third Policeman*'. *Irish University Review* 15.1 (1985): 56–72.

79 It is interesting to note that even O'Nolan disliked Joe and wrote in a letter to Pat Duggan that he intended 'to kill completely a certain repulsive and obtrusive character called Joe'. (7 September 1940 SIUC).

80 There are obvious repetitions and similarities between the narrator's exegetical remarks on de Selby and the content of his afterlife, as it is read through his desire to absorb the author. Thus, de Selby's description of a house as a ' "a large coffin", "a warren", and "a box" ' (TP 22) is realized in Mather's house, which is the narrator's coffin and a warren containing Fox's small police burrow. De Selby describes the Celtic ability to read roads, and we see that Fox has this skill. His theories on the direction of roads are repeated in the policemen's theories that the left is easier than the right (TP 158). His theories of names highlight the namelessness of the narrator. His thesis that journeys are hallucinations is echoed in the fact that the narrator's journey is not physically occurring, and that repetition

disallows movement. His theory that freedom lies above is echoed in the tale of the man who disappears in a hot air balloon, while his water-box is, like MacCruiskeen's chests, 'the most delicate and fragile instrument ever made by human hands' (TP 149). His theory of time writes itself into the temporal confusion of the afterlife, and his other stranger theories lead to the general unreason that characterizes the afterlife.

81   Booker *Menippean Satire,* 47.

82   Roy L. Hunt, 'Hell Goes Round and Round: Flann O'Brien'. *The Canadian Journal of Irish Studies* 14.2 (1989): 66.

83   This is in clear contrast to Clissmann's reading, which proposes that O'Nolan believed that 'order, pattern and harmony . . . are inherent in man's world even if the sophistries of philosophy seek to convince him that they are not. The emotional stress of the book lies always in the evocation of nature and in the belief that it is this kind of perception which defines what is best in man' (180).

84   Thomas F. Shea, *Flann O'Brien's Exorbitant Novels* (Lewisburg: Bucknell University Press, 1992), 120.

85   Hugh Kenner, *A Colder Eye: The Modern Irish Writers* (Baltimore: The John Hopkins University Press, 1983), 258.

86   Doherty, 58.

87   Camus, 108–9.

88   That is, politically ruined by an excessive Church response to his relationship with a woman separated from her husband.

89   Diarmaid Ferriter, *Occasions of Sin: Sex and Society in Modern Ireland* (London: Profile Books, 2009), 226.

90   It is hard not to read 'orifice' here.

91   Andrea Bobotis 'Queering Knowledge in Flann O'Brien's *The Third Policeman*'. *Irish University Review* 32.2 (2002): 248.

92   Bobotis, 250.

93   CL 29 October 1955.

94   BON to Hugh Leonard (hereafter HL) 14 November 1964, SIUC.

95   BON to HL 11 August 1965, SIUC.

96   Lir O'Connor, Letter, *Irish Times,* 12 June 1940.

97   Luna O'Connor, Letter, *Irish Times,* 19 June 1940.

98   Lee Edelman, *No Future: Queer Theory and the Death Drive* (Durham, N.C.: Duke University Press, 2004).

99   Čapec, Josef and Karel, *R. U. R and The Insect Play.* Trans. Paul Selver (Oxford: Oxford University Press, 1961), 124.

3

Ireland on trial

Tragi-farcical repetitions

As Karl Marx famously wrote, 'Hegel observes somewhere that all the great events and characters of world history occur twice . . . . He forgot to add: the first time as high tragedy, the second time as low farce'.[1] Marx argues that although history repeats itself, it does so through difference, showing a decline from the nobly pathetic to the basely ridiculous. While the collapse of the French regime, starting with the revolution of 1789, was *tragic*, as it was the disintegration of an established world order in the face of an emergent political system, the fall of the German *ancien régime* in the 1830s and 1840s was *farcical*, as it was

> an anachronism, a flagrant contradiction of universally accepted axioms [that] only imagines that it still believes in itself and asks the world to share in its fantasy. . . . The modern *ancien régime* is . . . the *clown* of a world order whose *real heroes* are dead.[2]

The farcical, anachronistic event that apes the potentiality, rhetoric and self-belief of its tragic precursor can be used as a heuristic for the picture of post-independence Ireland that O'Nolan presents. While the Irish political situation and the discourse of the Celtic Revival is a system rather than event, Marx's formula of bathetic mimesis evokes a country imagining commitment, imitating procedure and mimicking heroisms – the absurdist Ireland O'Nolan targeted in *An Béal Bocht* and *Cruiskeen Lawn*. De Valera's infamous 1943 St Patrick's Day speech typifies this picture of an Ireland out of time with itself and with the world; an Ireland of saints and scholars, of a spiritual, frugal people untroubled by material desires, a country whose future was an idealized, romanticized version of its past. But the past that de Valera wished to return to, and the Ireland of the Abbey Theatre and the Gaelic league never existed: neither the temperate past of innocence and noble poverty, nor the cheeky, divil-may-care Irish roguery were anything more than fictions created for political, ideological or theatrical ends. 'Playing up to the foreigner, putting up the witty celtic act, doing the erratic but lovable playboy, pretending to be morose and obsessed and thoughtful'[3] were all acts of compliant make-believe. The *Cruiskeen Lawn* articles returned frequently to what O'Nolan deemed to be 'the sham, self-delusion and evil pretences'[4] of romantic Ireland, and in February 1943 Myles neatly pre-empts de Valera's speech, describing the Irish as

> A humble community of persons drawn together in our daily round of uncomplicated agricultural tasks by the strongest traditional ties, closely woven on a diminutive leprechaun's loom, five and six a go and no coupons required. Our conversation – gay, warm, and essentially clean – is confined to the charming harmless occurrences of every-day life (and *not*, of course, every-night life, that undesirable Parisian phenomenon). The wild and morbid degeneracy of the outer world does not concern us (save, if you like, to provide mute evidence of the distinction between the Irish race and all others).[5]

This simulacrum, this 'farrago of childish pretences, ignorant opinions and plain lies'[6] is not only, O'Nolan argues, adopted from the stereotypes preceding or separate to an experienced past, but is created to mask an anxiety about the absence of any 'authentic' Irish heritage and culture:

> we are all Irish and we are in the parlour. Sweet Rosie O'Grady is pulling bottles of stout for us in the scullery. Mother Machree is in the kitchen knitting woollen shamrocks. Bould Phelim Brady is in the attic tearing the lungs out of his harp. The Colleen Bawn is below in the cellar.[7]

In mockery of the creation of a single ancestry and identity, Myles sends an expedition from the Royal Myles na gCopaleen Institute of Archaeology to 'the most remote Gaeltacht area in Ireland or anywhere else',[8] Corca Dorcha – which he anglicizes as Corkadorky – and finds the Corkadorky man, who not only predates all other homo sapiens, but in fact forged those archaeological discoveries, as he 'practiced the queer inverted craft of devising posterity's antiques'.[9] This 6000 BC forger, who had an unusually long right index finger – he tended to put things on the long finger[10] – was 'an Ice Age fly-boy and the progenitor of the present indefeasible Irish nation'.[11] Thus, the first Irish man was an indolent counterfeiter, a literati troublemaker. In attempting to repeat a past that never was, and becoming a version of itself that existed only in fiction, Ireland moves beyond bathetic mimesis to suffocating cycles of repetition, as recurrence is seen not to be a single replicated event but a tendency. This is not simply to comment on the inauthenticity of national identity or the fabrication of a history, but to establish that for O'Nolan, Ireland is and was predicated on fakes, copies, farce and anachronisms. While an 'authentic' foundational event – self-generating, present to itself, and singularly responding to the specifics of a historical moment – might not ever exist, for O'Nolan Ireland's political process and revivalist-based identity undid any concept of an Irish origin or Irish event not *a priori* locked in an originary repetition.[12]

Beginning with repetition, Blanchot maintains, places us within cycles of the unrelenting, the monotonous:

> what if the farce is in its turn repeated?. . . . What if what has been said one time not only does not cease to be said but always recommences, and not only recommences but also imposes upon us the idea that nothing has ever truly begun, having from the beginning begun by beginning again – thereby destroying the myth of the initial or the original, to which we remain unreflectively subject – and tying speech to the neutral movement of what has neither beginning nor end: the incessant, the interminable?[13]

For O'Nolan, we begin in the midst of a cycle of rain, potatoes, hardship and lamentation, we begin with the stage Irishman, who represents and repeats a stereotype that never existed, and we begin with adaptations and translations. In so beginning, we 'originate' with anachrony and farce, but this does not imply the absence of tragedy. Rather, the tragic and the farcical become indistinguishable: we 'begin' with a repetition that is tragically farcical, and farcically tragic. All does not simply disintegrate into a post-modern meaningless pastiche; the tragedy is the absence of the 'originary' step. Thus, the farcical cycles of poverty and lamentation, the imposed and perpetuated anachronisms of Irish, the insincerity, the ridiculousness, the inappropriate, become (also) tragic. In beginning with repetition, we dissolve the distinction between the farcical and the tragic, and thus we find, as Nell says in *Endgame*, that 'Nothing is funnier than unhappiness';[14] as Beckett wrote in a letter to Roger Blin, that 'nothing is more grotesque than the tragic',[15] or as Myles says, in throwaway style, that 'there is not a whole lot of difference between comedy and tragedy'.[16] In the works of Beckett and O'Nolan, the tragi-comic or tragi-farcical repetitions are wholly contaminated. As Eagleton explains:

> Tragedy is too highbrow, portentous a term for the deflation and debunker of Beckett's work. His farce and bathos may spell the ruin of hope, but they also undercut the terrorism of noble ideals, maintaining a pact with ordinariness which is a negative version of solidarity. They represent the grisly underside of the carnivalesque.[17]

The 'grisly underside of the carnivalesque' is precisely what O'Nolan has in common with Beckett; the physicality, the absurdity, and the excessiveness of the tragic farce. As Michael Booth writes, nineteenth-century farce proffered a world where the subject put 'the ingenuity of his own insanity against the massive blows of hostile coincidence and a seemingly remorseless fate'.[18] Farce is absurdist, harsh, often physical, a Marx Brothers romp of exorbitance: a tragic farce sees the unceasing repetition of the same fate, the same injustices, the same inanities. In beginning with repetition, in beginning with laughter and tears, we thus begin with *An Béal Bocht*.

An Béal Bocht is a *reductio ad absurdum* of Irish life, a carnivalesque stretching of tendencies, difficulties and prejudices to histrionic, hyperbolic conclusions. This it does by repeating, *in absurdum*, the straight representations – repetitions – of life on the west coast of Ireland found in Tomás Ó Criomhthainn's *An tOileánach* and Peig Sayers's *Peig*, as well as harshly critiquing – through repetition – the Irish peasant as insular and foolish, or

as a European 'noble savage', found in the works of the likes of
Yeats, Synge and Gregory. O'Nolan's respect for Ó Criomhthainn's
novel in particular is well documented, as is his passionate fury
at the figure of the stage Irishman. Both, however, become objects
of parody, both become part of Ireland's tragi-farcical repetitions;
repetitions of what never (wholly) was. The supposedly mimetic
and realist works of these writers represent and 'repeat' that which
never existed, offering a formulaic version of Ireland that is, Myles
argues, dangerously self-creating, as the Irish public themselves
began to repeat the repetitions, *becoming* Synge's falsehoods:

> when the counterfeit bauble began to be admired outside Ireland
> by reason of its oddity and "charm" ... [we], who knew the whole
> inside-outs of it, preferred to accept the ignorant valuations of
> outsiders on things Irish. And now the curse has come upon us,
> because I have personally met in the streets of Ireland persons
> who are clearly out of Synge's plays. They talk and dress like
> that, and damn the drink they'll swally but the mug of porter in
> the long nights after Samhain.[19]

This sense of repeating what never was, with the added danger
of *becoming* an incessant repetition, is excessively portrayed in
An Béal Bocht, in which characters live as hyperbolic fictions of
fictions. They live as characters from the good books, with Peadar
Ó Laoghaire, Synge, Yeats and Gregory as the writers of the gospels;
books which do not (simply) describe but *prescribe*, whose repetitive
descriptions of the way to live determine the mode of repetition of
life. The peasants in *An Béal Bocht* repeat books because they lack
the agency to change their lives, and they lack agency because the
books they repeat contain characters caged by their circumstances.
Thus, with perfect compliance, they sit, again and again, '*ag plé
cúrsaí an drochshaoil agus ag eadarchamánú an bhochtordaithe a
bhí, agus a bheadh feasta, ar Éirinn*' (AB 78).[20] Repeated as refrain
or chorus throughout the text are versions of the phrase 'our likes
shall be never seen again'.[21] While in isolation this phrase speaks of
a mode of existence on the brink of extinction, such is its excessive
reiteration that repetitions of the phrase – and the way of life – seem
infinite. Such is the passivity of the people, such is their unfailing,
unchanging mode of accepting their life that the words meant to
herald the end serve to make the end (seem) impossible. The endless

litany of expressions of finitude serves to render them infinite, and the cycle of poverty and punishment wholly unending. Thus, we find an apocalyptic sense of being the last line of a race on the brink of destruction mixed with an equally calamitous sense that this way of life will never end, that the indigence and the misery and the rain will go on and on and on.

Similarly, the novel's epigraph – 'Má caitear cloch níl aon réamhinsint ar an bhfód tíre don cloch sin' – indicates the farcical repetitions of fate and the inescapability of a destiny tied irrevocably to the restricting Irish language. The phrase, which masquerades as a *seanfhocal* or proverb, contains all the elements of a mock rural mysticism, the facile parading as the profound. The adage posits that all should be left up to fate, that futures are aleatory and open, and that life is beyond human control. And yet it prefaces a text whose lesson is precisely that we *do* have foreknowledge, because for the Gaels of Corca Dorcha we know exactly where the stone will land. It will land in precisely the same place as it always landed, though its like will be never seen again. It will land, and stay, on the edge of a mountain, although a perfectly good spot for building a house is right below. It will land, and stay, in a place of rain and hunger and poverty. It will land, and stay, in a place where all there is to fill mouths are sweet words of Irish. Satirizing the (country) wisdom that induces passivity, Myles thus prefaces *An Béal Bocht* with a fake proverb outlining the ways in which submissiveness and compliance are perpetuated; through repeated, inherited slogans whose danger is precisely their vague falsity.

While Blanchot, analysing Constant's *Adolphe*, wrote that 'repetition . . . makes monotony the principle of an extraordinary march towards catastrophe',[22] for the inhabitants of Corca Dorcha repetition makes monotony the principle of an endless shuffle towards an infinitely delayed extinction. There can be no tragic end, just tragi-farcical repetition. Hence, as Blanchot writes – and how can we not hear in this quotation the fatigue of the inhabitants of Corca Dorcha? – '*I do not really speak, I repeat, and weariness is repetition, a wearing away of every beginning*'.[23] The repetition of phrases by Bónapárt and the other inhabitants of the Gaeltacht robs of them of active speech; they recite their life in tired formulas that infinitely repeat, without beginning and therefore without ending. It thus denies all involved – speakers of Irish, speakers of English, the impoverished peasants in the Gaeltacht, the *daoine uaisle* outside it, the *Gaeilgeoirí*, the Gaelic Leaguers, the government, authors, poets and playwrights – any access to sincere, ethical, uninvolved tragedy. Instead, realities and fictions intertwine, and tragedy and farce become conjoined in harsh, almost nihilistic parody.

In keeping with a novelistic mode of tragic farce, in *An Béal Bocht* characters are caricatures and are expected to live as such. Thus, the phrase '*i mo thachrán ag imeacht faoin ngríosaigh*' (AB 13)[24] is taken literally. The Captain – whose story is told by Ferdinand in the Rosses with the loquacious delivery of modern Irish storytelling, and by Maeldoon with the repetitive Middle Irish bardic style – the Ultonian Jams O'Donnell and Bónapárt all live in houses built according to the same narrative formula: in the corner of the glen on the right-hand side as you go eastwards along the road.[25] Bónapárt, who is also Jams O'Donnell, is also addressed by the Ultonian Jams O'Donnell as 'Captain', and becomes a trinity of characters. All dwell in the same (kind of) house, all are the same (kind of) person. Individual identities are irrelevant before the overriding narrative structures and fates. The courtship of Nábla - Mabel - takes place, as the old books describe, in the middle of the night, and the marriage negotiations that took place between the Seanduine and Bónapárt are glossed over, because, we are told, they simply repeat the contents of the books. The Ultonian Jams O'Donnell is evidently '*Ultach de réir mar tá luaite sna dea-leabhair*' (AB 55)[26]: he recites the Lay of Victories, walks three steps of mercy and throws a tongs in the Seanduine and Bonapart's wake. In every cabin in the Rosses, there is a man called 'An Cearrbhach' - 'the Gambler' - who spends his days drinking and smoking, an old man ready to stick his feet in the fire and tell stories of the bad old days, and a pretty young girl called 'Nuala' or 'Babby' or 'Mabel' or 'Rosie' for whose hand men would come in the middle of the night. Should one wish to clarify these facts, one goes not to the Rosses but to the library, where the good books outline the destiny of the Irish, a destiny that is '*cinniúna liteartha*' (AB 58).[27] While in the Rosses – each 'Ross' as delightful as the other, each repeating the other in yellow sun and blue stream and brown bog, all reminiscent of the repetitions and fictions of *The Third Policeman* – the Seanduine and Bónapárt are able to hunt freely because, each evening, as outlined in the good books, the fishermen are in difficulties on the water and the women are on the beach lamenting their fate. The day may have been fine, the hill overlooking the sea untroubled by inclement weather, but on the shore the waves were high and the storm/story violent. In parodying the paucity of the skill of the writers of the good books, Myles presents a literary space so deliberately ill-constructed that the cracks are blatant. The generic, fictionalized status of the characters in *An Béal Bocht* can thus be thought of as performance of the theory of character borrowing outlined in *At Swim-Two-Birds*. Characters from the Gaeltacht autobiographies and the works of Synge, Yeats and Gregory are recycled, relocated to the wet fields of Corca Dorcha, and in its hyperbolic fictive space they play excessive, overwritten versions of themselves.[28]

The farcical repetition of great Irish myths is found again in *An Béal Bocht*, although the voyager Maoldún plays a smaller role than Fionn MacCumhaill both in Myles's text and in Irish cultural knowledge. But, as is the case in *At Swim-Two-Birds*, the great Irish hero is rewritten as a debased version of himself; the story the Seanduine tells is one of selfishness and theft, a tragi-farcical repetition of a Celtic romance and epic voyage viewed through the lens of the embattled and embittered country poor. According to his account of the tale, many years ago a great flood descended upon Corca Dorcha, and Maoldún was the only one who knew how to build a boat. And thus, like Noah, he built one, and survived the flood, but unlike Noah he did not save family members or animals, but used his boat to steal from the houses of the drowned. The Seanduine thus rewrites the tale to bring the hero in line with his own sense of self; as a storyteller, the Seanduine repeats his own life within each narrative, and Maoldún becomes the greedy, devious Noah the Seanduine would have been.

The original text, or texts, of *Immram (Curaig) Máel Dúin* – The Voyage of (the boat of) Maeldoon/Maildun (Patrick Weston Joyce)/ Máel Dúin (Whitely Stokes)/Maoldún (O'Nolan) differs radically from this, although the story does begin with violence. Máel Dúin's father, Ailill Ochair Ága, was killed soon after raping a nun while on a raid, and when Máel Dúin was born, he was given to the queen to raise as her own. Unlike the impoverished and physically unimpressive inhabitants of Corca Dorcha, Máel Dúin was very beautiful and talented at all manner of sports. It was this talent that caused a jealous youth to inform him that his parentage was unknown, which led Máel Dúin to find his birth mother and begin a voyage to avenge his father's death. But while a druid gave him exact instructions on what day to begin building his boat, what day to sail, and the exact number of men to take with him, Máel Dúin had to ignore these instructions when his foster brothers insisted upon joining them. This inauspicious start led them to drift from island to island for three years and seven months, encountering giants and monsters, beautiful women, magical animals, strange lands and miraculous foods. In the end, Máel Dúin and his crew return home, and following an encounter with a reformed thief turned hermit, are wise enough not to kill the murderers of Máel Dúin's father, but to love and respect life.

The beautiful, noble adventurer Máel Dúin is rewritten as the avaricious, self-interested pirate Maoldún, who in the great flood takes to his ship neither to avenge nor to save, but to steal from those who can no longer resist.[29] He ends his days drinking whiskey by the fire, an alcohol-preserved wretch. As the Seanduine says, '*más fírinneach inchreidte a bhfuil againn i gCorca Dhorcha de sheoda seanchais agus de bhéaloideas béal dorias ár sean agus ár sinsear*' (AB 93),[30] then he and his loot remain in Hungerstack. And because the stories tell it, then in Corca Dorcha it is so, but in repeating the old stories they are changed, and epic quests become ignoble robberies. The destiny of noble Irish heroes in O'Nolan's texts is to devolve into mumbling, dishonourable storytellers; in *At Swim-Two-Birds* the great warrior Fionn MacCumhaill is a rapist and an incessant reciter of old lays, and while Maoldún retreats to a hermit-like cell, its stark, religious austerity is undone by the presence of his stolen loot and an unending supply of whiskey. Importantly, he is awoken not by the theft of his gold, nor by Bónapárt's taunting or rock throwing, but by the word *story*. While the English translation simply gives Bónapárt's words as 'He has nothing to say' (PM 109), the Irish contains the far more telling '*Níl aon scéal aige*' (AB 100) – 'he doesn't have any story/news'. It is on hearing this word – *story* – that Maoldún awakes and replies in Middle Irish '*Ocus gá scél is ail duid?*' (AB 100), 'and what story would please you?' Bónapárt is too scared to reply, so Maoldún begins to settle himself in the way of the *seanachaí*: '*ag iarraidh é féin a shocrú ar a shuíochán cloiche, an dá spág á sá i dtreo na tine agus an sceadamán á réiteach chun seanchais*' (AB 100).[31] Maoldún proceeds to tell, in Middle Irish, exactly the same story as was told by Ferdinand, and thus represents what Ireland has become: a farcical, degraded repetition of itself, where heroes are now old tellers of tales; greedy, covetous and wholly unprincipled.

The tragic, farcical repetitions of fiction and fate are not, however, simply a harsh parody of representations of the Irish speaker, but a cutting depiction of the exclusion of Irish from the law, education and progress. The supposed impossibility of discussing the war in Irish, as it lacked the appropriate terminology, was the focus of the very first, bilingual *Cruiskeen Lawn* column, in which a child demands to know the Irish for 'Molotoff Bread-Basket'. This section concentrates on a scene of linguistic exclusion that is itself almost excluded from the text, so brief is its mention: Bónapárt's trial. The prosecution of Bónapárt Ó Cúnasa is undoubtedly unethical – he is tried and convicted in a court proceedings conducted in a language foreign to him. In *An Béal Bocht,* Irish is other to the law, and its speakers must bow to the decrees of a legal system wholly beyond their understanding. Justice, supposedly outside of language, theoretically wholly translatable and universal, is in this case absolutely anglophile and anglophone. Hence, in this short scene O'Nolan performs the sentiments written in the unpublished 'The Pathology of Revivalism': Irish is a 'prison of a language'.[32] For the English speaker there is the law, but for the Irish speaker there is only prison, only the restriction of a language other to justice and right. And compounding the exclusion of the Irish language from the law is the use of Bónapárt Ó Cúnasa's other name: Jams O'Donnell.

Over the course of *An Béal Bocht,* the question 'Phwat is yer nam?' is put to Bónapárt Ó Cúnasa three times. The first time, when he also learns the answer, occurs at school, as a bloody and violent event of rebirth as renaming. The second time transpires when the Seanduine wishes to fool an inspector into giving the family money, and so Bónapárt, to prove he can speak English, answers the question with the rote response: 'Jams O'Donnell'. The third time heralds the beginning of Bónapárt's 29-year jail sentence and is accompanied by a policeman's firm hold on his arm. The name Jams O'Donnell is thus associated with violence, trickery and arrest. But even more problematically, not only is Jams O'Donnell the name given to Bónapárt within an English-language context, it is the name given to *every* male Irish-speaking peasant operating within that context.

Bare life

Giorgio Agamben writes on the Greek division between *zoē* and *bios*, whereby the former designates simple, natural life – 'the simple fact of living common to all living beings' – and the latter a particular way of life – 'the form or way of life proper to an individual or group'.[33] *Bios* exists within the political realm, while 'simple natural life is excluded from the *polis* in the strict sense, and remains confined – as merely reproductive life – to the sphere of the *oikos,* "home"'.[34] In Ancient Greek society, natural life was relegated to the domestic, a private space separate from but still included within the public *polis*, and thus we find the inclusion, through exclusion, of *zoē*, and the foundation of Western politics on a complex relation between exclusion and inclusion.

While Aristotle may speak of *zōon politikon* – the political animal – it is in order to stress that the human, whose political and philosophical ability is paramount, is also an animal or, as Foucault explicates, 'a living animal with the additional capacity for a political existence'.[35] But while the living body of the subject was traditionally considered private and domestic, and as such excluded from the political, within the modern era, argues Foucault, 'man is an animal whose politics places his existence as a living being in question'.[36] In other words, the modern era is the period of the *biopolitical*, in which

> Power would no longer be dealing simply with legal subjects over whom the ultimate dominion was death, but with living beings, and the mastery it would be able to exercise over them would have to be applied at the level of life itself; it was the taking charge of life, more than the threat of death, that gave power its access even to the body.[37]

While sovereign power was the right to deal death, that is, 'the right to *take* life or to *let* live',[38] this 'ancient right' was 'replaced by a power to *foster* life or *disallow* it to the point of death',[39] or, as Agamben paraphrases it, the power to '*to make live and let die*'.[40] Biopower or biopolitics transforms the political body into a biological body, and an obsessive focus on the body, birth rates, life expectancies, health and so on becomes a point of control. Thus, *zoē* is politically foregrounded, and one's world is framed by one's physical or biological existence. This contamination of *zoē* and *bios* leads to what is referred to as *bare life*, as what is created 'is neither an animal life nor a human life, but only a life that is separated and excluded from itself – only a *bare life*'.[41]

Agamben equates bare life with *homo sacer* (sacred man), a curious figure in Roman law who '*may be killed and yet not sacrificed*'.[42] If one kills the sacred man one is not punished for murder or manslaughter, and yet the death will not have been a ritual sacrifice. One may kill without contamination and without committing sacrilege. The *homo sacer* is, therefore, outside both human and divine law, or, more accurately, included within the law as an exclusion, as he is neither executed under the normal functioning of the law nor sacrificed to the gods. The life of the *homo sacer* is thus a '*life exposed to death*'[43]: bare life. As bare life the sacred man lives a 'life devoid of value', a 'life unworthy of being lived'.[44] Neither *zoē* nor *bios* but a blighted and debased amalgamation of the two, bare life is 'a threshold of indistinction and of passage between animal and man'[45] – 'the slave, the barbarian, and the foreigner, as *figures of an animal in human form*' [emphasis added].[46] Bare life is linked by Agamben to Carl Schmitt's *state of exception*, that is, a period when the normal functioning of law is suspended in a time of emergency. Thus, for Agamben, the Nazi concentration camps exemplify the state of exception, and the inmates there the bare lives exposed to death. *Homo sacer*, or the bare life, is, therefore, a mode of political subjectification by dint of objectification: it is made an object of the cessation of the law in a space where distinctions between law and order, reason and chaos, innocence and guilt become meaningless. Different periods have given us bare life under different names: Jew, Palestinian, gypsy, homosexual, refugee, detainee; those who were 'lacking almost all the rights and expectations that we customarily attribute to human existence, and yet were still biologically alive, [who] came to be situated in a limit zone between life and death, inside and outside, in which they were not longer anything but bare life'.[47] Bare life names those who are designated anthropomorphous animals, human vermin whose lack of rights, lack of political place, lack of means of expression, and lack of a fully formed language 'prove' the legitimacy of the supposedly unconditional rights of 'real' citizens.

In 'The Indigent Sublime: Spectres of Irish Hunger', David Lloyd describes the victims of the Irish famine as bare life, whose extreme suffering, poverty, and sheer numbers caused the famine to be an 'excess of lack',[48] and those who starved to be the limit or threshold of the human. The famine victims

> pose the spectacle and the question as to the minimal limit of the human – the material, rather than the legal and political state of exception in which the bare human appears. Simultaneously, and with the relentless force of a surplus and redundant population, these "poor bare fork'd animals" reveal the deep connection between the rightless, politically unrepresented status of bare life and the process of a primitive accumulation that denies the dispossessed even the right to subsistence.[49]

Contemporary depictions of the victims likened them to spectres and animals, and 'The excessive spectacle of these starving bodies forces the viewer to the very threshold of humanity, to the sill that divides the human and the nonhuman, or, rather, the boundary that marks the division *between the human and the nonhuman within the human*' [emphasis added].[50]

The great hunger is a daily presence to those on O'Nolan's version of the West coast. The famine is referred to in Irish as *An Gorta Mór* (The Great Hunger) or *An Drochshaol* (lit: The Bad Life, The Hard Times).[51] The subtitle of *An Béal Bocht*, which Power translated as '*A bad story about the hard life*', reads in Irish as '*Drochscéal ar an drochshaol*' – a bad story about the bad life or *a bad story about the famine*. At the feis people die due to the '*tuirse na bpléaráca agus an gorta fíor Ghaelach a bhí riamh againn*' (AB 50).[52] The 'fear of *gort*' is omnipresent; as Bónapárt and Máirtín and the Seanduine sit and discuss *an drochshaoil* (the hard life, the famine) they address the '*ganntanas prátaí*' (AB 78)[53] that never goes away, no matter how good the year's crop. But while Bónapárt's weak and unhealthy frame can be likened to depictions of those suffering from malnutrition, it is in the body of Sitric Ó Sánasa that the bare life of the famine victims is most clearly portrayed. The '*iomad na hocrachta a bhí breactha ina aghaidh*' (AB 77-78)[54] exceeded everyone else, and he was

> *sleá ard fir a bhí chomh caol ag an ocras go dteipfeadh ar do shúil é a shonrú dá mbeadh sé ina sheasamh cliathánach leat. Bhí a chuma air go raibh sé baoth aerach, gan aon deariar ar na*

cosa aige de thairbhe na meisce a fuair sé as aer na maidine. Tar éis scaithimh ina sheasamh dó thit sé anuas na chnap laige ar an talamh. (AB 79)[55]

Sitric says he has nothing in front of him '*ach an síorchlábhar, an fliuchras agus an glasghorta*' (AB 81);[56] he eats turf to try to stay alive but that just makes him ill. In the West coast the famine never left, both in the tragic reality of the poverty of the people and in their farcical inability to escape the fear of cycles of lack. The responsibility for this farce is not, of course, theirs alone – although no one, in O'Nolan's texts, is ever wholly innocent – but primarily that of the English speakers who perpetuate a Gaeltacht trapped in the past.

Hovering on the line between human and animal, Sitric is described as often seen '*ag troid is ag coraíocht le madra fánach, cnámh coal cruaidh eatharthu mar dhuais san iomaíocht, an tsrannfach agus amhastrach chonfach chéanna ag teacht uathu araon*' (AB 78).[57] He lives in a hole in the ground – where passing strangers presumed him to be a badger – which he eventually exchanges for a cave in the sea. There he lives as a seal, cannibalistically consuming seal flesh. While the famine saw a people dehumanized by hunger and the control of an external power, in post-independence Ireland we see a country anthropophagously preying on itself; for Sitric the only escape from being consumed by a system to which he does and does not belong is to place himself at the head of an equally cannibalistic economy. The visiting gentleman who breaks Sitric's water bottle because 'spile *sé an* effect' (AB 77)[58] sees in Sitric nothing but bare life, a living statue representing the horrors of the past, whose poverty inspires little more than armchair reflections of history's inequalities. Sitric thus farcically and tragically represents bare life that is succumbing to the ontological embodiment of the category, becoming the drowned 'Muselmann' of the Gaeltacht.

While the empty eyes, the emaciated bodies, and the apathetic slouch of the body suffering extreme malnutrition makes the famine victims bare life 'whose death had begun before that of their body',[59] Lloyd sees their life exposed to death as a *material* rather than *legal* or *political* state of exception. That is, he sees the state of exception as one produced by a natural disaster rather than an active governmental policy, and the Irish bare life because their hunger demoted them, not a political or ideological strategy. But in presuming this, Lloyd fails to ask an important question: what occurs when bare life is created through a state of exception formed not by the suspension of the law, but by a policy of upholding, with minor exceptions, the normal ruling of the law, *at precisely the time when suspension is required*? In other words, the material cause of the famine, the potato blight, required political response in the form of the active creation of a mode of a state of exception, and yet none arose. What we have in the case of the famine is thus not the active creation of a state of exception by the cessation of the normal functioning of the law, but the resolute perpetuation of the usual treatment of Ireland, which turned the country into a zone of indistinction. As Cormac Ó Gráda writes:

> The Irish famine relief effort was constrained less by poverty than by ideology and public opinion. Too much was expected of the Irish themselves, including Irish landlords. Too much was blamed on their dishonesty and laziness. Too much time was lost on the public works as the main vehicle of relief. . . . Too many people in high places believed that this was a time when, as *The Times* put it, "something like harshness is the greatest humanity."[60]

Proving this very ideology, Thomas Carlyle wrote, just before the famine, that 'The time has come when the Irish population must either be improved a little, or else exterminated. . . . In a state of perennial ultra-savage famine, in the midst of civilisation, they cannot continue'.[61] As an article in *The Economist* argued in 1847, 'To convert a period of distress, arising from natural causes, into one of unusual comfort and ease, by the interference of government money, or of private charity, is to paralyse the efforts of the people themselves'.[62] In a continuation of this philosophy, the state of exception in Ireland was passively created, not by doing *nothing* but *not enough*, and the walking dead were the result of a state of emergency that was *insufficiently different from the normal running of the country*. This is not to suggest that the British government denied the existence of the famine, nor that they refused to instigate policies of relief, nor to conflate the policies of Sir Robert Peel and Lord John Russell, but to propose that the assistance offered was an ideological and political continuation of pre-existing harsh treatment of an impoverished nation.[63] Insufficient funds were allocated, the starving were made to labour for wholly inadequate wages,[64] workhouses were expressly designed to be only a slighter better option that death, grain, livestock, butter exports continued,[65] and evictions still took place when rent could not be paid.[66] In 1847, Sir William Gregory – Lady Gregory's husband – introduced what is known as the Gregory clause into the Poor Law legislation, which stipulated that any family that had more than a quarter of an acre of land could not be granted any relief until they gave up their land – a convenient way to introduce land clearance.[67] Much could be gained from the famine by the British government, the British and Irish landlords, and by a certain class of Catholic farmers. In fact, David Nally argues that the famine was used to continue a project of radical biopolitical control begun with the Irish Poor Law of 1838. The Great Famine, and the Poor Law that preceded it, enabled the British government to take absolute biocontrol of what they, through 'racialized notions of poverty and biological understandings of overpopulation', had turned into bare life.[68] Ireland was turned into a zone of indistinction, a country as camp where state power was organized and implemented through discipline, objectification and biopolitical control. The creation of a state of exclusion through inaction is precisely what occurs in Bónapárt's trial, although the situation is a complex one. The states of exception that were the concentration camps were a site of ethnic cleansing, where the 'purity' of the German race could be secured by the removal of lesser, bare life. In *An Béal Bocht*, however, the state of exception that is the Gaeltacht is a site of an inferior people, but an inferior people who prove the racial purity of the Irish not by being removed, but by being that purity itself. They are not the excluded *impure* that prove by *comparison* the purity of the general populace, but the excluded *pure* that prove by *association* the purity of the general populace. They are bare life because they are antiquated, inferior relics of the past, but that past proves the 'Irishness' of a rapidly changing country.

Bare life, language and the people

The division between *zoē* and *bios* is described by Aristotle and Agamben in terms of the difference between voice and language.

All life has a voice, but only *bios* has language, and so, as Aristotle writes,

> language is for manifesting the fitting and the unfitting and the just and the unjust. To have the sensation of the good and the bad and of the just and the unjust is what is proper to men as opposed to other living beings, and the community of these things makes dwelling and the city.[69]

Language manifests justice, and to use language is to be fully human. Without it, one is not of the law and of the city but of the wild, barbaric outside. The term 'barbarous' comes from the Greek, meaning one who does not know how to speak: the savage or the barbarian is one whose language is not considered civilized or cultured. As bare life, straddling the divide between the human and that which is heterogeneous to the human, one does not speak, or, rather, one speaks in a barbaric, improper tongue, making the noise of animals. To refuse to recognize the legality of a language is to refuse to recognize the humanity of the speaker.

Throughout *An Béal Bocht,* the position of the Irish language is problematized. While it is a human language that fills mouths with sweet words – although English is noted to be better protection against the difficulties of life (AB 40, PM 48) – it is also confused with the grunting of pigs. The ethnographer who comes to Corca Dorcha joyfully records the words of Bónapárt's pig because, as Bónapárt explains, '*Thuig sé go mbíonn an dea-Ghaelige deacair agus an Gaelige is fear beagnach dothuigthe*' (AB 36).[70] An inhuman language, it is spoken by those indistinguishable from animals. If these people who speak Irish resemble pigs, and the language they speak confused with the grunting of pigs, how can it truly be a language at all, but simply the sounds, spoken by one on the border between animal and human? And how then can Irish and the Irish speaker ever be given the full rights of *bios*, legally, politically and socially? The Irish become animals under the law, bare life proving the full rights of the other. They are *zōon*, but not *zōon politikon.*

The use of a pig to represent Ireland was a common theme in late nineteenth- and early twentieth-century weekly comics such as *Punch*, *Fun* and *Judy*: 'The pig represented Ireland's status as an agricultural, rustic and backward nation, as well as the Irish peasantry's supposed indifference to filth and muck'.[71] But if for Joyce Ireland is the old sow that eats her farrow, for Myles Irish is, for those who do not speak it, the language of pigs. And the emblematic pig of *An Béal Bocht*? Ambrós. Ambrós was the runt of the litter, and because he was too weak to fight for a place at his mother's teat, he was fed cow's milk by hand by the Seanduine. Weak and unnatural, Ambrós became excessive; huge, and possessed of a smell defying oral and written description. Swollen, unresponsive, the pig rotted from the inside, becoming a living corpse. His stench nearly killed Bónapárt's mother, and in the end, hesitant to slit his throat, they allow a neighbour to block the windows and doors so that he suffocates on his own odour. Reading Ambrós as an allegorical representation of the Irish language, we understand it as a language rotting from within, harmed by and harming those who would seek to protect it, detrimentally insulated from the life that would enable it to live properly. A living-dead language speaking through the rotting horror of the undead tongue, in the end it asphyxiates itself. Thus, Myles presents a complex – and noisome – contamination between the treatment the Irish language received by those who wished to protect it, and those who saw it as an anachronistic remnant of poverty and insularity.

Against, or in addition to, the representation of Irish as the 'pig-language' and Irish speakers as ignorant animals dwelling in squalor and filth are 'the baby-brained dawnburst brigade who are ignorant of everything',[72] that is, the *Gaeilgeoirí*, English speakers who chose to learn and preserve the bestial tongue. O'Nolan's attitude to the *Gaeilgeoirí* is rarely positive: 'It is common knowledge that certain categories of Irish speakers are boors. They (being men) have nun's faces, wear bicycle clips continuously, talk in Irish only about *ceist na teangan* [the question of the language] and have undue confidence in Irish dancing as a general national prophylactic'.[73] But what is clear in *An Béal Bocht* is that while the *Gaeilgeoirí* are academically interested in the Irish language, and theoretically devoted to preserving a way of life, this language and life are literary inventions valued over the actual poverty and suffering of their objects of study. They come as pseudo-linguists with a mild anthropological bent, determined to have the accuracy of the good books proven, their preconceived notions of picturesque poverty reinforced, and their sense of being members of a noble lineage secured. Thus, the death of the Gaels is irrelevant before the importance of long speeches at the feis, the thirst of Sitric unimportant before the visual aesthetics of his poverty, and the possibility of the death of Irish impossible as '*Nee doy lom goh vwill un fukal sin 'meath' eg un Ahur Padur*' (AB 42).[74] The *Gaeilgeoirí* view the inhabitants of the Gaeltachts as bare life, and as such the language spoken in the Gaeltacht is an animal language, a dead language, a fossil spoken by the walking dead. A language spoken by bare life cannot be a living, human language, and a dead language is one in which '*it is impossible to assign the position of a subject*'.[75]

Such is the treatment of the Irish speakers that Bónapárt is eventually called to question not simply his own identity, but his very humanity, asking the Seanduine: '*An bhfuilir cinnte . . . gur daoine na Gaeil?*' (AB 90).[76] Unsurprisingly, his grandfather is unable to confirm the inclusion of the Irish speakers in the category of the human; he knows they are simply alive, but what manner of life it is, and what rights they have are unknown to him. Hence '"*Tá an t-ainm sin amuigh orthu, a uaislín," ar seisean, "ach ní fritheadh deimhniú riamh air. Ní capaill ná cearca sinn, ní rónta ná taibhsí, agus ar a shon sin is inchreidte gur daoine sinn*"' (AB 90).[77] The inhabitants of Corca Dorcha are bare life, living/dying half animals with none of the privileges and defences of humanity. As bare life they are not human, but a sub-class, a group of undesirables, and their inferiority is reflected in the deeply racist overtones of the name *Corca Dorcha* itself. According to P. W. Joyce's work on Irish place names, *corc* and *corca* mean race or progeny,[78] and while *dorcha* is usually translated as 'dark', according to Dinneen it also means 'hidden, secret, mysterious, shy, distant, malignant, blind'. Hence, Corca Dorcha means secret race, malignant race, blind race, but most importantly, *dark race*, or dark progeny. While in 'Corca Dorcha' one hears overtones of Mary Shelley's 'hideous progeny', a deliberate play on a racist slur is being made. If the Irish speakers are people, they are the dark race, the 'niggers' of Ireland, with all the overtones of racial difference, inferiority and immaturity that term implied/implies.

The trial and the proper name

On the 17th of August, 1882, the quiet Galway village of Maamtrasna saw the brutal killing of John Joyce, his wife Bridget, his mother, his daughter Margaret and his son Michael. The family were shot and beaten, and dogs ate the flesh from the arm of the dead grandmother. Of the accused – and sentenced to death – was one Myles Joyce, a man for whom the trial was incomprehensible, as he spoke no English. Joyce spent his trial with his head leaning on his arm, and when the jury returned after six minutes of deliberation and the judge declared him guilty, understood nothing.[79] When the interpreter eventually explained, he spoke of his innocence in a language that few present understood.[80] As the *Freeman's Journal* of the 20th of November 1882 wrote, "The condemned man . . . turned slowly away, and with a step, lingering and sorrowful, and a heavy sigh, with which there was an indistinct exclamation in Irish . . . he descended to the cells."[81]

While walking to his hanging Myles

> turned to every official of the jail he met, . . . and, with the fiery vehemence of the Celt, declared, in a language which nearly all those who surrounded him were strangers to, that "he was innocent. He feared not to die. But he felt the indignity of being put to death as a murderer."[82]

Even with the blindfold over his eyes Myles continued to proclaim his innocence – in Irish – but his death was treated with no more respect than his trial:

> The rope caught in the wretched man's arm, and for some seconds it was seen being jerked and tugged in the writhing of his last agony. The grim hangman cast an angry glance into the pit, and then, hissing an obscene oath at the struggling victim, sat on the beam, and kicked him into eternity.[83]

Prior to Myles's execution, two men, also due to be hanged, wrote dying confessions proclaiming both their guilt and Myles's innocence. One of the witnesses publically confessed to the Archbishop of Tuam that his testimony was false and that Myles was innocent. While this was corroborated by a further witness, the authorities refused to reopen the case. As George Trevelyan, Irish Chief Secretary from 1882 put it, cavalierly equating all involved, 'What earthly motive could we have in hanging one peasant more than another for the murder of another peasant?'[84]

What difference indeed, in executing one Jams O'Donnell or another? At issue in both the trial of Myles Joyce and the trial of Bónapárt Ó Cúnasa is the problem of language and of the proper name. For those of Trevelyan's mentality, whether Bónapárt killed the old man or not becomes irrelevant: an Irish peasant killed, so an Irish peasant must be punished. Once an Irish peasant is incarcerated, justice has been served. The enactment of a trial is sufficient to ensure that justice is done, and thus the process of law is privileged. Addressing the Maamtrasna trial in a Triestine newspaper, *Il Piccolo della Sera*, in 1907, James Joyce wrote that Myles Joyce, 'the figure of this dumbfounded old man, a remnant of a civilization not ours, deaf and dumb before his judge, is a symbol of the Irish nation at the bar of public opinion'.[85] In *An Béal Bocht,* Myles places the Gaelic League, the government, the English-speaking public and the Gaeltachts themselves before the law, in a novel whose status as farce or parody belies a vehement indictment of representations of Irish and the Irish speaker, and the dehumanizing effects this treatment produces. The Myles Joyce trial was held under British rule, and in it the Irish in general are the other necessitating an enforceable law; in the Bónapárt trial Irish *speakers* are that other. English-speaking Irish re-enact the exclusion and separation that all were subject to under British rule, filling the vacant position of excluded other with those from the Gaeltacht. While Irish as symbol of independence and individuality was constitutionally enshrined, in practice it was treated as the language of backward peasants, and Irish speakers as anachronistic, troublesome lives – bare lives – included, through exclusion, within the law. Hence, in Bónapárt's trial Bónapárt utters not one word, as the trial is conducted in a language proper to the law: in English. Bónapárt can only speak Irish, a bestial, barbaric language unrecognized by the judicial system, and he is, therefore, forced to act simply as a silent presence, a body or bare life there to satisfy the writ of *habeas corpus* but not partake or defend himself. It is at this point that the state of exception passively created in the famine is found at the trial. The law is not suspended for Bónapárt, rather, at precisely the point at which the law *should* be interrupted, and when it should acknowledge (linguistic) difference, it *absolutely and resolutely functions as normal.*

A hyperbolic portrayal of the gulf between the language of the law and the language of defendants is found in *An Cruiskeen Lawn.* In the District Court and the Cruiskeen Court of Voluntary

Jurisdiction, Myles contrasts a monoglot legal system, firmly entrenched in the English language, with polyglot defendants whose responses move easily between English, Latin, German, French and Irish. But while within *An Béal Bocht* the privileging of English over Irish is predicated on a hierarchy that sees English as the language of progress, learning and cosmopolitanism, within the *Cruiskeen Lawn* trials the use of English as the language of law reveals an utter debasement of the legal process. Judge Twinfeet, for example, calls repeatedly for the proceedings not to be confused by too much jargon, as 'justice is a simple little lady . . . not to be overmuch besmeared with base Latinities'.[86] This call does not reveal a desire for a universally accessible justice, but demonstrates the anti-intellectualism of the 'Plain People of Ireland': 'Philologo-juridical obscurantism sits ill upon the mantle of Dame Justice and will not be permitted to besmirch the fair name of this court (Laughter)'.[87] The law is entrenched in monolingualism, blind particularity, self-congratulatory inanity, and defiant homogeneity. It is relentlessly bureaucratic and obsessed with a fatuous mode of logical and linguistic 'precision': the case of a man suing a surgeon for needlessly removing his hand is thrown out, as it is revealed that the man's hand was already missing two fingers, and therefore not, according to strict definition, a hand, but a 'hand'.[88] If justice transcends the vagaries and idiosyncrasies of language, then justice is wholly absent from the cases tried by these courts; the trials are founded on a legality that realizes and recognizes itself only in the overdetermination of sign systems. Puns, spoonerisms and ambiguities are rife, and the majority of the trials concentrate on the mockery of legalese and the clichés of courtroom-reporting, on typographic jokes using inverted commas and parentheses, and on the movement between languages.

When Myles na gCopaleen himself appears before the District court on the 19th of June 1944, it is on a charge of 'begging, disorderly conduct and with being in illegal possession of an arm-chair. He was also charged with failing to register as an alien'.[89] His multilingual defence is met with hostility and suspicion, as the court fails to understand erudition, disrespects learning – he quotes from Cicero, Horace and Thomas Aquinas – fears difference and adheres to a twisted logic based in naïve word play. The courts have neither the value of being superior in learning – they do not speak Latin and demand plain, non-academic language – nor specifically designed for the needs of the Irish situation – they do not speak Irish, and the English they employ is simply an excessive copy of the old Imperial system. They are inappropriate in every way, an anachronistic, tragic farce of a justice system following outdated, inapt and inept codes. The simple suggestion to use a translation system made by an American judge present at Myles's trial is gratefully received and immediately ignored. These trials are as farcical, and as tragic, as the trial of Trellis in *At Swim-Two-Birds*, of K. in *The Trial* or of Alice in *Alice's Adventures in Wonderland*, but their excessiveness does not, by comparison, serve to prove the logic and sense of the trials of Bónapárt and Myles, but reveals the same lack of justice throughout.[90]

In depicting a law incomprehensible to the Irish speaker, O'Nolan echoes a similar event in *An tOileánach*, in which men from the island, having been forced at gunpoint to crew a man's ship, are taken to Belfast and then to court by the nefarious captain. The trial was held in English, and as in Bónapárt's and Myles' cases, they understood nothing: 'They didn't understand what was going on, and nobody understood them, for they had no English'.[91] This tale, however, had a happier conclusion, as an Irish-speaking passer-by heard of the affair, translated for them, and the villainous man was fined. Interestingly, in 1936 an instance arose in which the presiding judge refused to allow testimony given in Irish to be translated into English for the non-Irish-speaking defendant.[92] However, while instances of non-translation were more common from English to Irish, a 1929 murder case of the Attorney General versus Joyce and Walsh does establish the ethical obligation of the court to translate. In this trial, nine witnesses and both of the accused gave evidence in Irish, which was then translated by an official translator provided by the state. As Kennedy C. J. wrote,

> It would seem to me to be a requisite of natural justice, particularly in a criminal trial, that a witness should be allowed to give evidence in the language which is his or her vernacular language, whether that language be Irish or English, or any foreign language; and it would follow, if the language used should not be a language known to the members of the Court, that means of interpreting the language to the Court (Judge and jury), and also, in the case of evidence against a prisoner, that means of interpreting it to the prisoner, should be provided.[93]

Importantly, Kennedy adds that given the special position of Irish within the constitution, 'whether it be the vernacular language of a particular citizen or not, if he is competent to use the language he is entitled to do so'.[94] Native Irish speakers have therefore a 'double right' to speak in Irish, both as it is their vernacular, and as it is their constitutional right.[95] In ignoring this right, Irish speakers are doubly oppressed by a deaf legal system that to this day contains 'no statutory provision for the general right to an interpreter in Ireland for non-English or Irish speakers to date'.[96] Other than indirectly through the European Convention on Human Rights Act 2003, 'the international obligation to provide free interpretation services to those unable to understand the criminal process has never been enshrined specifically in law in Ireland'.[97]

The term 'bare life' – *la nuda vita* – stems from Benjamin's *das bloße Leben*, usually translated as *mere life*, and understood by Derrida to be 'life pure and simple, life as such'.[98] Law, argues Benjamin, is affirmed in 'the exercise of violence over life and death',[99] and in it we see a 'mythical violence' that is, a 'bloody power over mere life for its own sake'.[100] This is violence that founds a law rather than enforces it, which is arbitrary and unpredictable, which is founded in the act of transgression, and which is the privilege of the great and the powerful. As Derrida describes it, 'the mythological violence of law is exercised for its own sake (*um ihrer selbst willen*) against mere life (*das blosse Leben*), which it causes to bleed, while remaining precisely within the order of life of the living as such'.[101] The law punishes mere life, and the law is predicated on violence and force.[102] It is a lawmaking based on the capriciousness of a reactionary and tyrannical politics desperate to retain power, and is exemplified in the gods' punishment of Niobe for her pride in her children. The violent reaction of the gods 'establishes a law far more than it punishes for the infringement of one already existing':[103] the law Niobe transgressed did not predate her act, but was formed in the act of her transgression. Niobe did not break public law but tempt fate with private boastfulness; Benjamin argues that modern law and the police wield the same intrusive and inescapable power and are based on the same impulsiveness as fate. The law that Bónapárt comes before is not a law working towards just ends but a power-making of mythical violence, and the force of the law is brought to bear on him. He can no more escape the heavy clasp of the policeman's hand on his arm than he can fate; for the Irish speaker, the law and fate are inseparable. As bare life, Bónapárt is that *against which* the law can be enforced, the point against which the law is imposed, and therefore shown to operate. The purpose of Bónapárt's trial and conviction is to prove that the law functions: he is within and yet without the law. In the Greek myth Niobe is punished by being turned to stone; silenced and robbed of the power to protest. In *An Béal Bocht*, the Irish-speaking Bónapárt is *a priori* silenced, always already petrified by the violent exclusion/ inclusion of the English-language legal system. But if Bónapárt is no more than bare life, a being outside the law, then how can he be prosecuted? How can the force of the law be brought to bear on someone wholly exterior to it?

'Jams O'Donnell', we are told, is the '*gall-leagan a ainm féinig*' (AB 27),[104] that is, the English form of Bónapárt's name, and on the few occasions that Bónapárt is involved with the (English-speaking) authorities, be they educational or law enforcing, this is the name he has violently been taught to use, a name which nominally includes him within the juridical process. Thus, we see that rather than change the law, and make bare life – the Irish speaker – a fully functioning member of the polis, biopolitical control is exerted over Bónapárt by renaming and recategorizing him. Recognizing the potential need to legally include bare life, and desiring to punish the life pushed outside the law, the bare life that is Bónapárt Ó Cúnasa is given the name Jams O'Donnell, a marker in the language of the law that signifies that bare life may be legally penalized, momentarily included within the law in order to suffer its violence, but not feel its protection. When Bónapárt is tried as Jams O'Donnell he is tried as a life, but a life that is outside (proper, legal) language and outside the proper name. He is subject to the normal functioning of the law, and he has the right to a trial, but a trial in which he cannot participate, a court case in which he has no speech. He is, therefore, not subject but *object* located inside and outside the law; it functions around him, including and excluding him.[105]

'Jams O'Donnell' is not a name given solely to Bónapárt, but to every Irish-speaking male on his first day of school by the vicious schoolmaster Aimeirgean Ó Lúnasa. In this O'Nolan returns to the *Lebor Gabála Érenn* (*Book of the Taking of Ireland*), as Amorgen – also spelt Amergin – was the Milesian who named Ireland after the goddesses Ériu, Fotla and Banba, and who also made the first judgement on Irish shore. Thus, from the birth of Ireland we see the act of naming implicated in legality and inclusion/exclusion, but also note the sense of degradation prevalent in O'Nolan's works: from Chieftain, judge and poet we descend to sadistic schoolteacher, who names not in homage or honour, and certainly not to ennoble, but to subjugate and silence.[106] The name beaten into Bónapárt – 'Jams O'Donnell' – does not denote an individual, but the *category* or *genus* of 'male, Irish-speaking peasant'. In English, therefore, the inhabitants of the Gaeltachts do not have individual proper names, but are designated simply by a generic term. 'Jams O'Donnell' becomes a cog within the machine of the law, a law that turns around him, ignoring any points of alterity. If Kafka's man from the country cannot pass through the open gates to the Law, it is nonetheless his gate, his doorkeeper, all in his name. For Bónapárt, there is merely a gate for Jams O'Donnell, a gate for a category rather than a unique individual, and neither the doorkeeper nor the law itself deigns to speak his language. He is not before the law, he is beneath the law; beneath its notice as an individual but nonetheless under its control. His position in relation to the law can only be negative: he can transgress but he cannot be protected. As Bónapárt is tried as Jams O'Donnell he is, therefore, not tried as a unique individual, but as a member of a social group. His function is representative: he represents – in the eyes of English speakers – the unlawfulness of the Irish peasant and the subsequent functioning of justice. Because the system must act, at the very least, as the simulacrum of legality, Bónapárt is not wholly picked at random, but as a peasant suspiciously in possession of gold coins. Beyond that, however, further investigation is – apparently – unnecessary. As in Kafka's penal colony 'guilt is always beyond question';[107] what needs to be proven is not Jams O'Donnell's culpability but the unfailing justice of the law. Neither the condemned man nor Bónapárt is to be given the opportunity to defend himself, as defence is not necessary: the law holds a trial simply to perpetuate and prove itself.

If 'Jams O'Donnell' refers to each male, Irish-speaking peasant, then it may masquerade as a proper name, but it very clearly functions instead as a common noun. A proper name, according to John Stuart Mill, is 'utterly unmeaning . . . a word which answers the purpose of showing what thing it is we are talking about, but not of telling anything about it'.[108] In other words, 'Proper names are not connotative: they denote the individuals who are called by them; but they do not indicate or imply any

attributes as belonging to those individuals'.[109] Derrida agrees: a
proper name has 'no meaning, no conceptualisable and common
meaning', and when pronounced 'can designate [viser] only a single,
singular individual, one unique thing'.[110] A name denotes a distinct
individual; regardless of the number of times newborns are given
the Irish name 'Bláthnaid', for example, in each case it refers to a
specific and singular 'Bláthnaid'. Each instance of 'Bláthnaid' exists
in homonymic relation to every other instance; while they may
sound the same, they designate a wholly different signified. Derrida
writes that proper names 'designate individuals who do not refer to
any common concept';[111] proper names do not mark a particular
category. In beating the name 'Jams O'Donnell' into every male
child, each is effectively robbed of a proper name in English; their
Irish name is not recognized, and their English name is not a proper
name but a common noun marking a category rather than an
individual. Unique subjectivity is effectively denied them, and they
are made instead to be no more than homogeneous instances of
controlled bare life. As Derrida writes, 'Mastery begins . . . through
the power of naming, of imposing and legitimating appellations':[112]
in the act of renaming, the Irish speakers of Corca Dorcha are
subjugated, and their inclusion within the legal and political is
improper and wholly restricted. Markers of individuality and
potentiality are removed and replaced with a common designator
of passivity – 'Jams O'Donnell' is a 'name' for one not worthy of
a name. While the *Gaeilgeoirí* take Irish names voluntarily and
individually, the Irish speakers have a single English name thrust
upon them. Significantly, the names taken by the *Gaeilgeoirí*
are predominantly common nouns operating as proper names –
An Fód Móna (The Sod of Turf), *An Bata Damhsa* (The Bout of
Dancing), *An Chiaróg Eile* (The Other Beetle) – which, as Kiberd
notes, mocks *An Craoibhín Aoibhinn* (The Pleasant Little Branch),
the name taken Douglas Hyde, founder of the Gaelic League and
first President of Ireland, and points to the idea that for English
speakers, Irish names are not 'proper' names but antiquated
appellations taken by a primitive people.[113]

When O'Nolan translated Brinsley MacNamara's play *Margaret
Gillan*, one of the major issues was the proper name/title. In
letters between the publishers and O'Nolan, different names were
suggested; Maighréad Gilion, Maighréad Gillan, Máiréad Gilion
were proposed, and O'Nolan became quite heated in making the

distinction between Maighréad Ní Ghilleáin (this would imply
that she was unmarried) and Maighread Bean Uí Ghilleáin (this
implies that she was married).[114] When discussing the translation
of *An Béal Bocht*, Evelyn O'Nolan showed concern regarding the
transition of names between languages, writing to O'Keeffe that
'Power translates "Corca Dorcha" as "Corkadoragha". Somewhere
Brian himself referred to the same place as "Corkey Dorkey"
which is much better'.[115] Similarly, when Kevin O'Nolan wrote to
Evelyn O'Nolan to comment on possible translators for the text,
he criticized the attempt made by Maurice Kennedy, focusing in
particular on Kennedy's odd translation of the name of Bónapárt's
townland – *Lios na bPráiscín* (the fort of the apron) – as 'The
Mound of Mashed Potatoes'.[116] Much work was done on finding a
translator that could capture the 'verve and "go" of Brian's Irish',[117]
but even Power's was not deemed perfect, Kevin O'Nolan writing
that 'the translation [Power's] is a little too easy going. It is not
always faithful in detail and though this may not always matter there
is danger of overlooking small points'.[118] This is particularly clear
in the list of the titles taken by the *Gaeligoirí*. Power mistranslates
some, excludes others and adds ones that O'Nolan never included
in either the manuscript or published versions of *An Béal Bocht*.
Interestingly, in the manuscript of *An Béal Bocht* Jams O'Donnell
is *Jams Gallagher*. Jams Gallagher is a play on James Gallagher
from Máire's (Séamus Ó Grianna) novel *Mo Dhá Róisín*, in which
a pupil learns of his official name – James Gallagher – for the first
time when he went to school. Thus, even in employing a generic
term for a group deprived of all singularity O'Nolan chooses a
more innovative term – his stereotype for the generic had to retain
the original, and the tension between the proper name/common
noun is further intensified.

While the anglicization of Irish proper names has a long history,
the decision to alter names within a literary text is, while not without
precedent, extremely problematic. From *An Béal Bocht* to *The
Poor Mouth*, Bónapárt Ó Cúnasa becomes Bonaparte O'Coonassa,
Feardanand Ó Rúnasa becomes Ferdinand O'Roonassa, Aimeirgean
Ó Lúnasa becomes Osborne O'Loonassa, Seanduine Liath becomes
Old Grey Fellow, Máthair becomes Mother, Sorcha becomes Sarah,
Nábla becomes Mabel. Why, in a text so engaged – parodically
and earnestly – with the treatment of the Irish language, would
the translation present proper names according to English spellings

and English equivalences? Why transcribe and anglicize proper names?

Brian Friel's *Translations* addresses the consolidation of colonization through the appropriation and assimilation of names. In an act undecideably poised between translation, mispronunciation and anglicization, mirroring the 'standardisation' or 'correction' of the Irish place names, Owen is called 'Roland' by the English soldiers. When the villagers point out their mistake, Owen says 'Owen – Roland – what the hell. It's only a name. It's the same me, isn't it? Well, isn't it?'.[119] Undoubtedly, the answer is 'no'. As the tension in *An Béal Bocht* is located in the movement between Irish and English, and specifically in the movement between names, the alteration of the names makes a darker point that phonetic transcription. It is generally accepted by continental and analytic philosophers alike, that, as proper names do not refer to a concept, 'personal proper names cannot be translated. They are sometimes adapted, in pronunciation or transcription (like the proper names of cities: Londres, London . . . but Londres is not a translation of London), but they cannot be translated'.[120] Hence a proper name

> does not belong to . . . language, . . . not only is not translatable [*traductible*] from one language to another but is not translatable [*traduisible*] in the very language "in" which it seems to function normally. With what does one replace a proper name; how can one find an equivalent for it in any language at all?[121]

Proper names do not mean, proper names do not describe or signify attributes, proper names cannot, therefore, be translated. A proper name is not a proper part of language, but that which is included through exclusion. In order to label an included/excluded other, a name is given, as names themselves operate on the border of language, included through exclusion. But as a name's exclusion is also a marker of individuality, a name is given that borders a borderline category: a name which is not quite a name but a name impossibly translated into a category.

Remaining first of all simply within the Irish text, *An Béal Bocht* is about impossible, reductive and controlling instances of translation: the movement from Bónapárt Ó Cúnasa to Jams O'Donnell is an act of inexecutable and violent translation, one in which the alteration of the signifier instigates a radical shift in the signified. *Bónapárt* is a singular subject in possession of an untranslatable proper name, but *Jams O'Donnell* is a homogeneous object within the law labelled by a translatable common noun. In other words, the 'translation' from Irish to English creates a wholly different signified. English cannot recognize the untranslatable individual and proper name that is Bónapárt, all it can see is the translatable bare life and common noun that is Jams O'Donnell.

However, this movement is complicated when *An Béal Bocht* is translated into English, and everything, even untranslatable proper names, become altered. Within *The Poor Mouth*, the movement from Bónapárt Ó Cúnasa to Bonaparte O'Coonassa may simply be, or have been intended to be, an uncomplicated transcription that enables non-Irish speakers to pronounce Irish names, but its operation as translation is impossible to ignore. If a text that establishes that a subject in Irish becomes no more than object in English is translated into English, and the very site of the point of opposition – the proper name/common noun – becomes a site of translation/transcription, then a performative contradiction is created. The tension between the language in which the text is written – Irish – and the language of education, biopolitical control and the law – English – is lost when the entire text is written in English, and particularly if the names are altered. The name which marks a locus of singularity – albeit a name not 'originally' Irish – cannot mark the same degree of difference from Jams O'Donnell when it is already in the same language/phonetics as Jams O'Donnell. The vital linguistic distinction and shock of the eradication of the name in the native tongue is lost.

Furthermore, Bónapárt – in Irish – is a playful parody of the Irish-language characters of the West of Ireland autobiographies, and a harsh satire of the representations of Irish speakers in (predominantly) English texts. Bonaparte – in English – is still a parody and a satire, but a parody of the *translated* autobiographies, and a satire whose proximity to that harshly mocked is radically increased. In other words, the distance between satirically representing an Irish stereotype, and *being* a stereotype, is drastically reduced when read in English. How many Irish literary stereotypes are actually presented speaking wholly in Irish? Within the context of English, Bónapárt/Bonaparte is, even prior and separate to being named 'Jams O'Donnell', too much a stereotype, too much a stage character, too much a farcical repetition to be anything but a common noun designating a concept. In English, the language through which Irish speakers are understood as anachronistic and inferior, *Bónapárt/Bonaparte is always already Jams O'Donnell*. Bonaparte is not the direct and simple *equivalent* of Bónapárt, the same signified in a different language, but a wholly different mode of stereotype. While Bónapárt cannot be translated, Bonaparte can. While names are of untranslatable individuals in Irish, in English they are markers of translatable category types.

As Bónapárt is taken off to jail as Jams O'Donnell, he sees a man who looks familiar, a man '*cromtha, briste, agus chomh tanaí le tráithnín*' (AB 112).[122] Speaking the English sentence beaten into his head long ago, he asks, 'Phwat is yer nam?', and receives the expected reply: 'Jams O'Donnell!' (AB 112, PM 123). With joy Bónapárt shakes the old man's hand and exclaims, '*Is é an ainm* [sic] *agus sloinne domsa féin* . . . Jams O'Donnell *freisin, is tusa m'athair agus is follas go bhfuil tú tagtha as an gcrúiscín!*' (AB 113).[123] Fresh from a trial he didn't understand and the news that he has a 29-year sentence, Bónapárt sees an old man, and asks his name, not in Irish but in *English*, doing so with a question that has only one answer. The old man gives it, replying with the generic common noun rather than proper name, and the little boy who looked in the milk jug for his father meets him at last. That is, meets *Jams O'Donnell*. The ambiguity regarding Bónapárt's guilt is repeated in his reunion with his father: does he meet his father or does he meet another Jams O'Donnell? The situation must remain open and undecidable. Should Bónapárt meet his birth father, then the unending cycles of inescapable destiny are reinforced: as his father served 29 years, so too does he. Jams O'Donnell will always serve a 29-year sentence, regardless of the crime, because that is his fate.[124]

Should, however, he simply meet another Irish peasant, then the repetition of fate remains unchanged, but a slightly darker point is made. This darkness doesn't merely lie in the fact that Bónapárt deludes himself, but in the fact that Bónapárt now self-identifies not by proper name but common noun, and allows the repetition of that common noun to denote 'father'. All sense of specific lineage is undone, and the consanguinity denoted by family names is suppressed before the overwhelming strength of the larger taxonomic category: Jams O'Donnell. Exact family ties and units become irrelevant as each male, Irish-speaking peasant is reduced to a member of the set of 'male, Irish-speaking peasant', and the unique characteristics denoting the specificity of each subject and each family unit are lost. The inhabitants of Corca Dorcha and the Gaeltachts become a homogeneous, incestuous mass: any frail old man from the Gaeltacht can be Bónapárt's father because as Jams O'Donnell he is Bónapárt's father and cousin and neighbour and friend and *Bónapárt himself*. By treating all members of the set of Jams O'Donnell as ostensibly the same, as living animals, speakers of the pig language, the incest prohibition no longer applies, although it is not without effect: Jams O'Donnell can marry the daughter of Jams O'Donnell, who gives birth, it should be noted, to a piglet, only to die a year and a day later among the pigs.

While common noun 'Jams O'Donnell' is a debasement and a point of absolute biopolitical control of a manufactured category of included/excluded bare life, there is a group within *An Béal Bocht* who are not even included in the category of exclusion. Women. Women never figure prominently in O'Nolan's texts, and when they do it's rarely to their advantage. Women in *An Béal Bocht* are distant literary stereotypes wailing on the beach for their Mikey, women to be married whose names are 'Nuala nó Babaí nó Nábla nó Róise' (AB 56),[125] or a mother who embodies a dull country cliché. The two main female characters in *An Béal Bocht* are unsurprisingly domestic; Bonapart's mother, who remains nameless, and his wife, Nábla – Mabel in the English text – so generically named as to be effectively nameless. Against the generic category that is Jams O'Donnell, the included/excluded male, Irish-speaking peasant, we have women, whose exclusion is such that they are not even included in the category of exclusion. They do not go to school, and so they do not receive an English name. Their names are common nouns designating *roles,* dissipated plurals which never combined into a larger taxonomic category: mother, or Nábla as synonym for woman-to-be-married. While Nábla's father's name is Jams O'Donnell, which places him firmly within a definite set, she is in the category of '*Nuala* nó *Babaí* nó *Nábla* nó *Róise*', that is, the category of 'or'. The category of other, the category for those not in a category. The category, should we follow Borges's 'Celestial Emporium of Benevolent Knowledge's Taxonomy', of *etcetera*.

They are bare life that does not need to figure before the law, before education, before the authorities: they are bare life wholly excluded.

Argument for the prosecution

While Bónapárt's trial, *as it is presented to us*, is an undeniable travesty, clouding the transparently unethical conduct is a deep ambiguity. The conceit of *An Béal Bocht*, it cannot be forgotten, stipulates an author and an editor: the author is Bónapárt himself, writing from jail, and the interfering hand of the editor – '*Tá an scríbhinn seo go díreach mar a fuair mé í ó láimh an údair ach amháin go bhfuil an mhórchuid fágtha ar lár*' (AB 7)[126] – that of Myles na gCopaleen. While Bónapárt's lack of English makes the legal proceedings a painful farce, it also means that he can honestly and convincingly fail to present any evidence that might demonstrate his guilt. Writing from jail, his version presents his innocence, but this innocence is rendered suspect by a series of repeated structures and inconsistencies in his account. Did, we must ask, Bónapárt take the money from Maoldún as he avows, or did he in fact murder and rob the gentleman in Galway, as the law courts insist? One might protest that Bónapárt is too weak and cowardly to kill, but O'Nolan's texts repeatedly feature the execrable abilities of the pathetic, and the evidence against him is, at the very least, highly suggestive.

The entire Maoldún incident bears remarkable continuity to events already encountered, in that the Maoldún Bónapárt meets is an extension of the Seanduine's version of the tale, not the middle Irish saga. While Maoldún does speak in Middle Irish – and here we have to detect the help of one editor, Myles na gCopaleen – the story he tells is the same story related to Bónapárt by Ferdinand. While the otherworldly features of Bónapárt's 'voyage' mean that it conforms to the mystical elements of the heroic cycles, it also means that Bónapárt can present a highly interrupted narrative. The episode thus combines the stylistic devices of the Middle Irish tale with the confusion and interruptions of a dream work, ending, unsatisfactorily, with the equivalent of 'and then I woke up'. Hence, the oneiric quality of the descriptions – '*aibhneacha colgacha buí ag gluaiseacht eatarthu, ag líonadh mo chluas le dordán diabhalta díshaolta'*, *'sráidbhaile de charraigeacha bána'*, *'criathar de phoill béaldorcha díthónacha ina raibh na huiscí luatha ag titim go síorthitimeach'* (AB 96)[127] – are coupled with repeated accounts of Bónapárt's overwhelming fatigue. While on the summit he says *'Ní fheadar ná gur ligeas tharam gan fhios tamall den lá faoi shuan nó ar chaolchéadfaí'* (AB 97),[128] and all is concluded when he wakes up suddenly at the bottom of the mountain, with no memory of the descent, naked and clutching a bag of gold. Bónapárt's clothes may have been stripped from him by the tumultuous waters; they may also have been discarded as they were covered in blood, which, a year later, as Bónapárt deliberates on how to spend the money, washes through the house. Thinking that the apocalypse was nigh – and judgement day with it – Bónapárt anxiously asks his mother about the source of the *'ceathanna dearga'* (AB 104).[129] It transpires that it had come from the Seanduine. Echoing the words of the guilty and troubled Lady Macbeth, Bónapárt breaths, *'Ní raibh aon choinne agam . . . go raibh an oiread seo fola sa tSeanduine'*,[130] and thus decides to spend his money. Money, it should be noted, that is later perfectly acceptable in a shoe shop. While the shopkeeper might raise an eyebrow at a peasant's possession of gold, his reaction would undoubtedly be greater had the peasant attempted to pay him with an archaeological artefact.

Bónapárt's voyage to the top of Hungerstack hovers between a true, if supernatural, event, a pathology concocted to repress guilt, and an attempted alibi. But while the case for Bónapárt's guilt or innocence can be extended almost infinitely, and arguments for the defence able to include temporal ambiguities – the Maoldún incident occurred a year ago, while the murder was committed *'go déanach'* (AB 110)[131] – or structural devices – the repetition of the story of the captain simply part of O'Nolan's interest in narrative redoubling – its significance lies not in finding a definitive answer to the problem, but the openness or undecidability itself. Bónapárt is the victim of an indifferent and unlawful system, but he is not an unambiguously innocent victim. Myles's parody allows for no idealism or romanticism; the people of Corca Dorcha cannot be statically depicted as fallen nobles enslaved by the English tongue. *An Béal Bocht* writes against homogeneity and static sameness, be it biased or simplistic representations, the racial, social and linguistic purity of the *fíor-Ghael* (true Irish) valued by the Gaelic

League – and enforced with all the blind determination of adherents of eugenics – or the equally reductive and negative creation of the lower caste that is Jams O'Donnell.

Notes

1   Karl Marx, 'The Eighteenth Brumaire of Louis Bonaparte', trans. Terrell Carver. In *Marx's Eighteenth Brumaire: (Post)modern Interpretations.* Ed. Mark Cowling and James Martin (London: Pluto Press, 2002), 19.

2   Karl Marx, 'A Contribution to the Critique of Hegel's Philosophy of Right'. In *Early Writings*, trans. Rodney Livingstone and Gregor Benton (London: Penguin, 1992), 247–8.

3   CL 28 August 1942.

4   Brian O'Nolan, 'The Pathology of Revivalism', 17, BC.

5   CL 15 February 1943.

6   O'Nolan, 'Pathology', 1, BC.

7   CL 8 December 1950.

8   CL 29 May 1942.

9   Ibid.

10 CL 17 June 1942.

11 CL 29 May 1942.

12 One could argue that the anachronistic quality of the Irish language was one imposed by those who did not speak it, who saw it as a dead language, out of touch with the realities of modern life. In a cutting parody of this, O'Nolan writes that Irish cannot even report on the war that was raging in England, as it lacked the vocabulary. He did, of course, offer to remedy this by presenting an idiosyncratic glossary of his own. See CL 4 October 1940. Irish becomes a language falsely segregated, insulated from the 'dangerous' ideological implications of alien tongues.

13 Blanchot, *Infinite Conversation*, 342–3.

14 Samuel Beckett, *Endgame, Samuel Beckett: Complete Dramatic Works* (London: Faber and Faber, 2006), 101.

15 Letter to Roger Blin, 9 January 1953. As quoted in Deirdre Bair, *Samuel Beckett: A Biography* (New York: Touchstone, 1990), 428.

16 CL 9 January 1945.

17 Terry Eagleton, *Sweet Violence: The Idea of the Tragic* (Oxford: Blackwell, 2003), 64–5.

18 Michael Booth, *English Melodrama*, as quoted in John Docker's *Postmodernism and Popular Culture: A Cultural History* (Cambridge: Cambridge University Press, 1994), 255.

19 CL 28 August 1942.

20 'discussing the hard life and debating the poor lot which was now (and would always be) Ireland's' (PM 89).

21 Itself a repetition of the phrase used throughout Tomás Ó Criomhthain's *An tOileánach*: '*mar ná beidh ár leithéidí arís ann*' (because our likes won't be around again).

22 Maurice Blanchot, *The Work of Fire,* trans. Charlotte Mandell (Stanford: Stanford University Press, 1995), 242.

23 Blanchot, *Infinite Conversation*, xx.

24 'a child among the ashes' (PM 16).

25 As is the destiny of every inhabitant of the Gaeltacht.

26 'an Ultonian according to the formula in the good books' (PM 64).

27 'literary fate' (PM 67).

28 One could argue that while the conditions in which they 'work' in Corca Dorcha are worse than anything Trellis might have imposed, they don't rebel, first of all, because of the passivity of the people they play is overwhelming, but also because *An Béal Bocht* doesn't have an external, dictatorial author. Preserving the conceit with which the book is presented, Myles na gCopaleen edits *An Béal Bocht*, but it is written by one of the characters themselves: Bónapárt.

29 In even sharper contrast is Tennyson's loose ballad reworking 'The Voyage of Maeldune', which opens by emphasizing the nobility of Máel Dúin and his men:

> I was the chief of the race – he had stricken my father dead –
> But I gather'd my fellows together, I swore I would strike off his head.
> Each of them look'd like a king, and was noble in birth as in worth,
> And each of them boasted he sprang from the oldest race upon earth.
> Each was as brave in the light as the bravest hero of song,
>   And each of them liefer had died than have done one another a wrong.

No doubt O'Nolan would have found this reworking in parts amusing and distressing (Alfred Tennyson, *The Major Works:*

Including The Princess, In Memoriam and Maud. Ed. Adam Roberts (Oxford: Oxford University Press, 2000, 2009), 449).

30 'if what we have in Corkadoragha of storytelling-gems and next-door folklore from our ancestors is true and believable' (PM 102).

31 'endeavouring to settle himself on his stony seat, to shove his hooves in the direction of the fire, and to clear his throat for storytelling' (PM 109).

32 O'Nolan, 'Pathology', 3, BC.

33 Giorgio Agamben, *Homo Sacer: Sovereign Power and Bare Life,* trans. Daniel Heller-Roazen (Stanford: Stanford University Press, 1998), 1.

34 Agamben, *Homo Sacer,* 2.

35 Michel Foucault *The Will to Knowledge: The History of Sexuality Vol. 1,* trans. Robert Hurley (London: Penguin 1990), 143.

36 Foucault, 143.

37 Ibid., 142–3.

38 Ibid., 136.

39 Ibid., 138.

40 Giorgio Agamben, *Remnants of Auschwitz: The Witness and the Archive,* trans. Daniel Heller-Roazen (New York: Zone Books, 1999), 83.

41 Giorgio Agamben, *The Open: Man and Animal,* trans. Kevin Attell (Stanford: Stanford University Press, 2004), 38.

42 Agamben, *Homo Sacer,* 8.

43 Ibid., 88.

44 Ibid., 138.

45 Ibid., 105.

46 Agamben, *The Open,* 37.

47 Ibid., *Homo Sacer,* 159.

48 David Lloyd, 'The Indigent Sublime: Specters of Irish Hunger'. *Representations* 92.1 (2005): 160.

49 Lloyd, 161.

50 Ibid., 163.

51 For example, Cormac Ó Gráda's Irish-language text on the famine is called *An Drochshaol: Béaloideas agus Amhráin* (translated as *The Famine: Memory and Song*) (Dublin: Coiscéim, 1994).

52 'fatigue caused by the revels and the truly Gaelic famine that was ours always' (PM 59).

53 'potato scarcity' (PM 89).

54 'amount of famine which was delineated in his person' (PM 89).

55 'a tall spear of a man who was so thin with hunger that one's eye might fail to notice him if he were standing laterally towards one. He appeared both gay and foolish, lacking any proper control over his feet because of the inebriation caused to him by the morning air. Having stood for a while, he collapsed in a weakness on the bog' (PM 90).

56 'but constant muck, the wet and raw famine' (PM 92).

57 'fighting and competing with a stray dog, both contending for a narrow bone and the same snorting and angry barking issuing from both' (PM 89).

58 'it spoiled the effect' (PM 88).

59 Primo Levi, as quoted by Agamben, Remnants, 34.

60 Cormac Ó Gráda, Black 47 and Beyond: The Great Irish Famine in History, Economy and Memory (Princeton: Princeton University Press, 2000), 82–3.

61 Thomas Carlyle, 'Chartism'. In English and Other Critical Essays (London: J. M. Dent & Sons, 1900) Ed. Ernest Rhys, 183.

62 The Economist, 16 January 1847, as quoted by Ó Gráda, Black 47, 77.

63 Russell took over as Prime Minister from Peel in 1846.

64 'On one level the creation of employment on such a scale and at such short notice was an administrative achievement that historians have justly considered astonishing. On the other hand, over its full range of operation . . . the public works are more astonishing still as a reflection of the lengths to which the ideologically driven government of Lord John Russell was prepared to go rather than actually feed the starving' Ciarán Ó Murchadha, The Great Famine: Ireland's Agony 1845–1852 (London: Continuum, 2011), 67.

65 See Ó Gráda, 122–7.

66 Differing views on the apportioning of blame and the reading of statistics can be found by comparing books such as Tim Pat Coogan's The Famine Plot: England's Role in Ireland's Greatest Tragedy (London: Palgrave MacMillan, 2012), James Donnelly's The Great Irish Potato Famine (Stroud: Sutton Publishing, 2001), essays in Carla King's Famine, Land and Culture in Ireland (Dublin: University College Dublin Press, 2000).

67 Colm Tóibín, 'The Irish Famine'. In The Irish Famine: A Documentary (London: Profile Books, 2001), 4.

68 David Nally, ' "That Coming Storm": The Irish Poor Law, Colonial Biopolitics, and the Great Famine'. *Annals of the Association of American Geographers* 98.3 (2008): 733.

69 Aristotle, *Politics* (1253a, 10–18), as quoted in Agamben, *Homo Sacer,* 12.

70 'He understood that good Gaelic is difficult but . . . the best Gaelic of all is well-nigh unintelligible' (PM 44).

71 Michael de Nie 'Pigs, Paddies, Prams and Petticoats: Irish Home Rule and the British Comic Press, 1886–93'. *History Ireland* 13.1 (2005): 44. See too Joseph P. Finnan, 'Punch's Portrayal of Redmond, Carson and the Irish Question, 1910–18'. *Irish Historical Studies* 33.132 (2003): 424–51.

72 BON to Sean O'Casey, 13 April 1942, SIUC.

73 CL 23 April 1940.

74 'I don't think that Father Peter has the word *decline* in any of his works' (PM 49).

75 Agamben, *Remnants,* 160.

76 'Are you certain that the Gaels are people?' (PM 100).

77 This is an instance of problematic translation. While the Power text reads 'They've that reputation anyway, little noble, said he, but no confirmation of it has ever been received. We're not horses nor hens; seals nor ghosts; *and in spite of all that, it's unbelievable that we're human*' [emphasis added] (PM 100), the clauses in italics should be: 'and so it's plausible we're human'. O'Nolan doesn't unequivocally equate Irish speakers and animals, but argues that their humanity is only negatively presumed by comparison – the fact that they're not animals – rather than positively asserted.

78 Patrick Weston Joyce, *The Origin and History of Irish Names of Places* (Dublin: McGlashan and Gill, 1869), 113.

79 Report of the Maamtrasna Murders in *The Freeman's Journal*, 20 November 1882, as presented in T. Harrington, 'The Maamtrasna Massacre: Impeachment of the Trials (with appendix containing report of trials and correspondence between Most Rev Dr M'Evilly and the Lord Lieutenant)', (Dublin: Nation Office, 1884), 29.

80 The trial had been moved from local courts to Dublin.

81 Harrington, 'Maamtrasna', 35.

82 Ibid., vi.

83 Ibid.

84 Hansard's Parliamentary Debates, Third Series (London: Cornelius Buck, 1884), 234, as quoted in Jeanne A. Flood, 'Joyce and the Maamtrasna Murders'. *James Joyce Quarterly* 28.4 (1991): 883.

85 James Joyce, 'Ireland Before the Bar'. In *The Critical Writings of James Joyce*. Eds. Ellsworth Mason and Richard Ellmann (London: Faber and Faber, 1959), 198.

86 CL 30 November 1942.

87 CL 28 December 1942.

88 CL 1 December 1942.

89 CL 19 June 1944.

90 Brooker's '"Grand Playsaunce"' is interesting on law within the Cruiskeen Lawn articles.

91 Tomás O'Crohan, *The Islandman*, trans Robin Flower (Oxford: Oxford University Press, 2000), 67.

92 *State (Buchan) v. Coyne*, in Ivana Bacik, 'Breaking the Language Barrier: Access to Justice in the New Ireland'. *Judicial Studies Institute Journal* 7.2 (2007): 116.

93 *Attorney-General v. Joyce and Walsh (1929)* I. R. 526, reprinted in *Irish Cases on Evidence*, ed. J. S. R. Cole (1972), 126. Quoted in Bacik, 'Language Barrier', 116.

94 Kennedy, Cole, 127, as quoted in Joseph Brooker, '"Grand Playsaunce"', 28.

95 Kennedy, Cole, 127, Brooker, 28.

96 Bacik, 'Language Barrier', 117.

97 Ibid.

98 Jacques Derrida 'Force of Law: The "Mystical Foundation of Authority"', trans. Mary Quaintance. In *Acts of Religion*. Ed. Gil Anidjar (Routledge: London, 2002), 288.

99 Walter Benjamin 'Critique of Violence'. In *Reflections*, trans. Edmund Jephcott (New York: Schocken Books, 1986), 286.

100 Benjamin, 297. Opposed to mythical violence is divine violence, 'pure power over all life for the sake of the living' (297), which sacrifices to save the living.

101 Derrida, 'Force of Law', 288.

102 Jacques Derrida, 'Force of Law', 228–98.

103 Benjamin, 294.

104 'foreign form of his name' (PM 34).

105 While we are presented with no direct evidence that Bónapárt trial is conducted under the name Jams O'Donnell, in every English-speaking instance in the text this is the name employed. In English, his name, like every other Irish speaker, is Jams O'Donnell. If the trial is in English, then that is his name during the trial.

106 I am grateful to Jonathan Ó Néill for this point, which he develops in his PhD thesis 'Invoking Irish: A Cultural History of Irish in English-language Discourse', currently being researched at Australian National University.

107 Franz Kafka, 'In the Penal Colony'. In *The Transformation and Other Stories*, Ed. and trans. Malcolm Pasley (London: Penguin, 1992), 132.

108 John Stuart Mill, *A System of Logic: Ratiocinative and Inductive*, Vol. 1 (London: Longmans, 1872), 34.

109 Mill, 33.

110 Jacques Derrida, 'Who or What Is Compared? The Concept of Comparative Literature and the Theoretical Problems of Translation' trans. Eric Prenowitz. *Discourse* 30.1 and 2 (2008): 36.

111 Derrida, 'Who or What', 36.

112 Jacques Derrida, *Monolingualism of the Other, or, The Prosthesis of Origin*, trans. Patrick Mensah (Stanford: Stanford University Press, 1998), 39.

113 Declan Kiberd, 'Flann O'Brien, Myles, and *The Poor Mouth*'. In *Inventing Ireland: The Literature of a Modern Nation* (London: Vintage Books, 1996), 501–2.

114 Letters May 1943 between O'Nolan and Sean McLallan, BC.

115 Evelyn O'Nolan (hereafter EON) to TOK 28 November 1969, BC.

116 Kevin O'Nolan to EON 29 November 1969, BC.

117 EON to TOK 22 October 1969, BC.

118 Kevin O'Nolan to EON 29 November 1969, BC.

119 Brian Friel, *Translations, Plays 1* (London: Faber and Faber, 1996), 408.

120 Jacques Derrida, 'Who or What', 36.

121 Derrida, 'Who or What', 39.

122 'bent and broken and as thin as a stem of grass' (PM 123).

123 'The name and surname that's on me . . . is also Jams O'Donnell. You're my father and it's clear you've come out of the jug' (PM 124).

124 Of course, we should note that while fulfilling his destiny, Bónapárt writes from the jug (crúiscín). The jug full of Jams O'Donnells (crúiscín lán), or anglicized, Cruiskeen Lawn . . .

125 'Nuala or Babby or Mabel or Roise' (PM 65).

126 'This document is exactly as I received it form the author's hand except that much of the original matter has been omitted' (PM 7).

127 'yellow fretful rivers flowing between them and filling my ears with an unearthly mysterious humming', villages of leaning white rocks', 'a mesh of bottomless dark-mouthed holes where rapid waters were falling incessantly' (PM 106).

128 'I don't know whether I allowed a large part of the day to slip by in sleep or in semi-consciousness' (PM 106).

129 'red showers' (PM 113).

130 'I never thought . . . that the Old Fellow had that much blood' (PM 114); 'Yet who would have thought the old man to have had so much blood in him' William Shakespeare, Macbeth, V. i.

131 'lately' (PM 119).

4

A hard life for women

In a 1962 interview with the BBC, O'Nolan announced that

> women are not important in Ireland in any sense of the social
> determinative, if there's such a word. . . . What I mean is they
> make our breakfast and they make our beds, but they're not
> really formative . . . they're not really a social force in this
> country . . . you can't leave them out but you mustn't allow them
> to intrude too much. It would be a very artificial book that gave
> women a big role.[1]

While the misogynistic complacency, the lazy relegation of women
to the domestic, and the disingenuous dismal of women as a
credible literary study are indefensible, O'Nolan's sexism must be
positioned within – but not excused by – the wider, instutionalized
misogyny operative within Irish society. Ireland's isolation from
Europe, the authority of the Church, the State's construction of
an idealized Irish identity, urban slums, remote rural farms and a
tendency towards large families collectively worked to severely limit
the position of Irish women, so that from 1922 to 1970 women
were conspicuously underrepresented in the political scene. While
the Irish Countrywomen's Association and the Irish Housewives'
Association did labour to improve women's often arduous daily
lives, they made few moves to alter women's roles beyond the
domestic, and numerous ecclesiastical and legal proclamations
reinforced women's restriction to home and hearth. Article 41.2
of the Irish Constitution (1937) made specific provisions for the
family, situating the woman within the home and stipulating not
only that it is a woman's natural place, but that governmental steps

should be taken to prevent a woman from 'neglecting' her duties there:

1 In particular, the State recognizes that by her life within the home, woman gives to the State a support without which the common good cannot be achieved.

2 The State shall, therefore, endeavour to ensure that mothers shall not be obliged by economic necessity to engage in labour to the neglect of their duties in the home.[2]

This wording, which to date remains unchanged, not only equates women with the maternal, but formally binds the woman to the hearth, where she is to fulfil the duties of nurture and care that should come naturally. Leaving the home, it is implied, becomes an unnatural act of abandonment that the State should help discourage, as a woman's role was to support the state, protect the family and uphold Catholic values by remaining in the house, thereby providing a calm and comforting private space to which men and children could retreat from the stress of public life. But while women were expected to be content within the sphere of the domestic, they had few rights over property and their children – children's allowances were paid to their husbands, a woman's consent was not required to sell her marital house and they were allowed no functioning methods of controlling family size. Nor could they protect themselves and their children from an abusive husband by ejecting him from the home. As Scannell puts it,

Laws based on the premise that women's rights were inferior to those of men survived in, and indeed even appeared on, the statute books. Despite the constitutional adulation of marriage and motherhood, the legislature preferred to keep women in the home by foul rather than fair means.[3]

Both the Church and the State resolutely placed the woman within the home as wife and mother, thereby equating 'woman' with 'reproduction', and the female body became a site of political significance and distrust. The image of the virginal Irish colleen was upheld both as an ideal and an expected norm, and women were made to act as the trustees of modest, Irish, Catholic society. Inappropriate dress and behaviour were denounced from the altar, and 'fallen women' with illegitimate children, whose presence was an uncomfortable reminder of moral and sexual 'aberrations', were incarcerated in Magdalen Asylums, thereby instilling a cultural understanding of premarital sexual activity as a social crime necessitating isolation and internment. Maria Luddy notes that prior to the departure of British garrisons in Ireland venereal diseases were attributed to the laxity of foreign morals, but their increase following independence required a reassessment of this prejudice.[4] Recognizing that sexually transmitted diseases were rife in all parts of Ireland, urban and rural, all women began to be seen as potential threats to the male body, and women became a dangerously double-edged sword, as they 'had the ability to destroy or recreate, to foster sterility or to make fertile, to be the agent of contamination'.[5] The female sphere was not simply inferior but polluted, as its reproductive role – a role supposedly so precious that Censorship laws forbade even literary allusions to abortion – could at any moment lead to the apex of promiscuity and disease.

In *Occasions of Sin*, Diarmaid Ferriter quotes a 1941 article in *The Bell*, in which a contributor argues that 'the average Irish mind has not, and perhaps never had, a properly balanced outlook on sex. Either it runs away from sex or it runs after it; it never seems able to stand and look at it objectively'.[6] The *Playboy* riots, which O'Nolan was worried *The Saints Go Marching In* would repeat, sprang not from modest horror at the public mention of Irish women's underwear, but, as Yeats put it, from a hypocritical 'defence of virtue by those that have but little'.[7] As Yeats recounts, during one such protest Synge came to him and said, '"A young doctor has just told me that he can hardly keep himself from jumping on to a seat and pointing out in that howling mob those whom he is treating for venereal disease"'.[8] Sex, pregnancy, abortion, motherhood and the body were subject to a confused and contradictory 'protection' – women's modesty was to be protected, and yet when, through rape, coercion, financial necessity, bad luck or sexual preferences 'modesty' was not an option, women became a threat from which others were to be shielded – Ferriter gives the example from 1936 in which two teenage girls being used for sex in the backstreets of Cork city were described in the *Cork Examiner* as 'two little girls who were a positive danger to the people of Cork'.[9]

The contamination within the virgin/whore dichotomy meant that the Virgin Mary had to be separated from all things sexual, which also meant denying the very thing that that resulted in her

worship: her motherhood. Gerardine Meaney attributes 'the peculiar
stillness and singularly unmaternal figures of the Virgin Mary
which predominate in Irish churches and grottoes' to the 'refusal to
countenance any representation of the mother's body as origin of
life'.[10] Mary was a 'disembodied mother',[11] designed to emphasize
virginity and repress the physicality involved in motherhood. In a
country where sin and sex were synonymous, and even sex within
marriage deemed problematic, particularly in regard to female
pleasure, motherhood was to clothe itself in robes of patience, love,
passivity, modesty and, to all appearances, chastity. Furthermore,
the latent peril at the core of every Irish virgin and mother also
meant that images of nationhood were effected, as Mother Ireland
was not only a trembling maiden to be protected from the might of
the colonizer, but was also the 'monstrous maternal' wherein the
woman as mother/land becomes 'paradoxically ... both nurturer and
destroyer, demanding the ultimate blood sacrifice from her sons'.[12]
Given, then, as Bacik writes, that the 'virgin/mother stereotypes so
embedded in Irish law and culture portray women as de-sexualised,
monstrous, colonized and maternalized',[13] it is hardly surprising
that the women and domestic spaces within O'Nolan's works are
highly problematic, exhibiting a sustained, misogynistic distaste,
escalating in *The Hard Life* to palpable disgust.

Domestic spaces and bodily functions

Despite, or rather, because of the formal emphasis laid on the
domestic as a nurturing space, O'Nolan's homes are marked by
absence and death, and in his texts the familial becomes synonymous
with lack and incompletion. *The Third Policeman*, *The Hard Life*,
Slattery's Sago Saga and *Th'oul Lad of Kilsalaher* feature orphaned
protagonists, while the narrator in *At Swim-Two-Birds* lives with his
uncle and the only mother in the text – Sheila – dies of complications
arising from her pregnancy. In *An Béal Bocht* Bónapárt's father is in
jail and his wife and son die, in *The Hard Life* Finbarr and Manus's
guardians are dead by the end of the text, *Rhapsody in Stephen's
Green* sees the death of ducklings and pregnant crickets, in *The
Dalkey Archive* Mick's father died of drink, and alcoholism killed
Margaret Crockett's father and husband in *Faustus Kelly*. While the
parents in *The Boy from Ballytearim* are alive and together, their

son abandons them – once to find his fortune, and again when his sweetheart dies. Couples too are rift with tension; when Peggy and Furriskey get married, there are hints of adultery, Divney's marriage makes him look haggard, while the Pooka continually insults his wife. Mick ends up marrying a woman pregnant with another man's child, Crotty's and Collopy's relationship is tainted by suspicious of illegitimacy, and Ned is quite happy for his supposedly beloved wife to spend as much time in Ireland, and away from him, as possible.

In O'Nolan's works, parents thus abandon their children through death and crime, and domestic scenes are rife with infidelity, falseness, betrayal and hostility. Each of the texts, no matter how fantastical or pseudo-realist the plot, contains some hint of family trauma, and O'Nolan adds to the uneasy, disturbed and *unheimlich* tones in his texts by dissecting families and casting characters off into the world, troubled and confused. But while the absence of fathers robs his characters of the authority and financial security that one might stereotypically associate with the paternal, more significant is the absence of women from the place specifically reserved for them in Irish society, religion and law books. O'Nolan's homes contain few women, as they haunt the peripheries like the ill Mrs Crotty, isolated in the bedroom with the door open so 'her cries, often faint, could be heard' (HL 27), or Finbarr's sister Teresa, who is mentioned once in passing and never heard of again, thereby becoming, as Taaffe writes, 'important for being of no importance . . . she might well be O'Nolan's most archetypical female character'.[14] When women do figure they are marginalized, stereotypical and problematic: the labouring rural mother (*The Boy from Ballytearim* and *An Béal Bocht*), the aged and ineffectual mother (*The Dalkey Archive*), the adulterous wife/girlfriend (*At Swim-Two-Birds*, *The Dalkey Archive*, *The Third Policeman*), the repulsive woman (*The Hard Life*), or the domineering wife (*Slattery's Sago Saga*). In the absence of women the domestic becomes a male space, such that, as Beckett's Molloy writes, 'I am in my mother's room. It's I who live there now. . . . I sleep in her bed. I piss and shit in her pot. I have taken her place'.[15] This is not to say that the home is positively reappropriated by the male – it remains a site of ambivalence, discomfort and dislocation – but it is emptied of any association with a 'fullness of presence, a fantasmic image of originary harmony'[16] that the idealized maternal traditionally provides.

As such, private space becomes not of the maternal and the familial, but of the (predominantly male) body, as the home simply becomes the site in which one eats, sleeps, talks, defecates, masturbates, recuperates and dies. The bodily functions that then become central to the home are normalized – 'familiarly' dirty male bodily functions, as opposed to the strange, 'unnatural' bodily needs of the female – but they are, nonetheless, never embraced without a sense of uneasy bravado. The home is an arena of the predominantly male body positioned in a liminal, incomplete domestic zone – a zone bereft of a mother figure that, within O'Nolan's texts, never existed. *The Hard Life* opens with a description of the maternal which is purportedly innocent and yet deliberately severing, as even when present the mother figure signifies absence and lack: 'It is not that I half knew my mother. I knew half of her: the lower half – her lap, legs, feet, her hands and wrists' (HL 11). As such the mother in O'Nolan's works bears resemblance to Kristeva's concept of the 'abject'; other, excluded, wrong, 'the untouchable, impossible, absent body of the mother' that leaves not maternal love but emptiness.[17] The home is a site or marker of exile, of original loss and homelessness, and the idealized depiction of the maternal offered by Church, State and stage is, in O'Nolan's works, a false image, a simulacrum of the mother.

Throughout O'Nolan's texts, the idealized Irish mother is rejected, with varying degrees of complicity with the sexist restriction of women's roles. When motherhood is directly engaged with, he incorporates the realities of sexual desire and of pain, acknowledging a complexity exceeding the Church and State's propaganda, without, however, subscribing to a positive, feminist perspective. 'The Martyr's Crown' (1950), for example, subtly undercuts this romanticized portrayal, but as it tends to be read through the story's playful substitution of 'dying for Ireland' with 'being born for Ireland', the depiction of the female protagonist is ignored, and the signification of the short story's title and closing line overlooked. Mrs Clougherty, a 'true daughter of Ireland' (SP 70) and a captain of *Cumann na mBan*, had been hiding members of the Irish Republican Army when members of the British army came to the house. Although a woman of strict religious observance and morality, she distracts the men by pretending to be a prostitute and sleeps with the officer. She is made pregnant by this, and O'Nolan is thus able to introduce the idea of her son being 'born for Ireland'. However, the tale is not named for the son, but for the mother; it was originally called 'For Ireland Home and Beauty', but O'Nolan changed the title, thereby highlighting Mrs Clougherty and the nature of her sacrifice. In the tale told by Mr Toole, Mrs Cloughtery is referred to as a saint and a martyr, who suffered the classical 'fate worse than death' and then died, one can infer, in childbirth. Her sacrifice is therefore double and her death twice, as first she saw the death of her 'honour', and subsequently the death of her body. Her martyrdom for Ireland is a specifically feminine sacrifice of death and life – pleasureless sex for the sake of Ireland, and dying by adding another son to the cause. She thereby becomes the perfect Irish, female martyr making the ideal feminine, domestic sacrifice. However, this martyrdom is undermined by the simple fact that, within the narrative, the woman doesn't exist, as Mr Toole as fabricated the history. Within O'Nolan's texts brave, saintly women making the perfect sacrifice are no more than tall tales told in pubs.

An earlier undercutting of the sacrosanct picture of virginal motherhood takes place in *Rhapsody in Stephen's Green*, where O'Nolan unconventionally calls attention to women's pleasure in the marital bed. In addition to this brief foray into female desire, pregnancy is represented not as the glorious fulfilling of a woman's destiny, but a painful burden outweighing any pleasure gleaned from fulfilment of her 'natural' role: 'If I'd known this is the way I'd be, not a bit of me would let you do it' (RS 48).

> Mrs Beetle: . . . sure many's the time I was in the same boat myself [pregnant] and I'd be in it this minute if I let his nibs have his way. But not me. I've learnt me lesson.
> Mrs Cricket: Well do oo know, tis nice, but tis a terrible price altogether to pay for the grand times you do have when you get married.
> Mrs Beetle: Ah the poor girl . . . and you so young. Sure 'tis only a mug's game. (RS 52)

The corresponding section in the Čapeks' *Insect Play* contains no reference to pleasure or to pain; Mrs Beetle euphemistically asks Mrs Cricket if she is pregnant, which Mrs Cricket confirms, and the conversation moves on.[18] For involving the maternal in the public acknowledgement of female pleasure and pain – albeit one in which the pain outweighs the pleasure – theatre critic

Gabriel Fallon deemed the adaptation an attack on motherhood, an opinion perhaps not little supported by the play's association of a certain delirium with pregnancy, a madness not included in the original: '*Mr Cricket prances round the stage in comic attitudes, humming and making outlandish noises. Mrs Cricket sits and laughs in a somewhat unbalanced fashion*' (RS 49). Fallon was correct; O'Nolan was attacking the virginal, unembodied depiction of motherhood, but was doing so without actively working to provide a more emancipated depiction. His works still resound with a suspicion of the female, the domestic and affect, and he conscientiously removes all direct mentions of love from the Cricket dialogue. Expressions of affection are invariably dismissed by O'Nolan as nauseating – in a *Cruiskeen Lawn* article Myles treats the notion of public marital affection with disgust, writing that 'you will sometimes encounter the author, uxorious and repulsive, who proceeds like this: "To my dear wife, without whose unflagging help and encouragement this book would never have been written". That sort of thing is usually found on books that are particularly bad'.[19] In a letter to Hodges Figgis providing a number of short book reviews, O'Nolan specifically targets domesticity and romance:

> *The Crying Land* is an Irish country-town tale concerned mostly with marriages, "romance" and the sundry trivial goings-on of a fairly large complication of characters. There is a repellent dwelling on domesticity, the style is banal and the characters are quite unreal. . . .
>   *Prizes and Surprises.* This is somewhat as "The Crying Land" above only worse. It is feminine chit-chat bearing on foreign travel and has no merit that I can discern.[20]

Perhaps remembering the reaction to his mention of pain and childbirth in *Rhapsody in Stephen's Green*, and hoping to profit from the wrath of the censors, the deliberately if unsuccessfully provocative *The Hard Life* also includes mention of male lust, female suffering and sex:

> – Do you not think women have enough suffering, as you call it, bringing babbies into the world? And why do they do it that? Is it because they're mad to sanctify themselves? Well

faith no! It's because the husband is one great torch ablaze
with the fires of lust!
- Collopy, please, Father Fahrt said in mild remonstrance.
That attitude is quite wrong. Procreation is the *right* of a
married man. Indeed it is his duty for the greater glory of
God. It is a duty enjoined by the sacrament of marriage.
- Oh is that so, Mr Collopy said loudly, is that so indeed. To
bring unfortunate new bosthoons into this vale of tears for
more of this suffering of yours, ah? (HL 33)

This scene reworks the debunking of the religious connotations of
motherhood and mocks the idea that 'the modest married woman is
the handmaid of the Lord' (HL 34). While O'Nolan was dismissive
of the banning of H. Sutherland's book *The Laws of Life* – a book on
the '"rhythm" system of limiting family increase . . . [which] bore the
imprimatur of the R.C. Archbishop of Westminster'[21] – interpreting
this contempt for the 'smut board' and the destabilization of the
idealized mother as promoting an enlightened idea of the role of
women would be inaccurate. Instead, the tendency was to undermine
a form of sentimentalized nationalism and gleefully alarm with a
'Trellisesque' technique of drawing in a readership through plenty
of shock and 'smut'. Hence, the romanticized depiction of Irish
domesticity is dismissed – 'They have only two uses for women,
Father – either go to bed with them or else thrash the life out of
them' (HL 39) – and even rural idylls shown, as in *An Béal Bocht*,
to comprise a 'banatee up at six in the morning to get ready thirteen
breakfasts out of a load of spuds, maybe a few leaves of kale, injun
meal, salt and buttermilk. Breakfast for Herself, Himself, the eight
babies and the three pigs, all out of the one pot' (HL 91). One the
rare occasion in *Cruiskeen Lawn* that a mother appears to conform
to society's expectation of the maternal – 'behold the lips that know
not of aught but prayer and poesy'[22] – she is revealed to be an
alcoholic. Similarly, in his early days of *Comhthrom Féinne* O'Nolan
undercuts the traditional representation of Ireland as a woman by
arguing that Caitlín Ní h-Uallacháin – Cathleen ni Houlihan – 'was
no angel! She changed her name fully twenty times and we have
two aliases, Róisín Dubh and Niamh Chinn Oir, to prove that the
courtesan's hair-dye was stored beside the bagpipes'.[23] In a later
Cruiskeen Lawn article, Myles argues that her name would be more
accurately written as 'Cathleen Ni Hooligan'.[24] There is no virginal

Cathleen ni Houlihan, no blushing maiden or capable mother, just corrupt women, for whom O'Nolan, particularly in later works, consistently expresses distaste.

Marriage and domesticity in the *Cruiskeen Lawn* articles fare little better. While wives do not figure prominently, when they are mentioned they are inevitably associated with stupidity, ugliness, dirt, misery and greed – 'Awful wife';[25] 'sullen wife';[26] 'red talons . . . ungrammatical approaches (I married beneath myself)';[27] 'dirty theatrical sobbing';[28] 'a bleak wife, both of you too bored and tired to have any more rows';[29] 'squaw-wife appears, [he] embraces her distastefully';[30] 'tiny, brown, hooked and toothless, a human face, probably female';[31] 'the wife takes it [milk] in, takes the cardboard cap off the bottle with her dirty thumb and pours the stuff into the jug out of which she had drunk barley wine last night and forgot to wash'.[32] The most positive treatment wives receive is complacent indifference:

> *The Dublin Man's attitudes to his wife and his pint are identical* . . . . He accepts both wife and pint as inevitable; he does not like or dislike either; under no circumstances will he take any notice whatever of either unless something extraordinary happens (e.g. if either is knocked over in his presence).[33]

Too often, however, Myle's Dublin man treats his marriage as a battleground of hostility and violence – 'he buries himself ever deeper in his newspaper, to emit a sullen, ambiguous growl';[34] 'Rises, winks broadly, takes up wife's handbag, opens it, stuffs in infuriated whistling rat, closes and replaces bag, which jumps about for a time';[35] '"Face" becomes livid with passion. Leaves room. Screams from basemen indicate he is beating wife'.[36] Even outside the 'vile' proximity of marriage women are a burden and a nuisance – 'the most potent sources of dissension among humans, i.e. womenfolk';[37] 'Women trying to look as if they had the remotest idea of Irish politics';[38] 'The Irish language reveals that Paddy had no word for love, home or wife, and went so far in disdain as to call girls colleens. Colleen (or *cailín*) is the diminutive of *cail*, a word which conventionally means "hag"'.[39] On the very rare occasions when female desire is alluded to, it is usually problematic: in one article a daughter allows her incestuous desire for her father to distract her from his (simple? euphemistic?)

request to relieve him of the 'humiliation of having to press [his] own trousers' and cries:

> Oh Poppa, I know, I know! I know what you are going to say. You ... you're not my Poppa at all. You found me one day ... when I was very small . . . and you brought me home . . . and cared for me . . . and now you find you have been in love with me all these years.[40]

The *Cruiskeen Lawn* articles form a disjoined corpus of fragmentary texts that interrupt, contradict and repeat each other, having no set beginning – the pseudonymic letters? the article by An Broc? – and an end that loops in on itself – the final *Cruiskeen Lawn* article printed, on the day of his death – 1 April 1966 – was a repeat of the Book Handling Service, and the penultimate one on 31 March, ends with pathos: 'These questions and more I will answer the day after tomorrow'.[41] They operate in a space of contaminated fantasy and reality, and present a hyperbolic version of Ireland whose own structural uncertainties and illogicalities are emphasized by the articles' contrived etymological and semantic misunderstandings. They mock and celebrate Ireland's emerging identities, offering alternative narratives of self to those proffered by Church, State and stage, albeit a self usually presumed to be male, educated, Catholic and from Dublin. While there are sustained targets subjected to varying levels of aggressive parody and attack – the Government, CIE, the ESB, *The Bell*, The Abbey, Universities, Joyce scholars, Corduroys, *Gaeilgoirí* – the conclusions of these diatribes often prioritize a pun or unexpected inversion rather than a consistent polemical position. When, for example, Maura Laverty objects to Myles's article on her play, and retaliates in a letter to the *Irish Times* implying that Myles is a bad playwright, his self-defence is elliptical and somewhat surprising: 'Mrs Laverty mixes up cookery and play writing. The two crafts are not dissimilar, but they are not to be confused. It is far easier to write a bad play that get a good dinner on the table'.[42]

The fragmentary form frees an author – or authors – from the logical requirement of consistency; as outlined in Chapter 1, fragments are too independent to contradict or support each other. Thus, Myles can be on whichever side of the argument appears most provocative or most humorous, and even his own personality need not be stable and consistent. Myles's defining characteristics are the equally fragmentary ones of mutability and volatility, as there is no single identity to which the name Myles na gCopaleen can be assigned – even the name itself changes. Over the course of the *Cruiskeen Lawn* Myles is rich and poor, handsome and repulsive, young and old, Irish and English, married and single, important and ignored, dead and alive, a scholar and a fool, an upstanding citizen and a thief. This narrative inconsistency is compounded by authorial ambiguity, as not all of the *Cruiskeen Lawn* articles were written by Brian O'Nolan.[43] This equivocality means that although the *Cruiskeen Lawn* is predicated on the provocative discourses of a single character, Myles is peripheral – he becomes the means through which an idea, pun, invention, argument, theory is voiced, and can provide whatever backdrop that theme requires. This marginality is performed in the positions assigned to Myles – even when he is portrayed as the greatest living novelist, advisor to the government and internationally renowned sage, he is usually a foreigner, external to the country's institutions. This distance permits him to present a picture of Ireland defamiliarized by absurdist or overly pedantic focus as one purportedly derived from the clarity of an exterior position. His is a border discourse.

While the fragmentary multiplicity of the *Cruiskeen Lawn* affords Myles excellent scope for parody and political commentary, it makes isolating a specific ideological position difficult, as the fragments express views that are often radically oppositional. Furthermore, given that Myles is not only a very different character/ author/structure/style to Flann O'Brien and Brian O'Nolan, but is often not penned by Brian O'Nolan, incorporating the *Cruiskeen Lawn* articles into an assessment of O'Nolan's positions and opinions becomes problematic. As fragments, the articles are a symphilosophical – perhaps sym-antiphilosophical – coming together of different voices which present commentaries on and performances of perceived societal tendencies, and Myles is neither O'Nolan, Montgomery or Sheridan but an assemblage of all three; a polyphonic yet highly subjective voice of – and on – Dublin. O'Nolan is not Myles, but he is to be held accountable for the ways in which *Cruiskeen Lawn* continued or consolidated misogyistic depictions of women. The majority of the *Cruiskeen Lawn* articles depict women and domesticity as foul, constrictive and draining, and men's violent and hostile reactions as the inevitable response to an impossible situation.[44] But it would be overly simplistic to label

Myles' vitriol a committed hated of women; he was not blind to 'The hopeless position of women in Ireland',[45] and the complicity of the Church, state and stage in this restriction of women. The hyperbole of his sexism – 'the whole lot of you can take your scarlet finger-nails off my typewriter and get back into the scullery'[46] – the sarcastic earnestness of his occasional (ironic) support – 'It cannot too often be pointed out that women are people',[47] and the conscious mimicry of the rhetoric of Church and state means that Myles's sexism is, while inexcusable, not uncontrived:

> How often must I point out that stories of sensational and ugly happenings, murder, divorce, bankruptcy, marriage, etc, are highly repugnant to the spirit and letter of our Constitution, subversive of public morality, contrary to holy charity and offensive in a special way to the metropolitan canons of good taste.[48]

At issue, however, is not the degree to which Myles's sexism exaggerates O'Nolan's, but the fact that through Myles O'Nolan used an awareness of inequalities for a humour that did little but reinforce disparities.

When Myles receives a letter whose 'contents re-open the whole sorry question of female mancipation and insuffrage [sic]', he announces that he is going to arrange a bill 'to provide for the enforcement of women's wrongs, female desuffragation and unilateral polygamy (whereby males can determine all such contracts at their absolute discretion)', as the letter demonstrates 'only too clearly . . . how completely "education" unfits or purports to unfit female persons for the finer things of life (cooking)'.[49] He argues that 'all this diversion of female activity from knitting, nagging and other nuptial activities is greatly to be deplored' and cries shame on those 'venal and abandoned politicians . . . who in their lust for votes did not hesitate to degrade and even enfranchise members of that sex, with results too patent to require enumeration'.[50] In an article on *Vogue*, he refers to women as 'unpeople' and 'non-men',[51] and in another writes that

> it is not seemly that our Irish womenfolk should occupy themselves with London (or even Parisian) concepts of what the "fashionable figure" should be. Let them be their own decent and lovely selves, unskilled in alien dietry, unversed in anatomical

wizardry. We rather decent Irish husbands and fathers are
prepared (without word of complaint) to spend a moiety of our
small incomes on having the floor boards strengthened. As if,
forsooth, we did not love them for themselves, for the truth in
their eyes ever dawning![52]

In 1942, Myles's Research Bureau launched an investigation
into woman's eyes, as according to the lyrics of *Mary, the Rose
of Tralee* Mary was loved for the 'truth in her eyes ever dawning'.
Myles decided to send a delegate to assess women's eyes for truth
'dawning, fully dawned, declining or otherwise'. The results,
however, were less than romantic, as 47 per cent were found to
have 'mild mydriasis, 21% Ptosis of the lids, 18% pronounced
hyperthyroidism . . .'.[53] This determined eschewing of idealization is
combined with an often pointed commentary on the constitutional
positioning of women in the home: 'Has the Imperial Government,
Merrion Street Upper, withdrawn from them the immemorial right
to . . . rock the cradle?'.[54] Similarly, when responding to an article by
Sean O'Faolain entitled 'The Irish Colleen is the Irish Coolie', Myles
fakes horror when O'Faolain and some foreign friends 'read through
our Constitution – apparently with the object of mocking at it!!'.
Quoting article 41.2.1 of the Constitution detailing the woman's
role in the home, Myles then cites O'Faolain's friends' comparison of
Ireland's treatment of women to the Nazi idea of 'Cookery, Kids and
the Kirk', and their argument that in countries where women were
involved outside the home industry and mining improved. Myles's
response, predictably enough, is: 'In the enlightened countries the
superior position of women is affirmed by sending them to work in
the mines. It is reasonable enough, in a way, but could they not find
time to scrub the floors before going out in the morning?'[55]
    And yet, in the midst of calls to keep women at work in the kitchen,
Myles emphasizes the lack of glamour involved in keeping house.
Thus, during a court case a man is said to have women's hands, that
is, hands that have never done any work. Myles calls this is an

infamous, vile and thrice-accursed assault upon the fair women
of Ireland. . . . You see the suggestion here . . .? That smooth
hands are characteristic of our excellent girls? That these same
girls do not do a "stroke" of work? . . . (rings bell and shouts
for crippled sister. Crippled sister enters and is sternly directed

to exhibit hands. Readers cautiously inspect hands, which are seen to be badly excoriated, scalded and deformed by arthritis. Crippled sister is sternly dismissed and leaves room weeping.) You see what I mean?[56]

Managing in a single image to debunk the myth of the home as a quiet refuge, present women as ugly and men as cruel, Myles avoids any possibility of a sympathetic stance by adding that the case had clearly been misrepresented: the man, having been married for nine years, is said to have had an easy time, despite the clear fact, Myles insists, that 'no man married for nine years has had an easy time'.[57] Whether it be the image of women, or of the country as a whole, in demystifying the illusion of Romantic Ireland Myles presents an alternative that contains little idealization. When a letter is written arguing that the Irish film *March of Time* portrays Ireland as a medieval society, he responds that the electricity might as well not work, the manufacturers are mainly foreign and not photogenic, the wheat campaign a euphemism for peasant farmers, and the 'ships' and 'new housing scheme' misprints for 'shops' and 'few housing schemes'.[58] Behind myths lies violence, and Myles demystifies, but without actively condemning the exposed reality: '**Irishmen respect women** – It is conceded that they strike women with clenched fist in the face only at home or in some place not public and inaccessible to the police' [emphasis in original].[59]

Myles takes the Constitution's equating of woman and the home, and reveals it to be a treatment of women as unpaid domestic help. Thus, when James Dillon says that foreign women should be given opportunities to work in Ireland, Myles writes that he will

continue to pay the thirty shillings a week to the Irish *colleen* who is my wife. I have had her in domestic service now for many years, I have not scrupled to deck her in exquisite sealskin and bootees befitting her station, and I have found her satisfactory in every way – she is scrupulously clean, an early riser, a hard worker, she has no "boy-friends" or followers, and her Thursdays off are spent with her relatives.[60]

But while calling attention to the unappreciated position of women, Myles notes that women are also equally guilty of undervaluing each other. What he renames as the 'Amalgamated Irish Housewives and General Consorts Association' is seen as equally guilty not only of a 'slavish passion for keeping our Irish girls not merely in domestic service but forever advertising to the whole world that that's all they're fit for . . . it's the old slave complex all over again'. This attitude, he writes, ignores the other jobs that women can take and is evidence that 'the Feudal System is still in operation'.[61] And when the Irish Housewives suggest that the domestic servants, who have been given good pay and comfortable rooms, are 'spoilt and indifferent', Myles points out not only are their hours longer and their pay less than a builder, the rooms in which they must sleep are cold and damp. The Irish Housewives Association is chastised for engagement in restricted fields – 'I wish the Housewives' League would look into questions which transcend doubts about the price of milk'[62] – and yet, when someone attacks women from the IHA in a dull and repetitive article Myles strikes back: 'I conceive that they [Tweedy and Sheehy Skeffington of the IHA] are the indefatigable and unpaid watch-dogs of the plain people vis-à-vis this new monster in the suede shoes known as the "Irish Industrialist". Maybe it is requisite that they should be publically insulted. But surely not by an unnamed lout who can't spell humorous'.[63]

In 1955, Myles protests with surprising clarity the unfair treatment of women, specifically addressing Aer Lingus's decision to force air-hostesses to leave their jobs after seven years. Given that the majority of women were hired at 18, this meant that their working lives were over at 25. Myles notes the sexism implicit in this decision:

> Women who want to earn a living are subject to a permanent male slander: that they don't really want or need a job – they are after a husband. . . . I think it is not unfair to say that the Aer Lingus order meant this: "Fair enough. You have had seven years within which to get your pilot or senior staff man. You haven't done so. Out! Get thee to a nunnery, for goodness sake!"[64]

Calling it 'damn nonsense', he notes that 'This thoroughly Irish transaction occurred at the same time as the British Government had publically agreed that women were entitled to pay equal to that of men for equal work'. This article stands out in a corpus notable for its misogynistic humour, and one is left to speculate as to its significance. Is it one of the articles written by Montgomery? Did O'Nolan feel that the target of Aer Lingus was worth some feminist rhetoric? Or does it indicate a greater sympathy with the female position and suggest that the previous misogyny was cutting satire? As tempting as the final position is, and as problematic as systematizing Myles's polemics must be, these minor counterpoints do little but reinforce the dominant theme: Myles was not blind to certain societal injustices, but found them a greater source of humour than a social ill: 'We have had indigenous ladies already in certain public offices and I say, with what is really startling mildness, that they were not a success. It is true that a woman's place is in the kitchen'.[65]

It is appropriate that a summary of Myles' thoughts on relations between the genders is submitted in a series of aphorisms which comments knowingly on male prejudices, and yet refuses to forgo – or condemn – a truculent misogyny:

Men don't understand women.
Women don't understand men. . . .
Women hate men, but that hatred is as nothing compared with the hatred women harbour for women. . . .
Men are convinced that women are not people.
Man is a great, important beast. *The stress on Man's importance is laid – in every science from anthropology to theology – by Man.*
Man regards Woman as an accessory. She is the spare tyre at the rear of Life's omnibus.
The mature Man's most generous assessment of the female is that she is a damn nuisance.
Women are customarily employed on tasks formerly assigned to slaves. . . .
When a man is half-mad from worry and trouble, the "consolation" and "help" received from women is as attractive to him as a dog's breakfast: and about as useful. [Emphasis added][66]

Myles is a thinner, Catholic version of Peter F. Murphy's formulation of the buffoon: a rotund, drunken, lawless misogynist – 'Women are in many ways the absent presence that haunts the buffoon's existence but . . . rarely ever appears'[67] – who uses his wit for acceptance within an overwhelmingly masculine sphere: 'Relying on his refined wit, his intelligence, and his comic abilities to make a clever joke, the buffoon laughs at himself, becoming a source of amusement for the intimate group in which he operates'.[68]

When assessed in relation to a career of 26 years, the amount of *Cruiskeen Lawn* articles engaging with women is relatively small – itself indicative of Myles's positioning of women as marginal. Despite his sustained criticism of the stage Irishman of the Celtic Revival, and its false depiction of the 'Irish Paddy', he treats women as stereotypes in much the same way: as a generic unit and a homogeneous other revolving around the single issue of the home. While this can be afforded a modicum of contextual leniency, and while he wasn't committed to keeping women subjugated to the conjugal and domestic, Myles, like O'Nolan, seemed incapable of conceiving of women as integral parts of Irish public life. Myles might not have thought that women belong in the kitchen, but he didn't seem to be quite sure where else to have them. Even when he engages with women as politicians or writers, he keeps bringing them back to the hearth, perhaps to infuriate and call attention to a lamentable trend, but primarily because he seemed incapable of locating an alternative. Thus, for example, in an article on Kate O'Brien Myles pretends not to recognize that a woman can be a novelist – 'What is hinted at in the phrase "the work of Miss O'Brien"? What work? . . . Could "work" be a mistake for, say, pork?'.[69] This joke might mock the attitudes of others, but its parody reinforces rather than undercuts.

In isolating Myles's depictions of women from those of men, there is the risk of masking the fact that the majority of his themes and characters were subjected to increasingly cantankerous invective. Given the range of subjects Myles wrote about, and the tendency of the tone of his engagements to be disgruntled and belligerent, particularly as he aged, it would be a greater insult had he never engaged with women at all, or afforded them a patronizingly soft touch. Despite this caveat, at issue is the fact that Myles's misogyny outweighs his misanthropy – that his treatment of women is more aggressive, less varied, and tends more towards an elision of individuality than his engagement with men. Despite the fact that the misogyny portrayed in his pieces is hyperbolic and often self-conscious, and despite the fact that the object of real derision is the Church and State's restrictive positioning of women, an equitable or enlightened replacement portrait of women is never presented. Continually depicting women in relation to dirt, violence, domesticity and ignorance may be an undercutting of Cathleen ni Houlihan, but it also maintains negative depictions of the female. Similarly, in repeatedly presenting a playful image of the Dublin man's prejudices and ideologies there was a tendency to embrace and regularize this character rather than problematize it; humour and excess cannot be allowed to excuse or dismiss collaboration in the normalization of violence or debilitating stereotypes. The *Cruiskeen Lawn* articles might be a humorous remarking on misogyny and mistreatment, but they must be faulted for their involvement in the standardization of that treatment.

Urinating women

Aligned to the attempted reconfiguring of the Irish woman and mother is *The Hard Life*'s lengthy conceit – urination. Not only is the Irish women not a naturally pure mother, she is an animal, which, to use Somerset Maugham's misogynistic formula, 'micturates once a day, defecates once a week, menstruates once a month, parturates [sic] once a year and copulates whenever she has the opportunity';[70] in other words, a beast ruled by cycles of base bodily functions, all of which produce disease and decay. *The Hard Life* is 'a treatise on piss and vomit'[71] attacking perfected representations of women, but presenting no positive picture in their stead. Instead it is a text luxuriating in the 'alien' operations of the female body, which is presented at worst as disgustingly repellent, and at best aesthetic but dull. In addressing a theme which O'Nolan termed 'the most preposterous in all the literature of the earth'[72] – female urination – the author does not work to stress that the female body is subject to the same, normal, boring needs as the male, but that the needs of the female body are dark and different. As has been often noted, the novel can be seen as a response to Bloom's ruminations: 'They did right to put him [a statue of Thomas Moore] up over a urinal: meeting of the waters. Ought to be places for women. Running into cakeshops. Settle my hat straight'.[73] But the meeting of the waters does not imply the mingling of streams of equality – to force the metaphor – as due to social conventions which permit(ted) men to urinate relatively openly but ask(ed) women to retreat to a private space, female urination becomes tied not only to the 'dirtier' defecation, but to the 'mysterious' menstruation.

Furthermore, since Collopy's euphemistic 'other business' (HL 34) conjoins female sexuality and urination, desire is deemed latently polluted: in providing public toilets for women, Collopy enables them to walk the streets – become streetwalkers. Thus, a project ostensibly addressing urination is also a project of blood, faeces and licentiousness, which O'Brien seemed to expect his readership to find disgustingly hilarious.

As the book progresses, Collopy's project is made increasingly ridiculous – he and his committee purchase a 'clinical hydrometer' so that the women can 'take careful readings day and night for a fortnight' (HL 96) of the amount of urine they produce. This will not only reveal 'very little difference in them, only slight variations' in the female animal but will also 'establish a great new scientific fact' (HL 97). The trams which are to assist the women with their bodily needs are to be a forbidding and deathly black, and the restrooms that form part of the Collopy Trust are mockingly named after male saints. This joke analeptically plays on Collopy's idea that the saintly is that which is removed from the female: 'They say piety has a smell. . . . It's a perverse notion. What they mean is only the absence of the smell of women' (HL 23). This means that in order for men to be virtuous and devotional, the distracting impurity of women simply need be removed, thereby implying not simply that chastity is godly, but that real virtue is a predominantly male preserve. In naming public toilets after saints, Collopy brings together the godly and the intimate scent of a woman in, to the novel, clear contradiction, a contamination foreshadowed in the manuscript of *At Swim-Two-Birds*, in which Trellis asks if a

> streetwalker makes £20,000 from her trade, saves it up over a period of 50 years, repents in her old age and builds a church with the money? Is it a church within the meaning of the act or what is it? Is it a brothel? Tainted money.[74]

But as ludicrous as O'Nolan finds the theme, the lack of public toilets made leaving the house to go shopping or do different errands a genuinely difficult task for women, because, as Caitriona Clear writes in an account of women's lives in Ireland, 'unless she had some friends or relations in the town, there was nowhere to have a cup of tea or to attend to bodily needs. Ordinary country women did not go into public houses, and there were very few cafes or restaurants'.[75] Genuine difficulties and injustices are reduced to points of easy, dismissive humour.

But while Collopy's obsession with women's toilets is meant to be entertainingly hilarious, it is a mania that embroils Collopy in a tragi-comic fate. Mrs Crotty dies of an illness that involves 'nocturnal diuresis (or bed-wetting)' (HL 118) which eventually rusts and rots the wire mattress of the bed and traps Collopy within it. Collopy becomes imprisoned, therefore, in a mesh of metal corroded by urination. He is caught in this repulsive embrace because he contracted severe rheumatism – more 'disease' – from standing in the rain shouting euphemistically about female toilets. Having been made ill from association with women's micturition, he is then treated with more water – gravid water – which makes him grossly heavy without visible difference to his size. When Collopy dies – falling through the floor in a theatre – he dies, effectively, of fluid retention, as his body cannot rid itself of the gravid water. On his gravestone is subsequently written the line, adapted from Keats, 'Here lies one whose name is writ in water' (HL 150): one whose name was made briefly known through urine and through gravid water.[76] While 'gravid' comes from the Latin *gravidus* meaning burdened or heavy, it most commonly means 'pregnant'. Thus, gravid water is both 'heavy water' and 'pregnant water', and Collopy dies under the weight of ingesting a very female liquid – a miscarriage, if you will. Inasmuch as he involved the lack of toilets in his wife's death – 'I will not say . . . that what-you-know was the sole reason for the woman's demise. Not the *sole* reason, mind you. But by Christ it had plenty to do with it' (HL 60) – the inability to void himself of this pregnant liquid became the indirect cause of his demise as well. Collopy dies because of an 'unhealthy' obsession with urination, and his body begins to decompose rapidly, revealing that contact with the female causes illness, death and rot.

Despite Collopy's sympathies for women's suffering, and the fact that he is rare in O'Nolan's works in that he shows genuine sorrow at a death, his investment in women's welfare is wholly limited. His interest in women's toilets take the form of an obsession rather than genuine concern, and his frequenting public meetings to shout euphemistically from the back about women's toilets brings his project closer to the perverse mania of 'a dirty old man' (HL 39). He casually likens a 'humble Jesuit' to 'a dog without a tail or a woman without a knickers on her' (HL 35), and attributes some women's dislike of going to mass to the fact 'They'd have to wash themselves. And darn their damned stockings' (HL 53). Having made toilets the focus of his energy, he sees filth – physical and moral – everywhere, except in himself. Thus, when he hears that Manus has books in the house he immediately presumes that they will be 'dirty books, lascivious peregrinations on the fringes of filthy indecency, cloacal spewings in the face of Providence, with pictures of prostitutes in their pelts' (HL 67). Similarly, he is hypocritically obsessed with the notion of cleanliness, thinking that one can contract 'syphilis and painful skin diseases' (HL 89) by using a public laundry, and yet shares his own unpleasant practices without hesitation: 'When you get back . . . tell Annie that there are two pairs of dirty socks at the bottom of my bed. They want to be washed and darned' (HL 127). Collopy's contradictions and entanglements mirror O'Nolan's own; the author may parody Church and State ideologies on sexual desire and women, but he latently subscribes to many of the positions he targets. The eccentric religious celibates that Hopper argues he lampoons[77] aren't too removed from O'Nolan himself, and while women's needs are a central motif, they are proffered as comedy rather than the real commentary on social injustice that Booker and Cronin say he presents.[78] Women's needs might be thematically incorporated into *The Hard Life*, but these bodily requirements are debased, and women themselves insistently marginalized and besmirched.

Disgusting women

All of O'Nolan's novels delight in the disgusting, and they resound with an obsession – more repressed than Beckett's – with pimples, boils, obesity, vomit, urine, masturbation, grease, sweat, dirt and stench. In *The Hard Life* in particular the world is one of contemptible squalor, slums and salaciousness, calling to mind a parable which Kant recounts, in which Earth is described as 'a *cloaca,* where all the excrement from the other worlds has been deposited'.[79] *The Third Policeman* pivots on desire, but was rejected by publishers and repressed by the author, and so the later works embrace disgust. Disgust, Menninghaus writes, is

> a state of alarm and emergency, an acute crisis of self-preservation in the face of an unassimilable otherness, a convulsive struggle

. . . . The fundamental schema of disgust is the experience of a nearness that is not wanted. An intrusive presence, a smell or taste is spontaneously assessed as contamination and forcibly distanced. The theory of disgust, to that extent, is a counterpart – although not a symmetrical one – of the theory of love, desire, and appetite as forms of intercourse with a nearness that is wanted.[80]

That which provokes disgust is that which aesthetically offends, sensorially disgusts, physically pollutes and seems so wrong as to invoke nausea. Baudelaire's mixture of physical decay and corrupted sexuality in his poem '*Une Charogne*' ('Carrion') evokes perfectly the disgust that focuses on the female body in *The Hard Life*, and which culminates in Finbarr's 'tidal surge of vomit' (HL 157) in response to the concept of marrying Annie.

> *Les jambes en l'air, comme une femme lubrique,*
> *Brûlante et suant les poisons,*
> *Ouvrait d'une façon nonchalante et cynique*
> *Son ventre plein d'exhalaisons.*
>
> . . .
>
> *Les mouches bourdonnaient sur ce ventre putride,*
> *D'où sortaient de noirs bataillons*
> *De larves, qui coulaient comme un épais liquide*
> *Le long de ces vivants haillons.*[81]

Disgust is what is felt at the sight of the rotting carcass, particularly a rotting carcass that emulates the body of a woman, as it assumes a state which mocks arousal, and gives birth to maggots in a putrescent masquerade of life. This conflation of Eros and Thanatos not only calls to the sexuality and desire of *The Third Policeman*, but makes an association between normal female sexuality and rot, which is made explicit as the poem continues. The association of the female body, particularly the aged female body, and disgust is consistent throughout reflections on the revolting, with the ugly old woman deemed the apogee of the disgusting:

> This phantasm conventionally brings together folds and wrinkles, warts, larger than usual openings of the body (i.e. mouth and anus), foul, black teeth, sunk-in hollows instead of beautiful swellings, drooping breasts, stinking breath, revolting habits, and a proximity to both death and putrefaction.[82]

Kristeva writes that 'filth is not a quality in itself, but it applies only to what relates to a *boundary* and, more particularly, represents the object jettisoned out of that boundary, its other side, a margin'.[83] As spittle, urine, blood, faeces move from the inside to the outside they provoke disgust and defilement, not only because of the wrongness associated with boundary transgression, but because of an associated problematization of the boundaries themselves. As such, when women, already other, are made doubly other by a visible contamination of the inside and the outside – menstruation, sweat, urination – the disgust provoked (in the male) is greater. Disgust is, therefore, all too often formulated in terms of the male response and male gaze, and the disgusting body *par excellence* that which presents the tattered remains of the object of male desire – an entity is most disgusting when it retains the corrupted remnants of what used to attract, and thereby mocks attraction itself. Hence, when O'Nolan disparages the women working in Heath's offices in a letter to O'Keeffe, he describe them precisely in terms of the typical hag:

> I see Heath's as a sort of Mayfair boudoir peopled by ageing girls who wear hair-nets, Dunlopillo tits, print frocks though with jumpers, thin venomous legs encased in thick cashmere stockings the better to shroud varicose fantasy, the ghastly spawgs ending in tennis shoes. The eyes are shielded by pince-nez, anchored to the ear with tiniest and most delicate of gold chains. . . . At a top desk is the boss, Frau Hamilton. This terrible creature, the face in a permanent scowl due to palsy and the back all corkscrewed through polio, wears a dirty, torn brown dress and carries something which could be either a club or a crutch. She farts sulphurously every two minutes. You get the nearest summary if you call her a female antichrist.[84]

It's significant that one of the most visual pictures of women offered by O'Nolan is one which adheres to the conventions of the disgusting old woman.

Kant tells the story of an ugly man called Heidegger:

> Heidegger, a German musician living in London, was fantastically deformed, but a clever and intelligent person with whom aristocrats liked to associate for the sake of conversation. Once

it occurred to him at a drinking party to claim to a lord that he had the ugliest face in London. The lord reflected and then made a wager that he could present a face still more ugly. He then sent for a drunken woman, at whose appearance the whole party burst into laughter and shouted: "Heidegger, you have lost the wager!" 'Not so fast', he replied, "let the woman wear my wig and let me wear her headdress; then we shall see." As this took place, everybody fell to laughing, to the point of suffocation, because the woman looked like a very presentable gentleman, and the fellow looked like a witch. This shows that in order to call anyone beautiful, or at least bearably pretty, one must not judge absolutely, but always only relatively.[85]

While Kant refers to the relativity of the disgusting, the anecdote nonetheless points to the fact that, within societal conventions, a deformed man is still less ugly than an 'unfeminine' woman, and to make himself even more hideous the ugliest man in the world need simply take on the accoutrements of the female. The ugly woman is the pinnacle of the disgusting, and this view is firmly subscribed to by O'Nolan. This is not to suppose that O'Nolan considered the male body a thing of beauty, however: 'The Pathology of Revivalism' contains annotations, in what appears to be Montgomery's handwriting, commenting on O'Nolan's tendency to reject as distasteful the male body too: 'hardly any male has a comely figure (BO'N OBSESSION – HAVE YOU EVER SEEN ME?) . . . good tailoring is concerned with hiding the gross defects of most figures (ARE YOU MAD?)'.[86] However, when compared to the way in which women are presented, the unpleasant attributes of men tend more towards the comically distasteful. Neither Father Fahrt's name, a macaronic homophone for flatulence, nor his skin condition – 'some scaly skin disease (psoriasis?) which need not appear on the face but be conveyed by itching and scratching'[87] – render disgust; they are irreverent, and humorously objectionable, but not repulsive. Similarly, while Finbarr's vomitus reaction to the concept of marriage to Annie indicates the repulsive horror of the incestuous suggestion, when vomit is not related to the unattractive female it becomes amusingly crude. Hence, O'Nolan can describe *The Hard Life* as urine and bile in a wholly approbatory way: 'I do think this is a very funny book, though no dog is a judge of his own vomit. It is old, elegant, nostalgic piss'.[88]

While men are often dirty and noisome, a special type of disgust
is reserved for women, and Annie embodies women as 'naturally'
impure and fundamentally disgusting. Annie is introduced as
'a streel of a girl with long lank fair hair' who 'did not talk very
much and seemed to be in a permanent bad temper' (HL 11). She
feeds the boys a diet of 'mince balls covered in a greasy paste' (HL
12) and is described as a dull, dreary, dirty constant who 'never
changes. In fact she never changes even her clothes' (HL 108). She
shows scarce sign of intellect – the few instances of direct speech
she is awarded show her uttering short, irrelevant answers, and
apart from the death of her father she gives little response to
changes in the house. She, like Teresa of *At Swim-Two-Birds*, is
represented as a barely sentient domestic slave, and Finbarr speaks
of having 'trained Annie to bring [him] breakfast in bed' (HL 140).
But the lifeless, repulsive Annie is also working as a prostitute, and
thereby not only physically repulsive but, within the protocols of
the narrative, morally repugnant. Thus, O'Brien is able to introduce
not only the disgusting female body, but the disgusting, diseased
female body, as knowledge of her occupation leads Manus to
speculate on her ability to protect herself both from pregnancy and
infection. The symptoms of two of the more visually distressing
sexually transmitted diseases are described, infections that involve
particularly noticeable ulcers and lesions on the genitals, before
Manus settles on the more standard gonorrhoea and syphilis.
While Manus' eventual decision that Annie is 'a cute and cunning
handful' (HL 115) and not in any trouble may imply that she is free
from contamination, the implication is instead that her venality
is so fundamental to her construct that she knows how to avoid
pregnancy – here the notion of contraception is smuggled in – and
disease.

While we are presumably to be surprised at the possibility of
Annie working as a prostitute (HL 110), the implication that Manus
was paying Annie for sex figures earlier in the narrative.

In the last eighteen months or so, she was asked to undertake
another duty to which she agreed willingly enough. The brother
had given up the early-rising of his schooldays but would often
hand Annie some money for "what-you-know" from his bedside.
He was in need of a cure, and the poor girl would slip out and
bring him back a glass of whiskey. (HL 89–90)

While the overt, eventual meaning is that Annie had simply been procuring whisky for him, the wording of the passage is deliberately suggestive. Annie is thus an older,[89] unattractive, unclean, dull prostitute, hardened to liquor (HL 61) and 'fucking on the banks of the Grand Canal',[90] who is Finbarr's half-cousin and possibly his brother's mistress. When Manus finally suggests that Finbarr marry Annie, and the book closes with Finbarr's 'tidal surge of vomit' (HL 157), the disgust he exhibits is in response to all that is fundamentally wrong about Annie. But, while Annie is presented as the zenith of the repugnant, she is also a form of the Everywoman, or 'Anywoman': she is a replacement mother for the boys, a virgin – Miss Annie – and an unattractive prostitute.[91] As virgin/mother/whore she embodies in a single, repulsive form all the traditional aspects of woman and portrays them all as equally disgusting and corrupt.

In representing the female as intrinsically damaged, all dealings between men and women become tainted with the implication of a dark and perverse sexuality. The 'Eternal City is full of brothels' (HL 129), and the women of England 'are nearly all prostitutes' (HL 156). When Irish women go to London assaults by men make them decide that if unmarried sex was the 'custom of the country, [they] might as well get paid for it' (HL 103). If the club 'composed mostly of women who met every afternoon to play cards or discuss household matters' that Annie joined, a club which helped her come 'out of her shell' (HL 65) was either a bordello or a group which encouraged her to become a prostitute, then, by implication, all women's groups are tainted with the same corruption. If, therefore, the only women at outdoor public meetings are prostitutes (HL 39), groups of women meeting up indoors also prostitutes, and men think that woman are objects on which to focus aggression and lust (HL 39), then we are left with a society saturated with despicable violence and corruption. Even the 'sacred union' of marriage is contaminated, as while Mrs Crotty and Mr Collopy are married she has not changed her name from that taken in her first marriage, and introduced into their relationship are the implications of the inappropriate masquerading as the legitimate: 'An ill-disposed person might suspect they were not married at all and that Mrs Crotty was a kept-woman or resident prostitute' (HL 20). Furthermore, if the disgusting Annie is a prostitute then it is because there are men willing to pay to have sex with her, and not only are women fundamentally immoral and impure, those who wish to sleep with them equally foul and diseased. Annie is a sex-worker 'of the very lowest cadres' (HL 110), the men who sleep with her 'dirty merchants' (HL 113), and the men and women frequenting the area she works 'poxed up to the eyes, drunk on methylated spirits, flooding the walks with contaminated puke' (HL 115).

The single instance of a physically attractive female in comes in the form of Penelope, who is 'a good hoult, with auburn hair, blue eyes and a very nice smile' (HL 89), who dresses neatly and well, and who operates, ostensibly, as the antithesis to Annie – a young, pretty, friendly, clean, virginal girl of no family relation. But not only is Penelope never again mentioned after a single evening of 'trivial and pointless' (HL 110) conversation, when Finbarr sees Annie at work as a prostitute his association with Penelope becomes, by association, equally soiled.

> What was the meaning of this thing sex, what was the nature of sexual attraction? Was it all bad and dangerous? What was Annie doing late at night, standing in a dark place with young blackguards? Was I any better myself in my conduct, whispering sly things into the ear of lovely and innocent Penelope? Had I, in fact, at the bottom of my heart dirty intentions, some dark deed postponed only because the opportunity had not yet presented itself? (HL 111)

While Finbarr's self-reflections are no doubt intended to make him appear self-indulgent and self-obsessed, underlying them is the concept that heterosexuality corrupts all. In O'Nolan's works, sexual congress rarely reflects well on either party, and had O'Nolan written sex scenes the few instances that were not rape would resemble Frieda's and K.'s rolling on the floor 'in the puddles of beer and the rubbish'[92] in Kafka's *The Castle*. Awkward, confusing, and associated with dirt and disgust. It is indicative both of people's thoughts on O'Nolan's relation to Joyce and his attitudes to sex and women that when *The Dalkey Archive* was given a theatrical adaptation by Allan McClelland, and Mary reads out part of a book she's writing, we are treated to Molly Bloom's final monologue, but with the Molly's masturbatory affirmations replaced by Mary's firm negations.[93] There will be no embracing of women's sexuality here.

Scheming women

While the main female characters in O'Brien's last novels – *The Dalkey Archive* and the unfinished *Slattery's Sago Saga* – are not as physically disgusting as Annie, they are nonetheless deeply problematic. In *The Dalkey Archive*, O'Brien takes the name of the virginal mother par excellence and places it on a woman whose surface charm masks duplicity and promiscuity. Her pregnancy becomes not a blossoming into motherhood, but evidence of the manipulation and immorality of the female. In *Slattery's Sago Saga* Crawford MacPherson, a woman closer to hag, is 'an elderly woman clad in shapeless, hairy tweeds, small red-rimmed eyes glistening in a brownish lumpy face that looked to Tim like the crust of an apple-pie' (SP 25), and is the epitome of the neo-colonialist, a presumptive and arrogant intruder who is utterly confident of her right to interfere: a form of colonial mother-in-law.

As is frequently remarked upon, when Niall Montgomery read an early draft of *The Dalkey Archive* he was perplexed by Mary, until he decided that Mary was a surname, and that she was in fact Mr Mary.[94] While Montgomery makes a playful point, the possibility of gender confusion arises in part from the simple fact that nothing about Mary matches O'Nolan's previous representation of women: she is clever, educated, witty and lively, and her interests span politics, literature, music and high fashion. But despite all these virtues, be they lauded or insulted by Mick, Mary is unconvincing both as a romantic interest and as a woman. Scott wrote to O'Nolan saying that 'Mary should be one of the principal characters but is in actual fact merely a shadow, a girl whose even outward appearance the reader cannot envisage'.[95] Mary may possess more talents and spend more time 'loiter[ing] enticingly around the fringes' (DA 8) of the text than O'Nolan's other female characters, but she is nonetheless an indistinct brown mass on the margins of the plot, 'a nuisance yet never far away' (DA 8).

O'Nolan's skills never lay in the creation of rounded, appealing characters – Montgomery suggested that not every personality in the text needed to be quite so obnoxious nor so ill-defined and could be given 'fleeting moments of self-awareness',[96] but O'Nolan replied: 'I don't think De Selby shd. [sic] be made into a firmer, more real character. The most I can do is make JAJ's [Joyce's] speech and manner more authentic'.[97] Nonetheless, while the other characters are easy character-types – the aggressive friend, the deaf proprietor, the mysterious man of knowledge – they are as a result satisfactory. Mary, on the other hand, is an awkward, indistinct mass too central to be so out of focus. When Montgomery suggested that Mary was a man and that the 'heterosexual agony'[98] was in fact homosexual, he was, no doubt, being playful, but a genuine point underlies: it is not simply that Mary is an unconvincing female character as she exceeds the usual confines of O'Nolan's women, and/or intrinsically feminine qualities – whatever they might be – but because she is constructed so awkwardly that one can only presume that there is another, deeper layer to her, and that O'Nolan is presenting a carefully constructed pun or joke. Only a shaggy dog story or final surprising twist should allow for lines of such agonizing awkwardness as 'Believe it or not, light or no light, they kissed as privately as possible under that tree' (DA 57). While these painfully awkward romantic scenes were most likely envisioned as evidence of Mick's prudishness, they lack the intimations of authorial control that attribute bad writing to narrator or character rather than author, and thereby appear to repeat O'Nolan's discomfort with romance and the female rather than introduce Mick's. While O'Nolan was capable, as Myles, of writing entertaining mimicries of bad love scenes in the short, fragmented form of *Cruiskeen Lawn* – 'Would she give up this man, deny herself forever the charming conversation he was wont to dispense, for aye? Or follow Love's beckon, the summons of Cupid, knowing that what is natural must be good?'[99] – the novel's demands for sustained characterization and credible interactions constricted him. Despite O'Nolan's claims that *The Dalkey Archive* was an 'essay in derision' rather than a novel – see Chapter 5 – it adheres primarily to the conventions of the realist novel, whose love scenes, even selfish love between obnoxious individuals, require a greater control than O'Nolan was able to provide. Myles's parodies of the realist novel comment on its emphasis on detail and the visual – 'my duty . . . is to give the atmosphere of the bathroom, not sloppily, not "impressionistically" nor sketchily, but by a concentrated barrage, an intensity of analysis, a pitiless searching description of the objects which most give . . . quality to the scene'[100] – but in the longer text O'Nolan proved incapable of getting close enough to the details to be convincing or far enough away to easily lampoon.

While the faint lines with which Mary is drawn are an irritation and a distraction, it is not the vagueness of O'Nolan's women that is troubling, or the fact that they are too often conceived of as no more than '"fringe-benefit[s]"'.[101] It is, as O'Keeffe wrote with telling insight, the violence underlying their depiction: 'The scenes with Mary are great but I feel a bit uneasy about the tone – which strikes me as hating rather than one of development'.[102] Mary, and women in general, are portrayed not only as strange, distant others, but as strange, distant, inferior others, objects to be assessed in terms of the mysteries of their gender rather than individuals:

Mary was not a simple girl, not an easy subject to write about nor Mick the one to write. He thought women in general were hopeless as a theme for discussion or discourse, and surely for one man the one special – *la femme particulière*, if that sharpens the meaning – must look dim, meaningless and empty to others if he should talk genuinely about her or think aloud. The mutual compulsion is a mystery, not just a foible or biogenesis, and this sort of mystery, even if comprehensible to the two concerned, is at least absolutely private. (DA 52)

Women are not the subjects of worthy intellectual inquiry, as it is merely the strange aberration of physical attraction that causes them to be interesting, and then only to the one whom the mystery of reproductive necessity has made fall. It is not only the sexual act which becomes a taboo subject, but love, as the attraction between two people is expressed with deep unease as a strange fetish. Heterosexual mechanics, the narration implies, simply requires a male and a female – specifically preferring one instance of the female over another indicates an odd but necessary perversion, useful for a healthy gene pool but otherwise best left unexplained. Thus, the pinnacle of love is expressed as follows: 'He was, he thought, very fond of her and did not by any means regard her as merely a member of her sex, or anything so commonplace and trivial' (DA 52). The demon love makes one believe that in the object of desire one sees more than just a woman, but, *The Dalkey Archive* shows, in the woman one finds only manipulation and control. Significantly, to return to the *Cruiskeen Lawn,* Myles writes: 'It is of the nature of man . . . to be predatory in his relations with women in general; women attribute this to their overwhelming charm.

In fact, the man's sole desire is to best and spite a fellow male'.[103] While the mechanics of reproduction require a male and a female, love and desire remain transactions conducted between men. It is not surprising that O'Nolan's female characters are disappointing throughout his works – they are little more than pawns in masculine games.

When revising the manuscript, O'Nolan made changes to scenes involving Mary, but the changes do not remove or reduce the levels of blatant hostility; they increase them. In the following quotation, the manuscript ends at the point indicated by the double slash:

> Yet work at the fol-the-lols of couture did nothing to impair Mary's maturity of mind. She read a lot, talked politics often and once even mentioned her half intentions of writing a book. Mick did not ask her on what subject, for somehow he found the idea distasteful.//Without swallowing whole all the warnings one could readily hear and read about the spiritual dangers of intellectual arrogance and literary freebooting, there *was* menace in the overpoise that high education and a rich way of living could confer on a young girl. Unknowingly, she could exceed her own strength. Did she find his own company a stabilizing pull? Mick had to doubt that, for the truth was that he was not all too steady himself. Confession once a month was all very well but he was drinking too much. He would give up drink. Also, he would make Mary more of his own quiet kind, and down to earth. (DA 53)

Female aspiration is compared to the ills of excessive drinking, which O'Brien's manuscript was replete with; 'What harm if, on my lone walk to the station, I entered another house to have an ultimate final absolutely last one, to reflect on that evening's strange talk?',[104] causing Montgomery to ask: 'Could you have the typescript fed into a computer to find out – to the nearest 1000 litres – the amount of drink consumed?'[105] In reducing Mick's alcohol intake, O'Nolan increases his misogyny, equating liquor with 'sinful reveries of the carnal kind' (DA 60). Added to this addition is the intimation that educated woman are dangerous and sinful. O'Nolan's personal library contains few books written by female authors; Woolf's *The Waves* seemed like an exciting exception until the inside pages revealed Evelyn's ownership. The dislike of the female writer is played upon in the *Cruiskeen Lawn* when Myles is twice 'replaced'

by women – Myles's sister, Shookra na Gopaleen and later Shuecra
O'Sleveen of the National Advertising Universal Sales Energising
Agency (NAUSEA). The homophonic qualities of their names evoke
Myles's opinion of the homogeneity of women – all that differs
is levels of education. Shookra is decidedly Myles's unintelligent
sister: 'I can cuk, I can write very finely, I can play the piana',[106]
and her articles are littered with multiple exclamation marks
that Myles would have found the height of vulgarity – '(!!!!!)'. As
Donohue puts it, 'the Sister represents a view of women common
in such a paternalistic society, insular, depressed, and suppressed
by the moral force of the Church into long celibacy and late
marriage',[107] with the added stain of a lack of intelligence. Sheucra
is better schooled, but is still made to repeat lines such as 'weak
woman that I am', and is no more than a foil for Myles's genius
and eccentricity,[108] affirming female subordination and reinforcing
the gender hierarchies running throughout the columns. While
Mick's overt misogyny was presumably intended to emphasize his
negative, small-minded prudishness and make him 'an even more
obnoxious prig than he is',[109] once again we encounter Myles and
O'Brien's preference for sexist situations and protagonists, and an
aggressive treatment of women whose supposed parody offers little
subversion of patriarchal norms. Performing a sexist scene is not
the same as exposing it, and as in the case of *Cruiskeen Lawn*,
O'Brien effectively promotes misogyny rather than undercutting it,
particularly when many of Mick's more hysterical concerns about
Mary are revealed to be accurate.

As *The Dalkey Archive* progresses Mick's devotion to the
Church increases in line with his decreasing respect for Mary. He
systematically undermines Mary's positive qualities, finally deciding
that his 'virgin Mary' (DA 111) is 'a gilded trollop . . . with plenty
of other gents who were devout associates. Or slaves, marionettes?'
(DA 133) Associating sexual subterfuge and intellectual dishonesty,
Mick's childish prejudices would seem deliberately designed to
belittle him and conflate religious vocations with misogynistic
attitudes were it not for the fact that the book's conclusion reveals
them to be true. As is often noted, the manuscript ends with the
lines: '"I'm sure enough I'll marry you. And I'm perfectly certain I'll
have a baby." There you are. I always knew that Mary was a girl in
a thousand'.[110] The published version of the text – '"I'm certain I'm
going to have a baby"' (DA 192) – implies not that Mary will have a

baby at some future date but that she is currently pregnant. Thus, her choice to push Mick's hand by revealing an association with Hackett seems born of a need to get him to marry her immediately. The fact that she blanches (DA 190) when Mick tells her that her relationship with Hackett 'doesn't matter' (DA 190) turns her into a woman who played around with a man who was more fun, and now faced with pregnancy tries to force the hand of the man who is more reliable. Thus, the novel ends with, as O'Nolan put it, the narrator's exit in 'a nightmare fug of doubt'.[111] Interestingly, when Montgomery read the text he didn't think of it in terms of a simple act of infidelity, but as the intercourse conducted without awareness raised in *At Swim-Two-Birds*. He writes: 'Ending gas – how could protagonist have had it out of sight unbeknownst to himself? (Remember wonderful Dinneen gloss – *sleith* – copulation with a woman without her knowledge or consent)'.[112] This reading presents Mary in an even more manipulative light. She ceases to become a woman forcing a man to father another man's child, but a woman who has managed to make a man father his own child without his comprehension. Thus, Mick's fears that Mary treats men like slaves or puppets is realized, as Mary begins to resemble a succubus, able to seduce a man into fatherhood without his awareness or sanction. O'Brien ends *The Dalkey Archive* with the death of freedom, as Mick is trapped in a repetitive relationship with a woman whose ability to control and manipulate is daunting. He may have foiled De Selby's plan, but he was incapable of escaping Mary's devious clutches.

Slattery's Sago Saga, O'Brien's final, unfinished novel is interesting primarily for the prominence of a female antagonist, a domineering, whiskey-drinking American with plans to prevent another famine, and subsequently another wave of Irish immigrants, by replacing Ireland's staple crop of potatoes with sago. But, as O'Nolan's early summary of the novel outlines, after twenty-five years of a concentrated sago diet, the Irish begin to suffer ill-effects, and as illegal immigration into America continues, sago-induced diseases begin to attack the population there. MacPherson, having thrown the world into chaos, dies of 'sagosis', and it is left to her husband and the Kennedy-like Tim Hartigan to lead the world back to the noble potato. MacPherson represents a development in the primacy and importance of female characters in O'Nolan's works, and Asbee deems her to be 'the most dynamic female character O'Brien ever created',[113] but this dynamism is by no means positive: Amy

Nejezchleb describes MacPherson as 'a stereotype of aggressive American feminists of the 1960s',[114] and inasmuch as the feminists in *The Hard Life* want to blow up City Hall, the feminist position in *Slattery's Sago Saga* is presented as aggressive and thoughtless.

Asbee rightly compares MacPherson to *The Dalkey Archive*'s De Selby, noting how her 'plans to change the pattern of nature and society recall the mad scientist'.[115] But, while MacPherson is a daunting adversary and crazed visionary – intelligent, well-travelled, instinctive, and with De Selby's determination in the execution of madly daring plans – she is, nonetheless, a highly circumscribed version of the male philosopher-scientist. While De Selby's wish to rid the world of all life is based on philosophically and theologically derived misanthropy, her desire to contain the Irish within Ireland is bred of a small-minded but venomous racism, which causes her to view the Irish as an infestation bringing 'crime, drunkenness, illegal corn liquor, bank robbery, murder, prostitution, syphilis, mob rule, crooked politics and Roman Catholic Popery' (SP 28). While De Selby employs a mysterious chemical with dramatic metaphysical and temporal implications, she makes recourse to a starchy crop and a change in diet. While De Selby is courteous and reflective, she is rude, impatient, meddlesome and tiring. Her retention of her maiden name does denote independence and self-reliance, but it also has the same misogynistic associations of the illicit and unnatural that are tied to *The Hard Life*'s Mrs Crotty. While both De Selby's and MacPherson's plans fail, De Selby is allowed to return to his wife, while she is punished with death. And while De Selby, although eccentric, is allowed dignity, she is tainted with intimations of incontinence.

O'Nolan's summary of the novel leaves little doubt that MacPherson is to be deemed a manipulative, interfering and dangerously short-sighted woman, in short, 'a fearful virago'[116] who marries Ned Hoolihan because she recognizes oil in his fields and who causes large-scale but unintended global damage. O'Nolan's inability to conceive of a convincing strong female character leaves MacPherson as an oddly androgynous one, with stereotypically negative feminine traits of bossiness and interference grafted on to the masculine – her androgynous names, her whiskey drinking, her aggressive mode of speech, her refusal to be addressed with female titles – and we are left, to allude to Montgomery's confusion regarding *The Dalkey Archive*, with an evil Mr Mary.

Supplementing O'Nolan's chauvinism and discrimination in relation to women is an undercurrent of xenophobia. Anderson notes the conflating of promiscuity and black skin in the kidnapped maids from the Western section of the *At Swim-Two-Birds* manuscript, and the ease with which any refusal of sexual favours on the part of the maids would lead to 'lynch[ing] a Sambo ofa tree'.[117] Later letters pertaining to *The Dalkey Archive* contain distressingly racist content, as O'Nolan gleefully investigated the possibility that Augustine might have been black: 'He was an African (Numidin) and what I have yet failed to be certain about is whether he was a nigger. I hope he was, or at least some class of a coon'.[118] O'Nolan's interest in Augustine's ethnicity stems from a belief that it would shame the Church if Augustine was revealed to be black, and he repeated this question in a number of letters, receiving no satisfactory reply. In the published text, De Selby reiterates O'Nolan's question directly, asking Augustine '*Are you a Nigger?*' [emphasis in original] (DA 40),[119] and the matter rests, flat and listless, until O'Nolan and Hugh Leonard correspond about a theatrical adaptation of *The Dalkey Archive*. O'Nolan was concerned about some of the terms that Leonard planned to use and wrote to Con Leventhal saying that 'there will be outsized riots but not of the right smell to be classified as publicity. "Jesus!" is used as a solitary expletive and John the Baptist (I almost wrote Bastard) is shown as an awfully comic clown'.[120] O'Nolan repeatedly asked Leonard to moderate the language used, fearing a '"Playboy" sort of row',[121] as there were rumblings in the Dáil about 'Foul language besmirching the eyes and ears of innocent children, immoral mouthings, depravity, degenerate writers etc.',[122] but was insistent about the retention of 'nigger'. When Leonard replaces it with 'black', O'Nolan objects, writing that 'I can't see why 'nigger' (De Selby is deliberately jeering) is replaced by 'black', which is a neutral, humbug term'.[123] Leonard repeatedly tries to get him to remove it from the script, but O'Nolan insists, until eventually Leonard seeks an outside opinion:

"Nigger": as I mentioned before, we know very little about De Selby's views re racialism; and it will be impossible to convey that the character rather than the authors is sneering. For myself, I detest the word for its latter-day contemptuous meaning. I am putting this up to Phyllis for her opinion, as you are obviously dead-set on using "nigger."[124]

O'Nolan respected Leonard and had written to O'Keeffe stating that Leonard's ending to the play was a 'brainwave (and tidal wave) [which] would much improve the book'.[125] That he would continue to insist on the term, in the face of active resistance by one who had his grudging respect, shows a very problematic attitude to racial equality. This is heightened – and the defence that it was voiced by a character dismissed – when in another letter to O'Keeffe, written during the African-American civil rights movement, O'Nolan mentions black voter registration in utterly disparaging terms. Annoyed that Cecil Scott thought him ignorant of US policy regarding the birthplace of an American President – this was to be an important plot point in *Slattery's Sago Saga* – he wrote: 'Who does he [Cecil Scott] think I am – a nigger seeking registration being quizzed in Selma on the Constitution?'[126] Coupling this with a 1963 *Cruiskeen Lawn* article on illiteracy, in which Myles writes 'One can overlook his [the 'black man of South Africa'] tuberculosis, glaucoma, syphilis and leprosy but his illiteracy and his feral twitterings in place of speech put him in a class lower than the chimpanzeesial',[127] places O'Nolan in an indefensible position. While Ireland in the 1960s was certainly not a bastion of equal rights for women or for non-Caucasians, O'Nolan's sexism and racism make his defence of Irish underclass in *An Béal Bocht* hypocritical and blind.

Notes

1   O'Nolan, interview broadcast by the BBC on the 7 March 1962, as quoted by Sue Asbee *Flann O'Brien* (Boston: Twayne Publishers, 1991), 107.

2   Article 41.2 of the Irish Constitution (1937).

3   Yvonne Scannell, from 'The Constitution and the Role of Women'. In *The Irish Women's History Reader*. Eds. Alan Hayes and Diane Urquhart (London: Routledge, 2001), 73.

4   Myles plays on this association of soldiers and venereal disease – ignoring the proportion of the civilian population infected – when he says that Julius Caesar's reference to the Gallic wars was 'Veni, VD, Vici!' (CL 8 August 1949).

5   Maria Luddy, 'Sex and the Single Girl in 1920s and 1930s Ireland'. *The Irish Review* 35 (2007): 86.

6 C. B. Murphy, 'Sex, Censorship and the Church'. *The Bell* 1.6 (September 1941) as quoted by Ferriter, *Occasions,* 5.

7 W. B. Yeats, *Synge and the Ireland of His Time and Four Years* (Fairford, Glos.: The Echo Library, 2010), 7.

8 Ibid., 7.

9 Ferriter, *Occasions,* 175.

10 Gerardine Meaney, 'Race, Sex and Nation'. *The Irish Review* 35 (2007): 52.

11 Meaney, 53.

12 Ivana Bacik, 'From Virgins and Mothers to Popstars and Presidents: Changing Roles of Women in Ireland'. *The Irish Review* 35 (2007): 102.

13 Bacik, 'Roles of Women', 103.

14 Taaffe, *Looking Glass,* 193.

15 Samuel Beckett, 'Molloy'. In *Three Novels* (New York: Grove Press, 2009), 3.

16 Rita Felski, *The Gender of Modernity* (Cambridge MA: Harvard University Press, 1995), 39.

17 Julia Kristeva, *Powers of Horror: An Essay on Abjection*, trans. Leon. S. Roudiez (New York: Columbia University Press, 1982), 6.

18 In fact, the original contains more references to the Cricket's desire to be a mother.

19 CL 2 October 1950.

20 BON to Allen Figgis, 28 November 1960, SIUC.

21 BON to TOK 27 November 1963, SIUC.

22 CL 24 February 1958.

23 CF 7.1 January 1934.

24 CL 9 April 1953.

25 CL 7 July 1944.

26 CL 17 May 1946.

27 CL 16 November 1942.

28 CL 2 November 1942.

29 CL 18 September 1950.

30 CL 21 August 1944.

31 CL 31 March 1947.

32 CL 6 December 1944.

33 CL 25 September 1950.

34 CL 3 September 1954.

35 CL 17 June 1944.

36 CL 3 May 1944.

37 CL 23 September 1946.

38 CL 23 June 1943.

39 CL 1 July 1953.

40 CL 7 March 1958.

41 CL 1 April 1966. This confusion of beginnings is also performed in an article that ends with the opening line, forcing to the reader to read the last line first (CL 24 May 1950).

42 CL 30 March 1951.

43 In a letter to the Department of Finance (13 November 1946, BC), O'Nolan names Niall Montgomery and Niall Sheridan as his substitutes. For more on this see Taaffe, *Looking Glass,* 126–7.

44 The few exceptions to this are the occasions when Myles's aristocratic standing requires an equally cultured or attractive female companion.

45 CL 28 July 1954.

46 CL 3 July 1945.

47 CL 4 April 1944.

48 CL 3 July 1945.

49 CL 30 May 1945.

50 CL 6 November 1945.

51 CL 13 November 1946.

52 CL 7 December 1943.

53 CL 14 September 1942.

54 CL 3 July 1945.

55 CL 13 June 1947.

56 CL 19 December 1945.

57 Ibid.

58 CL 9 September 1944.

59 CL 6 March 1959.

60 CL 28 April 1947.

61 CL 25 July 1947.

62 CL 13 February 1954.

63 CL 6 July 1951.

64 CL 11 February 1955.

65 CL 27 February 1960.

66 CL 23 September 1954.

67 Peter F. Murphy, 'Living by his Wits: The Buffoon and Male Survival'.
    Signs 31.4 (2006): 1125.

68 Murphy, 'Buffoon', 1130.

69 CL 5 November 1945.

70 W. Somerset Maugham, *A Writer's Notebook* (Melbourne: William
    Heinemann, 1949), 14.

71 BON to TOK 6 November 1961, SIUC.

72 BON to Mark Hamilton of A. M. Heath (hereafter MH) n.d.
    December 1960, SIUC.

73 James Joyce, *Ulysses* (London: Oxford, 2008), 155. Myles alludes
    to the location of the statue in a *Cruiskeen Lawn* article: 'Mr. James
    Joyce has made a facetious comment on its location but not one we
    can mention here' (CL 28 November 1961).

74 O'Nolan, *At Swim-Two-Birds* Manuscript typescript 1, 18, HRC.
    As quoted by Simon Anderson, 'Pink Paper and the Composition
    of Flann O'Brien's *At Swim-Two-Birds*'. Unpublished MA thesis,
    submitted to Louisiana State University, 2002: 18.

75 Caitriona Clear. 'Hardship, Help and Happiness in Oral History
    Narratives of Women's Lives in Ireland, 1921–1961'. *Oral History*
    31.2 (2003): 37.

76 Keats' line features in CL 30 June 1943.

77 Hopper, *Portrait*, 53.

78 Cronin, 217, Booker, *Menippean Satire*, 86.

79 Kant, 224.

80 Winfried Menninghaus, *Disgust: Theory and History of a Strong
    Sensation*, trans. Howard Eiland and Joel Golb (Albany: State
    University of New York Press, 2003), 1.

81   Legs in the air like a woman in heat,

        Spread-eagled, bare belly and arse

        Shamelessly oozing a venomous sweat

        With a primeval gas.

        . . .

        Flies sizzled as the putrefying guts

        Disgorged a noxious flood of fresh

        Troops – a viscous, thick river of maggots

        To plunder the last flesh.

Charles Baudelaire, *Complete Poems*, trans. Walter Martin (London: Routledge, 2002), 74–5.

82 Menninghaus, 84.

83 Kristeva, 69.

84 BON to TOK 28 May 1965, SIUC.

85 Immanuel Kant, *Anthropology from a Pragmatic Point of View*, trans. Victor Lyle Dowdell, Ed. Hans. H. Rudnick (Carbondale, Ill: Southern Illinois University Press, 1996), 212–3, as quoted by Menninghaus, 85.

86 O'Nolan, with Montgomery's insertions handwritten in capitals. 'Pathology', 11, BC.

87 BON to MH 20 February 1961, SIUC.

88 BON to MH n.d. December 1960, SIUC.

89 As she was in sole charge of the boys at the beginning of the book she must have been at least 15, thereby making her at least ten years older than Finbarr.

90 BON to TOK 3 October 1962, SIUC.

91 Her name also figures repeatedly throughout the *Cruiskeen Lawn*, as maid, friend, shop assistant, girlfriend.

92 Franz Kafka, *The Castle,* trans. Andrea Bell (Oxford: Oxford University Press, 2009), 40.

93 *The Dalkey Archive* (play), adapted by Allan McClelland (BC). Not to be confused with Hugh Leonard's adaptation.

94 NM to BON, undated, SIUC. In 1955, Myles claims to be working on a novel, but that progress was slow and hampered by the fact that his typist changed the name of a character Mary to Murray.

95 Cecil Scott of Macmillan (hereafter CS) to BON, 2 January 1964.

96 NM to BON 8 January 1964, SIUC.

97 BON to NM 9 January 1964, SIUC.

98 NM to BON, undated, SIUC.

99 CL 29 May 1950.

100 CL 5 August 1954.

101 BON to CS 11 February 1964, SIUC.

102 TOK to BON 22 October 1963, SIUC.

103 CL 23 September 1954.

104 Dalkey Archive MS 203, BC.

105 NM to BON undated, SIUC

106 CL 3 December 1956.

107 Keith Donohue, *The Irish Anatomist: A Study of Flann O'Brien* (Dublin: Maunsel & Co., 2002), 172.

108 CL 25 February – 2 March 1959.

109 BON to NM 6 January 1964, SIUC.

110 DA MS 224.

111 BON to NM 9 January 1964, SIUC.

112 NM to BON, undated, SIUC.

113 Asbee, 110.

114 Amy Nejezchleb, 'A Saga to Remember: Flann O'Brien's Unfinished Novel'. *Review of Contemporary Fiction* 31 (2011): 207.

115 Asbee, 111.

116 BON to TOK 29 October 1964 SIUC.

117 O'Nolan, *At Swim-Two-Birds* Manuscript, Pink Section 3, HRS, as quoted by Anderson 40.

118 BON to TOK 4 November 1962, SIUC.

119 Hackett also uses the word in relation to Mick's proposed religious career: 'Are you going to be a foreign missions man, preaching the Gospel to the niggers in Zanzibar or some such place?' (DA 156).

120 BON to Con Leventhal 28 July 1965.

121 BON to HL 27 October 1964, SIUC.

122 BON to HL 14 August 1965, SIUC.

123 BON to HL 11 August 1965, SIUC.

124 HL to BON 5 December 1965, SIUC.

125 BON to TOK 6 July 1965, SIUC.

126 BON to TOK 18 March 1965, SIUC.

127 CL 28 November 1963.

5

Archival fantasies

In *The Dalkey Archive*, O'Brien employs the term 'archive' to present a loosely connected series of files, raiding the unpublished *Third Policeman*, his repository of Dublin vernacular and character types, his *Cruiskeen Lawn* articles, his engagements with Joyce, and local libraries of biblical history. *The Dalkey Archive* reads with all the random noise, inconsistencies and disorder of the archive, together with the archivist's desire for knowledge, origins and order, as debates with Augustine, Joyce and De Selby lead the reader deeper into archives of theology, etymology and alternative literary history. *The Dalkey Archive* is an archival research project on theological abstractions and biblical minutiae masquerading as literary fiction, and plays upon the tension between archival truths and paperback fantasy, as behind its humorous depictions of Augustine and Joyce it presents accounts whose accuracy O'Nolan defended as objectively true in the case of Augustine and church history, and deservedly true in the case of Joyce. 'Archive' thus imparts a veneer of legitimacy and authenticity to the work, and while its realism has been targeted as a reason for its failure, the 'realism' of the archive was exactly what O'Nolan played upon.

O'Brien's work is an archive replete with writers; Augustine and Joyce are brought back from the dead to discuss their works, and De Selby is borrowed from the stillborn *Third Policeman* to conduct involved biblical analyses, turn the world into a dead letter office by mailing the lethal DMP[1] across it, and write a 'recondite, involuted and incomprehensible literary project' (DA 111) with Joyce. Hackett plans to have 'part of the Bible re-written' (DA 63) to redeem Judas Iscariot, while Mick, initially hoping to offer 'A real book on Joyce . . . [which] could clear up misunderstandings and mistakes, and eliminate a lot of stupidity' (DA 96), decides instead that 'The true story of Joyce would be ideal material for the exercise of [Mary's] rich mind. She would produce her own unprecedented book' (DA 99). But in the end literary aspirations come to naught, and *The Dalkey Archive* is a repository of failed writers, aborted projects and an archive distrustful of archivization. Joyce denies writing all of his major works, the planned collaboration with De Selby never materializes, Hackett's plans never progress and Mary's literary creation is shelved for a more biological form of production. Even Augustine's *Confessions* are treated as lies and '*shocking exaggeration*' (DA 34), as Augustine argues that '*There is no evidence against me beyond what I wrote myself. Too vague. Be on your guard against that class of fooling. Nothing in black and white*' (DA 33). Those who write deny it, and everyone else fails to put pen to paper. The circularity of *cogito ergo sum* becomes the regress of '*inepsias scripsi ergo sum*' (DA 15) – I write ineptly therefore I am. That is, my maladroit existence is predicated on my inability to describe or understand that existence – I write ineptly therefore I am, ineptly.

While the period in which *The Dalkey Archive* is set is regressive – 'Women were not served in the Metropole Lounge; the side roads of Dalkey were empty and silent; trams still ran in the streets of Dublin'[2] – the text's most important step into the past is its cannibalistic incursion into the unpublished excesses of *The Third Policeman*. Here the archive is censored and restricted, as the unfathomable and the inconceivable becomes the ineffable, atomic theory becomes Mollycule theory, the insane de Selby is made manifest as the eccentric De Selby, the dead occupy the text's margins rather than centre stage, the infinite recurrences of a hellish afterlife become the monotonous repetitions of a dull relationship, and the impossibility of ending becomes the easy resolution of a threat. *The Third Policeman*'s cycles of the death drive thus become *The Dalkey Archive*'s thanatic archival tension, as the impossibility of the archive in the earlier work becomes simply the limitations of the archive in the later.

The archive and the death drive

In *Archive Fever*, Derrida writes that Freud desired to find the 'original' trauma or event that was stored within the psyche, despite knowing that this was impossible. Freud envisioned himself as an archaeologist reconstructing the past through fragments of signs, and yearned for an 'archive without archive', where the footprint of the dead, 'suddenly indiscernible from the impression of its imprint', speaks for itself.[3] This is a passion for the archive not as archive – a dead, cold remainder of a life, changed in the act of storage – but as immediate, true, living experience, undisturbed and undistorted by the medium of retention. The desire for the archive is thus also the desire to transcend the archive, and to commune directly with the past. Derrida exemplifies this with Jensen's *Gradiva*, in which a man meets a ghostly woman, animated from a bas relief, and travels to find her in Pompeii. The city of remains and ash is a place of living archive, where 'the singular imprint, like a signature, barely distinguishes itself from the impression';[4] a place of living history, where the footstep and the footprint are one, and event, memory, and archive identical. But this longing tells an impossible story, a fantasy of resurrection – just like that which brings Augustine and Joyce back from the dead. As such we can understand *The Dalkey Archive* as exemplary of the archival fantasy; it desires to step beyond the archive and replace dusty remains with living people. When De Selby, Mick and Hackett enter the timeless cave to speak directly with the past, they do not enter a 'live' archive, but pass beyond the archive into the presence of the past. Similarly, when Mick meets Joyce he leaves the Joycean archive behind to relate directly to the man himself. *The Dalkey Archive*'s desire to turn the archive into truth in the flesh undoes itself – one cannot archive the presence it yearns to attain.

However, before *The Dalkey Archive* can be accused of unabashed idealization of presence and a tendency to denigrate the written word, O'Brien destabilizes the apparent authenticity of the voice: the men may enter a timeless cave to conduct a 'live' debate with the encorpified Augustine, but De Selby later casts doubt on the legitimacy of the encounter, as he suspects that the figure with whom they spoke was Beelzebub (DA 43), acting under orders of Lucifer, real controller of heaven, time and knowledge. Similarly, Mick retains some doubts as to whether the man he met really is Joyce. At the text's conclusion is uncertainty, not only about the truth of the archive, but the truth of presence and the voice, and De Selby abandons his plans based precisely on interpretative reservations: did he commune with Church fathers or demons in disguise? In charge of heaven is the Polyarch, 'Christ's Vicar in Heaven' (DA 34), a title which alludes to the Pope – *Vicarius*

Christi – but also indicates an undecidability of geneses – 'polyarch' can be literally translated as 'many' and 'origin'. While the non-apocalyptic close, and the contrived *deus ex machina* of the fire implies that God is in control, no conclusive proof is offered. Even an archive made flesh cannot eliminate interpretative doubt.

The repetition and re-fabrication of a rejected novel can be read as a structural echoing of the repetitions and fabrications of the death drive, as Freud's texts on the thanatic, Derrida argues, 'explain in the end why there is archivization and why anarchiving destruction belongs to the process of archivization and produces the very thing it reduces, on occasion, to ashes'.[5] The texts explicating the death drive are texts on the conditions of possibility and impossibility of the archive, and thus, in *The Dalkey Archive*, we return to the drive explored in Chapter 2. But while *The Third Policeman* performed the death drive's daemonic recurrences, in *The Dalkey Archive* the drive operates as an (an)archival force of repetition and destruction. This, once again, does not present a pyschobiographical incursion into O'Nolan's motivations or intentions, but addresses the structural similarities between the re-inscription of *The Third Policeman* and the death drive's (an)archiving operation.

Freud initially formulated the death drive to explain the repetition, without conscious knowledge or memory, of traumatic events. When a traumatic event for which one is unprepared occurs, it overwhelms the psychic system and cannot be directly addressed. So it is repressed and stored in the memory in a way that appears to cause the least immediate trauma, and as such the death drive can be seen to be of the archive and of archivization – a safe storage to ensure a future. But this archivization is ineffectual, as the energy flooding from the excitement and distress caused by the event has not been bound, that is, cathected. Failing to cathect the energy, the death drive thus attempts to cope with the rejected and repressed trauma and returns to the quietude of a pre-traumatic equilibrium through the unreasonable and unreasoning repetition of a potentially harmful short-term coping strategy of denial and reinterpretation. In trying to progress and conserve it regresses and endangers, and its technique is one of inertial aggression. The death drive thus alters the tale of the event and archives it differently. It is of the anarchival.

In additional complication, the repetition involved in the death drive is not the simple repetition of an original trauma which can be eventually uncovered by a knowing analyst. The repetition of the death drive is an 'originary repetition', as the event which is archived is not the 'original' event, but an event changed in the act of retention. The act of remembering – writing, storing, archiving – an event is itself a creative and destructive event. As Derrida outlines in 'Freud and the Scene of Writing', 'there is no unconscious truth to be rediscovered by virtue of having been written elsewhere. . . . The unconscious text is already a weave of pure traces, differences in which meaning and force are united – a text nowhere present, consisting of archives which are always already transcriptions'.[6] The 'original' event is already the imprint or copy of an event, distanced and delayed in the act of being experienced. While the archival process can be seen to be a conservative event, it conserves by changing the event. The archive is not a place of living memory but of altered remnants, and thus,

> right on that which permits and conditions archivization, we will never find anything other than that which exposes to destruction, and in truth menaces with destruction, introducing, *a priori*, forgetfulness and the archivolithic into the heart of the monument. Into the "by heart" itself. The archive always works, and *a priori*, against itself.[7]

Furthermore, since there is constant tension to return the psyche to a pre-traumatic state, different ways of coping with and responding to traumatic events are archived for future use. As Andrea Hurst puts it,

> the defensive pressure of the death drive, in spite of its being a fundamentally inertial drive to return to an earlier state, promotes the development of the psyche as an archival web of facilitations. It is in this sense that the death drive, associated with repetition in the economic sense of conservation, makes the psyche (or archive) possible.[8]

But since the death drive tends to promote psychical inertia, it tends to repeat the same and follow paths and connections already made. The death drive saves through the creation of the archive, and through recourse to the archive, yet the death drive is that which negates the archive's sense of origin. The death drive's repetition is the condition of possibility of the archive, and yet the death drive is always 'archive-destroying'.[9] It violently and aggressively alters the event into something more immediately palatable, and thus the archive is a place of forgetting and of Thanatos; the death of an event as it is disavowed before it is retained. The archive, created through repetition, 'will never be either memory or anamnesis as spontaneous, alive and internal experience. On the contrary: the archive takes place at the place of originary and structural breakdown of the said memory'.[10] Furthermore, the event which is archived is thus not an external event but an internalized, personal version of the event. The 'outside stimuli' against which the psyche defends itself is not wholly outside, and the action of the death drive is autoimmune, as it aggressively tries to undo the violence of its own version of an event.

The Third Policeman presents a story of infinite repetitions saturated with archival longings. Its thanatographic self-archivization, underscored by an obsessive footnoting, works to map and position and narrate, but the text it produces fails to anchor or aid memory, as the narrator's thanatic archival inscriptions fade like spoken words. The text produced is the text of the death of memory, identity, narrative and origins, and its most tragic event – the narrator's death – is repressed in favour of an endless recurring that repeats a fabrication designed to conceal an unthinkable trauma.[11] The Dalkey Archive repeats The Third Policeman's thanatic recurrences, but its re-inscription distances the loss of life, identity and control. The floating archive of parenthetical reference is replaced with the voice and presence of the author, the nameless narrator is replaced with a man bestowed with an appellation generically and derogatorily marking every male Irish Catholic – another Jams O'Donnell – and its circling around death is reduced to momentary dialogues with the encorpified past. Its atheism is replaced with involved doctrinal debate and its thanatography is demoted to séance, as writing by the dead is replaced with speaking to the dead. The atomic theory so pivotal to the sexual and the somatic within The Third Policeman is expurgated to mere whimsy, and the idyllic rural scenes which served to emphasize the fabrication of the narrator's afterlife become comforting evidence of the stability of 'reality'. This step from high phantasmagoria to low realism/ fantasy is exemplified in the opening pages of the book: Dalkey, we are told, is approached though Vico Road, and we are asked if there is 'to be recalled in this magnificence a certain philosopher's pattern of man's lot on earth – thesis, antithesis, synthesis, chaos?' (DA 7–8). Vico believed in 'the ineluctable circular progression of Society'[12] – which Joyce alludes to in *Finnegans Wake* with the line 'The Vico Road goes round and round to meet where terms begin'[13] – and so, on the road leading to Dalkey, we stand at the threshold of the cycles of *The Third Policeman*, but those excessive cycles are denounced when O'Brien answers his question – do we see in this road an allusion to engagements with repetition? – with a negative: 'Hardly' (DA 8). The complex repetitive structures of *The Third Policeman* are repeated, but this time either as a denial of repetition or a circularity permitted solely by association with the divine: 'the soul of man is immortal, the geometry of a soul must be circular and, like God, it cannot have had a beginning' (DA 40).

One clear example of reduction is the relation to time in *The Dalkey Archive*. In this text, O'Brien returns to Dunne and argues that time does not move in a linear trajectory from the past to the present, but occurs simultaneously, as it is, De Selby argues, a plenum. 'Plenum' refers to a space which is full of matter, or, in De Selby's words,

> a phenomenon or existence full of itself but inert. Obviously space does not satisfy such a condition. But time is a plenum, immobile, immutable, ineluctable, irrevocable, a condition of absolute stasis. Time does not pass. Chance and movement may occur within time. (DA 16)

When De Selby creates an anoxic environment, time is recognized in its fullness, as oxygen – *pneuma*/breath: 'ponder that equation of breath with life'[14] – imposes a false seriality on time, and removing breathable air causes its fullness to be recognizable: 'a deoxygenated atmosphere cancels the apparently serial nature of time and confronts us with true time and simultaneously with all the thing and creatures which time has ever contained or will contain' (DA 21). In unbreathable space there is no longer the illusion of a sequence of time, and all that is required to speak to those who have died and those who are yet to be born is their agreement to encorpify. This loose reworking of Dunne's theory, which, as outlined in Chapter 2, argued that the apparently consecutive nature of time was due to the habits of consciousness, and that the true simultaneity of time could be accessed during the laxity of sleep, replaces sleep with oxygen, allows De Selby, Mick and Hackett to interact with long dead saints while awake. However, and significantly, in Dunne's theories time is never sequential; it is we who can only read it as such. In O'Brien's reworking, time is always sequential if oxygen is present, never if oxygen is absent. Human consciousness plays no part, and time becomes subject to chemical content. If De Selby, Mick and Hackett attempt to view a deoxygenated environment, they must do so from within an oxygenated one, or die. Thus, they employ oxygen tanks and effectively create breathable spaces within an anoxic one. That is, they must remain within an atmosphere in which time passes in a regular, progressive fashion, and from there observe time as simultaneous and full. While this does occur within the text, its logic is problematic, as presumably the oxygenated situation of the men would effectively act as a barrier preventing them from witnessing time in the anoxic one.

This new relation to time not only introduces the concept of controlled and delimited spaces – albeit dangerous ones – but also reduces the importance of human consciousness. The mind's abilities and inabilities are no longer central, and the human sense of time becomes not one of a controlling agency but simply that of an oxygen-breathing life form. This demotion exemplifies a denial of autonomy that runs throughout O'Nolan's works, and implies a greater distance between the human and the divine than is shown in *The Third Policeman*. When De Selby speaks to Augustine, the encorpified saint equates the plenary nature of time with God, saying that 'God is time. *God is the substance of eternity. God is not distinct from what we regard as years. God has no past, no future, no presence in the sense of man's fugitive tenure. The interval you mention between the Creation and the Redemption is ineffably unexistent*' (DA 39). As such, removing oxygen from the atmosphere and revealing the true nature of time becomes automatically a religious act of approaching God. Similarly, if all life requires oxygen, but oxygen suppresses the nature of time and God, then De Selby's opinion of the worthlessness of humanity can be grounded in the fact that the very substance that the human body needs to survive is precisely that which masks the existence of God. *Pneuma* may be the breath of God, but it is also that, in humans, which hides God.

The Third Policeman is not the simple presentation of an 'original' event which is then repressively re-inscribed as *The Dalkey Archive*, nor, of course, are either supposed to be actual psychic functions. Rather, their relation can be understood though the heuristic of the death drive's (an)archivization such that the earlier work represents a fabrication which is then re-fabricated – its narrative is re-presented but its strangeness, its sadomasochistic undercurrents, its clear undercuttings of identity, memory and 'reality' are repackaged and re-archived into a safer, but repetitive, fabrication. This fabrication is incapable of erasing *The Third Policeman* and under the guise of an acceptable 'strange' still remains an archive trapped in repetitions of stasis and failure: the hellish repetitions of death are replaced with the hellish repetitions of life as Mick does not win a happy ending but secures a monotonous relationship and a life of deadening civil service work. Similarly, the anarchival force of DMP, which halts time and allows the men to transcend the static archive to live presence, is in the end disarmed by archivization within the confines of the Bank of Ireland's vaults. Radical change is repressed by the archive.

The factual archive

Although O'Nolan was an important student at University College Dublin, 'sod-faced University know-alls'[15] and academic institutions became frequent targets of attack in *Cruiskeen Lawn*:

> The whole field of literature is a mass of misunderstandings, inaccuracies, whimsy and mumblings of all sorts. . . . Worst imposters are the "scholars," whose prestige derives from the fact that they burn their midnight oil in the graveyards of dead jargons in which normal people have no interest.[16]

Joyce scholars in particular were subject to repeated scorn, being deemed 'American illiterates and high school punkawns',[17] and a favourite accusation of Myles's centred around 'that least excusable of follies, being "literary"'.[18] His criticism of readers' Keats and Chapman submissions demonstrates a suspicion of 'fine writing' mixed with a sense of craft; he deemed them 'pretty bad' precisely because 'they are too good, too polished and refined, too "worked over" as Sean O'Faolain would say. They lack effervescence and spontaneity. They are "literary". They are too obviously contrived and usually omit the essential boredom of the build-up'.[19] But neither did O'Nolan wholly embrace the 'Plain People' side of the 'town and gown' opposition; his condemnation of the literary was not grounded in a rejection of aestheticism, as, Donohue writes, he praised the 'formal aspects of art, music, literature . . . [and] insisted on the need to judge a work of art on its own terms, as a thing itself and not a mimetic imitation of life';[20] he disparaged work where pretension was prioritized. His works resound with a pedantry employed as dark humour, light wit and serious complaint. As a contemporary reviewer wrote:

> His is a column devoted to magnificently laborious puns, remarkable parodies of De Quincey and others, fanciful literary anecdotes and erudite study of cliches, scornful dissection of the literary meaning of high-flown literary phraseology and a general air of shameless irony and high spirits. No one can build up a pun more shamelessly. No one can analyse the exact meaning of a literary flight of fantasy more devastatingly.[21]

The Dalkey Archive is no exception: while the book is usually considered to have failed to bring together its vignettes into a coherent plot, the differing scenes and sketches are linked by a sustained engagement with knowledge. At the work's early stages, O'Nolan responded to a letter from Timothy O'Keefe, stating 'It's amusing and even eerie that you should say "the new novel sounds like a *Summa*"'.[22] A *Summa*, meaning to 'sum up', is a compendium which summarizes and stores knowledge in a field, and as such, a *summa* is an archive, a repository for knowledge and information pertaining to a particular field, event or person. *The Dalkey Archive* is a summa or archive of accurate information of varying degrees of 'objective' truth, as the text's overriding engagement is with presenting, attributing and discrediting information and received wisdom; its scenes attempt to reveal fact, employ authentic etymology, present accurate details, ridicule error and short-sightedness, lament wasted ability, correct mistakes, mock an interest in minutiae, and use information to both witty and solemn ends. De Selby spends his days speaking with dead fathers of the Church and attempting to sift through conflicting and contradicting information for biblical truths. Joyce needs to find the real origins of the Church and correct doctrinal misreadings, while Hackett plans to discover and reveal the truth about Judas.

Sgt. Fottrell is the holder of the arcane knowledge of the Mollycule theory, and Mick wishes to solve all the problems he is presented with. Similarly, when characters and institutions are criticized it is primarily for their ignorance or their misuse of information. Thus, Mary's knowledge – sexual and intellectual – is attacked, Mrs Laverty's ignorant piety is mocked, priests are dismissed as ignorant, university life and students are deemed barren, and medicine demoted to record-keeping. If, as De Selby's Augustine says, God is knowledge (DA 39), then *The Dalkey Archive* is a religious record, a new gospel of alternative histories and archives.

However, it is precisely the position of learning within the text that provokes tension between the values it derides and those it adopts. While the abstract target of *The Dalkey Archive*'s satire is casuistry, be it of the Jesuits or Joyce scholars, and the text's object of attack those for whom the minutiae of doctrinal, biblical or literary scholarship was a vital task, not only did O'Nolan forge a career in the Irish Times based precisely on a humorous yet insistent use of pedantry, but the letters he wrote during the writing of *The Dalkey Archive* show an enormous pride in the accuracy of the details he uncovered. While the line to Montgomery – 'It will be a queer day when TDA is made required reading at Maynooth'[23] – apes modesty, it still indicates his assessment of the text as a humorous presentation of genuine research and esoteric knowledge. When Cecil Scott suggested that the religious content of *The Dalkey Archive* should be reduced or removed, as it 'may amuse or infuriate a learned Catholic Father but will merely bewilder the average American reader',[24] O'Nolan refused, arguing that the dialogues on Augustine, 'Petros', the whale, Judas Iscariot, and the creation of the Holy Spirit were both amusing and accurate.[25] While the Augustine character is excessive – he speaks with a broad Dublin accent, his father Patricius is renamed Patrick, and he speaks of his sexual past and other saints in ways orchestrated to produce nervous laughter in the Plain People of Ireland – for O'Nolan this excess was humorous precisely because, with exception of the Irishisms, it is grounded in accuracy. This, of course, offered deniability – the sexual past alluded to had already been made famous by Augustine's own *Confessions* – but it also allowed O'Nolan to showcase knowledge.[26]

In the Augustine/De Selby dialogue, O'Brien thus worked to present, beyond the archive, a comic, caricatured version of the living 'truth' of the *Confessions*, but this creates an internal tension, as the type of knowledge it attacks as a flawed and unnecessary obsession is precisely the type of knowledge its author employs and is most proud of. Hence there is the danger that the butt of the joke in *The Dalkey Archive* is *The Dalkey Archive*, as behind a veneer of humour is precisely the same interest in casuistry it attacks; like Yeats O'Brien chastises the 'Old, learned, respectable bald heads' who 'all shuffle there; all cough in ink',[27] while ignoring his own limping and hacking. In implying that Joyce's writings are Jesuitical, O'Nolan calls attention to his own nit-picking and pretension; as Mick seems blind to the fact that his religious vocation is even more farcical and self-indulgent than Joyce's, O'Brien seems blind to the fact that his assault on Joyce and the Jesuits places him within the field he attacks.

Yet, O'Nolan was not quite as committed to the labour true pedantry requires; while he claimed that he had 'read everything about Augustine published in English, French, German and Latin',[28] Cronin suggests that this was mere bravado, writing that O'Nolan 'would pretend that he had done exhaustive research on St. Augustine . . . . The truth is, however, that his knowledge of St. Augustine was quite sketchy and could easily have been derived from the *Catholic Encyclopaedia* and the Everyman edition of the *Confessions*'.[29] Precisely how much research O'Nolan conducted is difficult to say – the archives in Carbondale contain notebooks with jottings about Augustine, but by no means show evidence of exhaustive research in multiple languages. One quotation, for example, jotted down is found verbatim in a footnote in a translated edition of *St. Augustine: The Problem of Free Choice*,[30] which implies that he did at least read a little more than implied by Cronin, although perhaps not as widely as he claimed. This is undermined, however, the fact that the information O'Nolan 'discovered' on the name Petros comes from a letter written to him by Prof. Stanford of Trinity College Dublin, which he quoted verbatim in the dialogue between Augustine and De Selby.[31] While this is absolutely not conclusive proof, it does imply that O'Nolan's claim of intensive scholarly research was hyperbolic. Thus, not only does *The Dalkey Archive* pride itself on the exactitude it derides, but its exactitude is rather less exact than that of its targets: borrowed casuistry to mock casuistry, scrounged pedantry to mock pedantry.[32]

The text's object of derision is as elusive as its sources, however, as O'Nolan appears to wish to mock without offence, and affront either without a loss of sales or with the lucrative scandal of a Censorship Board ban.[33] Thus, irreverence is claimed not to 'jeer at God or religion; the idea is roast the people who seriously do so, and also to chide the church in various of its aspects',[34] and apparent blasphemy is presented as constructive criticism of the flawed, human interpretation of the divine, and not the divine itself. Similarly, while O'Nolan repeatedly expresses the wish to wholly ridicule Joyce – 'I'm not happy at all about the treatment of Joyce: a very greater mess must be made of him. Would one of his secret crosses be that he is an incurable bed-wetter?[35] – he also feels obliged to claim that 'The intention here is not to make Joyce himself ridiculous but to say something funny about the preposterous image of him that emerges from the treatment he has received at the hands of many commentators and exegetists'.[36] While he insists that 'You will find that Joyce and the Jesuit Order are drowned in the same repulsive pan of boiling suet',[37] he also seems to make drowning a mild splutter, repulsion a fleeting distaste and boiling suet a tepid tallow.

The vagaries of the satire in *The Dalkey Archive*, a point which O'Nolan admitted – 'My target here is not even crudely defined'[38] – cause the book to be unfocused and incongruous. The fragmentation so well-employed in *At Swim-Two-Birds* descends into an awkward jumble of scenes that fail to mesh into a coherent – or artfully incoherent – work. The paradoxes and contradictions of the fragmentary operate simply as indecisions, and it is arguably this vacillation, compounded with the carefully worded critiques of Cecil Scott and Timothy O'Keeffe, that caused O'Nolan to define *The Dalkey Archive* not as a novel but as an archive of styles, that is, 'an essay in extreme derision of literary attitudes and people', with the admitted fault of an 'absence of emphasis in certain places, to help the reader'.[39] As 'a study in derision, various writers with their styles, and sundry modes, attitudes and cults being the rats in the cage', the manuscript's 'want of definition and emphasis'[40] becomes less problematic than it might be in a novel. And yet, given the irresolution in O'Nolan's letters, and the absence of cutting caricatures or painful insights within the text itself, his disdain seems incapable of hitting its mark. One might expect an essay or study satirizing writers, styles, modes, attitudes and cults to read like *At Swim-Two-Birds*, but there is never any sense of the possibility of providing, as Clissmann does for O'Nolan's first novel, a list of the multiple styles found within *The Dalkey Archive*. The objects of the parody are complicated either by a retreat from a direct target – Joyce but not Joyce, Augustine but not Augustine, Religion but not Religion, God but not God – or by a complicity with the target – casuistry and scholarly engagement – and we are left with an unclassified and unclear 'spoofy canon',[41] an archive of desires and frustrations rather than a composite text. Given the repetitions and cannibalization of *The Third Policeman* that occurs in the text, it is fair to say, as Taaffe does, that 'it is not Joyce who is the true victim of *The Dalkey Archive*, but Flann O'Brien'.[42]

The Joycean archive

A biographical work on an author adds to, enriches, explains or subverts his or her corpus, as work on an author changes the body of work of the author. As Derrida writes, 'the interpretation of the archive . . . can only illuminate, read, establish its object, namely a given inheritance, by inscribing itself into it, that is to say by opening it and by enriching it enough to have a place in it. There is no meta-archive'.[43] As such, a book on Freud belongs to the corpus of Freud as it carries the name of Freud. And a book revising the history of Joyce's career is part of the corpus of Joyce. Thus, the archive grows:

> By incorporating the knowledge deployed in reference to it, the archive augments itself, engrosses itself, it gains in *auctoritas*. But in the same stroke it loses the absolute and meta-textual authority it might claim to have. One will never be able to objectivise it without remainder. The archive produces more archive, and that is why the archive is never closed.[44]

The archive is never static and can never be said to be complete. It is an authority and not, as it is always awaiting new work. Each text on the subject of the archive must be included in the archive, and thus Myles and O'Brien's texts work their way into the Joyce studies he claimed so fervently to dislike. By rewriting Joyce's history, O'Nolan writes himself into it, and the archive of the father contains the parricide committed by the son. It's interesting to note that when Joyce was used on the cover art of the US edition of *The Dalkey Archive*, O'Nolan was strongly supportive of it:

I think it is brilliant and certain to provoke sales-on-sight. It is of course a bit tendentious and suggests the book is a biography of Joyce or mainly about Joyce but I don't think that's any harm at all. If the samples we see over here complete with notebooks and camera are any guide, there must be several thousand Joyce "buffs" in the U.S., and they will surely think that buying this book is an obligatory religious duty. If only for that reason I strongly recommend that you should use the cover but it is a good cover anyway.[45]

While acknowledging that *The Dalkey Archive* is more than a simple or direct biography of Joyce, O'Nolan was quite insistent on the financial advantages of emphasizing the Joycean connection and capitalizing on inclusion within the canon.

In 'A Bash in the Tunnel' (1951), O'Brien presents the image of the Irish artist: one who is under the illusion of a voluntary retreat from the world, celebrating defiance and control by rebelliously drinking in his or her embraced isolation, all the while being moved around by a world unaware of and indifferent to his or her revolt.

Sitting fully dressed, innerly locked in the toilet of a locked coach where he has no right to be, resentfully drinking somebody else's whiskey, being whisked hither and thither by anonymous shunters, keeping fastidiously the while on the outer face of his door the simple word, *engaged*? I think the image fits Joyce: but particularly in his manifestation of a most Irish characteristic – the transgressor's resentment with the nongressor. (SP 173)

The voluntary withdrawing is an illusion behind a larger involuntary imprisonment, and behind the delusion of control is a slow, dark, blind drinking of the self to death, while waiting for the ending of a night artificially and permanently lengthened by the dark of the tunnel. An active and glorious retreat from the world is always a passive rejection by the world, and Ireland's 'splendid isolation' just a quiet assisted suicide, while the dawn for which the artist waits comes and goes. In linking Joyce to this image of the Irish artist, O'Brien ensures that Joyce's silence, exile and cunning is, like every other Irish artist, no more than an ultimately futile attempt at control and a denial of the pre-existing exile all Irish people feel: as Myles writes, 'ALL IRISH PERSONS LIVING IN IRELAND ARE EXILES. . . . They are more than exiles, they are refugees. Refugees from humanity. Their attitude is that not only are they not persons, they are not even people'.[46] For O'Nolan, the 'natural' Irish state is one of exile, alienation, bitterness and displacement. In leaving Joyce might have attempted the illusion of control, but he will remain in a dark Irish tunnel, angrily and unashamedly drinking someone else's whiskey.[47]

Much has been written on the ambivalence of O'Nolan's feelings towards Joyce; Myles delighted in denying Joyce authorship, attributing *Ulysses* to Gogarty,[48] *Finnegans Wake* to Vico,[49] claiming that Joyce had been invented by Quidnunc[50] or by Harvard,[51] and affording himself paternal authority.[52] But the belittling – 'Joyce was a bad writer. He was too skilled in some departments of writing, and could not resist the *tour de force*. Parts of *Ulysses* are of unreadable boredom. . . . Joyce was illiterate'[53] – is tempered with praise: 'Joyce was more fastidious about the notation of his work than any musician',[54] had a 'supernatural skill in conveying Dublin dialogue'[55] and was 'a great master of the banal in literature. By "banal" I mean the fusion of uproarious comic stuff and deep tragedy'.[56] O'Nolan was particularly aware that by engaging with Joyce he operated within Joyce's archive and in competition with Joyce's texts, and worried that 'the last quarter of the book is very badly written indeed, and the Joyce stuff is all uneven and quite lacking in the elegance which is essential where that damn man is dragged on the scene'.[57] Similarly, although he derided the casuistry that his Joyce displays, O'Nolan also claims to have worked hard to find knowledge that the real Joyce deserved, finding it in the *spiritus/pneuma/ruach* transition: 'I've done some further reading to find something worthwhile for Joyce, and I've certainly found it.'[58] In 'Enigma' (1962) and 'A Bash in the Tunnel' O'Brien writes that Joyce's blasphemy stems from credence, and, like O'Nolan, that his real target was never the church but certain of its idiosyncrasies, as Joyce is 'a truly fear-shaken Irish Catholic, rebelling not so much against the Church but against its near-schism Irish eccentricities, its pretence that there is only one Commandment, the vulgarities of its edifices, the shallowness and stupidity of many of its ministries' (SP 174). O'Brien's acts of irreverence against the master in

The Dalkey Archive are not specifically attacks his works but the man and academia. As he writes, 'all true blasphemers must be believers' (SP 170): O'Nolan's derision of Joyce is the disrespect of a disciple, albeit a disillusioned one.

Both Cecil Scott and Timothy O'Keeffe criticized the Joyce sections of *The Dalkey Archive*, and so O'Nolan rewrote sections of it, the most major change being the introduction of the 'ragged undergarments' scene. In the manuscript, Father Cobble simply suggests that Joyce could be a gardener, and Mick stands up, explains quickly what Joyce wants, and leaves. In later edits, he also makes Joyce reject his own works more fervently – in the manuscript when *Ulysses* is brought up Joyce simply says that he's never put his name to anything he's published, and what he has published are two-penny tracts. No mention is made of *Dubliners* or Oliver Gogarty, and Joyce is more amused than annoyed at Mick's interest in *Ulysses*. While both attribute the text to a consortium of writers – thus bringing Joyce's magnum opus in line with O'Nolan's planned *Children of Destiny*, and an earlier article in *Cruiskeen Lawn* which attributes works by 'Joyce' to a syndicate including Myles na gCopaleen, Samuel Beckett, Beirt Fhear, Freud, Jimmy Joyce, Niall Sheridan, Father Prout, and Gogarty[59] – only the published version calls these writers 'Muck-rakers, obscene poets, carnal pimps, sodomous sycophants, pedlars of the coloured lusts of fallen humanity' (DA 167). The entire section between Joyce speculating that he could become the Rector of Clongowes (DA 169) to asking to meet Father Cobble (DA 173) is new, and all the material on God's breath in man a later addition. In the manuscript, the Joyce section ends when Mick, about to hand Joyce over to De Selby, simply says, 'With no hint of Pilates' thought, I was about to wash my hands'.[60]

Although Mick's praise of Joyce's works emphasizes Mick's self-indulgent pretensions and links him to Myles's condemnation of posturing civil service men – 'Peasants, crowded into the file-chocked ghetto commonly known as the Civil Service . . . began reading James Joyce, wearing canary-coloured pullovers and gaudy tweed ties'[61] – Mick's respect for the author's works cannot be dismissed as merely a facet of his 'obnoxious' personality. It is significant that with the exception of the aftermath of the 'undergarments' meeting with Father Cobble, when he deems *Finnegans Wake* 'incoherent trash' (DA 187), Mick never uses his new knowledge of Joyce to devalue Joyce's works. In the manuscript, in fact, he echoes Myles's sentiments on Joyce scholars, and calls their works 'the snapping of jackals'.[62] Joyce's works – regardless of who has written them – are treated with respect, and as such the subject of *The Dalkey Archive*'s derision is not the literary output of James Joyce, but James Joyce himself. The text denies the man authorship of works whose quality Mick does not deny, as *The Dalkey Archive* expresses filial tension with the father, the legacy of the father, and the reception of the father, rather than specifically with the father's works. The dead father is resurrected so that parricide can be committed, but the murder does not include his writings.

O'Nolan's intrusion into Joyce's archive is compounded by resentment at being involuntarily brought into it by years of comparison to Joyce, and the sense of writing within a field dominated by the author:

> *Ignorant reviewers have messed me up with another man*, to my intense embarrassment and disgust, and he will be another character. I mean James Joyce. I'm going to get my own back on that bugger. (I suppose you know that, like Hitler, Joyce isn't dead at all. He is living in sort of retirement and disguise at Skerries, a small wateringplace miles N. of Dublin. He has been trying to screw up enough courage to join the Jesuits. [Emphasis added][63]

While O'Nolan's sense of living in Joyce's shadow is often addressed, O'Nolan's attitude could perhaps be better expressed in terms of the feeling that Joyce had, through his exile, his reputation, and his earlier birth, effectively stolen O'Nolan's position, and forced O'Nolan to be 'a kind of "poor man's" Joyce'[64] rather than a writer able to stand alone. Thus, it was not a case of being second to Joyce, or having his works unfavourably compared to his, but that Joyce's position was in fact O'Nolan's position, that the praise lavished on Joyce was due to O'Nolan, and that it was a simple case – figuratively speaking – of mistaken identity that had caused the confusion: *Ignorant reviewers have messed me up with another man*. Joyce had been named 'Dublin's incomparable archivist' (DA 124) when it should have been O'Nolan. Joyce was the leading Irish literary export when it should have been O'Nolan. Joyce was a man studied and admired when it should have been O'Nolan. If there is to be only one father of modern Irish writing, then it should be

O'Nolan, not Joyce, and those who think so have confused them. In an early article, Myles argues that a writer who temporally precedes another can in fact be accused of plagiarizing the later – Myles influenced Joyce, regardless of the chronology.[65] When O'Nolan gives a description of Joyce in 'A Bash in the Tunnel' it is the Joyce he sees in his mirror: a man of secretiveness, ambiguity, polyguity, leg-pulling, dishonesty, technical skill and – if only! – attraction for Americans (SP 175). Joyce's 'fabulously developed jackdaw talent of picking up bits and pieces'[66] is a wonderful description of O'Nolan's own style, and the one consistent aspect of Joyce's writings that Myles praises is his humour – 'Joyce was among the most comic writers who have ever lived'[67] – the skill Myles/O'Nolan thought most important and valuable in his own works.

Mistaken identity and unappreciated talent is the theme of O'Brien's short story 'Two in One' (1954, prefigured in *Cruiskeen Lawn* 26 May 1953), in which an assistant taxidermist – Murphy – beats Kelly, his 'swinish, overbearing mean boss, a bully, a sadist',[68] to death, and, using the skills of his trade, preserves the dead man's skin and puts it on over his own. But having spent a day and a night as his deceased employer, he finds that the dead man's skin had fused with his own. He is eventually arrested for his own murder, but awaits his hanging comforted by the fact that his execution will seal his fate in public memory as a hapless victim, and his vindictive employer a cruel murderer. The story ends with the final insistence that despite the 'real' events, what would remain in history was truer and more accurate than what had really occurred: 'He [Kelly] *was* a murderer, anyway'.[69] In murdering Kelly and assuming his identity, he had instigated a series of events which led to his employer's 'true' character – his violence and murderous cruelty – being revealed. 'Kelly' lives again to undergo a public hanging, as Kelly was a murderer in everything but the act. Murphy had the skills to bring his employer back to life and ruin his reputation forever, fiction thereby revealing 'fact'. Thus, the sense of a position usurped or confused that O'Nolan felt with his 'master' is prefigured, and in *The Dalkey Archive* Joyce lives again to be debased, ridiculed and rejected, in a fiction which, for O'Nolan, indicates not the truth as *The Dalkey Archive* presents it – that Joyce didn't write his own texts – but the truth that is more real than real life – that Joyce, 'a complete prig, a snob, and a person possessed of endowment unique in the archives of conceit,'[70] *didn't deserve to have written his texts*. Thus, the archive presents the 'truths' of alternative history, a history of what should have been the case, 'truths' whose comic aspirations makes them no less desired.

Similarly, atomic theory and its weaker repetition, Mollycule theory, is effectively a treatise on mistaken identities and role reversals. As noted in Chapter 2, constant contact with a bicycle will cause the rider to become a bicycle in everything but appearance, and a bicycle human in all but external shape. When murder is committed, one cannot trust visual evidence, and thus, against all reason, a bicycle can be revealed as the real murderer. Furthermore, if riding an English bicycle is an act of treason, as Irish molecules are replaced with English ones, then the Mollycule theory has implications beyond the directly physical, as there is 'more to it than the monstrous exchange of tissue for metal' (DA 82).[71] Could one not argue that the constant years of treading Joyce's path, of colliding with his style, and of having Joyce, as Sheridan wrote, 'in the very air we breathed'[72] caused an atomic transfer between master and disciple? In other words, can we not see in the Mollycule theory, particularly within *The Dalkey Archive* context, an allegory of the anxiety of influence, in which exposure to the master has caused the inheritor to take on his guise, and to therefore have all his talents and accomplishments attributed to the father figure? Thus, everything that O'Nolan wrote was placed in the incorrect archive, the Joycean archive, rather than his own.

Wishing to move beyond the written archive to the presence of the reanimated author, Mick actively searches out the man behind *Ulysses* and *Finnegans Wake*, as, he says, 'I believe the picture of himself he has conveyed in his writings in fallacious. I believe he must be a far better man or a far worse' (DA 96). The man he meets turns out to be both; 'better' as he is devote, softly spoken, and a mild drinker, and 'worse' as he is pious, small-minded, and abstentious. The revived Joyce deems *Ulysses* 'Pornography and filth and literary vomit' (DA 167), and says that when he read a section of Molly's monologue, he 'blessed [him]self and put the thing in the fire' (DA 167). The reborn Joyce is a repugnant censor, armed with a project to translate and expurgate French classics for the Irish public: '[I had] a plan to translate and decontaminate great French literature so that it could be an inspiration to the Irish' (DA 166). O'Brien's Joyce is systematically denied all creative talent and reduced to the position of a copyist of the great works of others.

Bereft of all originality and innovation, a 'lonely, even a snotty, sort of fabricator',[73] Joyce is locked away in Skerries, unabashed, impotently reproducing the work of others. *Dubliners* becomes no more than a book of 'Simple stories: Dublin characterisations' (DA 165), that is, verbal translations of city scenes, and his other texts, spiritual tracts 'on marriage, the sacrament of penance, humility, the dangers of alcohol' (DA 165) simply repeat lines of scripture or recap the lives of saints. The father figure becomes one who didn't produce, but transcribed, translated and transliterated, scrabbling for knowledge in histories and etymologies, but bereft of any real insight.

When not copying, Joyce wished to correct mistakes caused by mistranslations and alterations: 'I wish to reform, first the Society, and then through the Society the Church. Error has crept in . . . corrupt beliefs . . . certain shameless superstitions . . . rash presumptions which have no sanction within the word of the Scriptures' (DA 170). His project specifically focuses on the diachronic evolution of the Hebrew *ruach* into the Greek *pneuma*: the Hebrew term, Joyce argues, originally meant 'the Divine Being, anterior to man', but came to mean 'not the immanent energy of God but His transcendent energy in imparting the divine content to men' (DA 170). It was simply a conflation and mistranslation between 'thought and language' (DA 171) on part of the Holy Fathers that caused the Divine breath to be given physical, if ephemeral, form as the Holy Spirit during the Council of Constantinople in 381, and as such Joyce's project to correct this inaccuracy is a mission of 'translation into language of raw spiritual concepts. I stress here *translation* as distinct from *exposition*. It is a question of conveying one thing in terms of another thing which is . . . em . . . quite incongruous' (DA 125). Thus, *The Dalkey Archive* re-presents *The Third Policeman*'s engagement with objects and concepts that defy language and comprehension, but this time forces Joyce into the position of failed translator, undertaking an impossible assignment that *The Third Policeman* knew was productive of no more than madness. O'Brien's Joyce, a man 'rather at sea as to *language*' (DA 126), can only fail in his endeavour to thetically represent the non-thetic.

Ruach, or *ruah*, is the Hebrew for 'wind', 'breath', 'spirit', 'ghost' or 'soul'. In philosophical/theological terms, it is used to represent an immediate correspondence between breath and spirit, or speech and thought in God. As Derrida argues in *Of Grammatology*, philosophy in the Western tradition has long privileged speech over writing, as philosophy is a *pneumatology*, a science of breath, that is, the oral.[74] Thus, 'writing, the letter, the sensible inscription, has always been considered by Western tradition as the body and matter external to the spirit, to breath, to speech, and to the logos'.[75] In other words, speech was thought of as a translation of an extra-linguistic concept, and writing the translation of speech, which meant that writing, 'the anguish of the Hebraic *ruah*, experienced in solitude by human responsibility',[76] was a double step away from the immediacy of the thought and breath of God. In his fascination with *ruach* and *pneuma*, O'Brien's Joyce seeks the ineffable inspiration and exhalation that created life, speech, presence and immediacy. In wishing to bring the Church back to the original words of God, the Joyce of *The Dalkey Archive* wishes to bring the Church back to the breath of God, wherein speech, concept and creation are instantaneous and identical: in the beginning was the word, and the word was with God, and the word was God. Thus, not only does *pneuma* link Joyce, De Selby's pneumatic chemistry and Sergeant Fottrell's pneumatic tyres, it turns Joyce into a 'pneumatologist', a man for whom writing is secondary to speech, for whom presence is everything, religion is all, translation is the highest goal, origins are truth and censorship was vital. Joyce becomes a copyist tracing a paper trail beyond the archive into the presence of the divine breath, a parody both of the Jesuit and the Joyce scholar, devoted to the minutiae of the text, and rejecting his 'home-made chaoistry' for a good 'dose of Jesuit casuistry' (SP 174) – as Myles wrote, 'Who can be answerable for James Joyce if it be not the Jesuits?'[77] Inasmuch as the Church has mistakenly revered the Holy Spirit, so has the world mistakenly revered Joyce. If in *The Third Policeman* the narrator encounters his stronger, more powerful double, in *The Dalkey Archive* O'Brien attempts to establish his ever-present father/double as the weaker mirror image mistaken for him. O'Nolan was the true original, regardless of historical fact, and thus he presents the archive of a 'real' history to prove it, albeit a history presented though truths in the plural within pre-posterous, hyperbolic scenes. It is not quite, as Ronald L. Dotterer puts it, 'a new, more sound belief',[78] but rather, as Lucas Harriman writes, a demonstration of 'the instability of the original conception, and indeed, of all attempts to fully 'know' the Joycean corpus'.[79]

However, Harriman adds that 'In a deliberately fictionalized confrontation with the truth, O'Brien opens the possibility of a more humble approach to the literary text'.[80] O'Nolan's truths should not be thought of proffering a new, ethical and unassuming response – the transparency of *The Dalkey Archive*'s intellectual pretensions and academic jealousies means that a deeper or indirect meaning seems desirable, but this tendency towards an inverted Occam's razor is deceptive. In 'Jokes and their Relation to the Unconscious', Freud tells the joke of the two men on the train:

> Two Jews met in a railway carriage at a station in Galicia. "Where are you going?" asked one. "To Cracow," was the answer. "What a liar you are!" broke out the other. "If you say you're going to Cracow, you want me to believe you're going to Lemberg. But I know that in fact you're going to Cracow. So why are you lying to me?"[81]

Freud employs this rather poor joke to demonstrate humanity's ability to deceive by telling the truth, and its logic obeys, as Žižek is fond of pointing out, the same structure as the old Groucho Marx line – 'This man looks like an idiot, and acts like an idiot, but this should in no way deceive you: he *is* an idiot!'.[82] In other words, the truth can be concealed in situations where it will not be recognized as such, as a culture of deception will mean that when one tells the truth one will simply be presumed to be lying. O'Nolan's oh-so-apparent jealousy is not masked self-effacement or genuine humility, but jealousy.

The autobiographical archive

When O'Nolan describes his revenge-through-resurrection of Joyce to O'Keeffe, he makes a very revealing slip:

> I've had it in for that bugger [Joyce] for a long time and I think this is the time. . . . *My* search for him there [Skerries], ultimately successful, brings us into the genre of *The Quest for Corvo*. *Our* ludicrous conversation can be imagined but it ends with Joyce asking whether *I* could use *my* influence to get him into the Jesuits.[83] [Emphasis added]

This conflation of author and character – Joyce will ask *Mick* if *he* could use *his* influence to get him into the Jesuits – removes the thin, illusionary veneer of authorial distance. The novel becomes an archive of desire, as O'Nolan meets Joyce through Mick, but an intellectually impoverished Joyce, who failed to write his major works, and who has embraced religion with a facile devotion. As such, *The Dalkey Archive* becomes a rewriting of A. J. A. Symons's *The Quest for Corvo: An Experiment in Biography.*

The Quest for Corvo was written in 1934, and tells the story of Frederick Rolfe, self-titled Frederick William Serafino Austin Lewis Mary Rolfe, also known as Baron Corvo, Fr. Austin, Fr. Rolfe, Prospero (and Caliban). Rolfe was a converted Catholic who tried to join the priesthood, but whose homosexuality and artistic excesses led to his vocation being denied. For the rest of his life he tried to earn a living from his varied literary and artistic skills, but they were too eccentric and idiosyncratic to be a commercial success in Victorian England, and he finally died, alone and impoverished, in Venice. His most famous work is a highly autobiographical novel entitled *Hadrian the Seventh*, in which his protagonist George Arthur Rose has his religious vocation cruelly ignored until, twenty years after his application, his saintliness and continued devotion to the Church causes a bishop to take his case to Rome. There he is not only welcomed into the fold, but made Pope. Until his tragic assassination the wise, worldly and knowing Pope embarks on a campaign of rewarding his friends and punishing his enemies, all of whom are clearly identifiable as figures from Rolfe's past.

Symons's text is ostensibly a biography, but rather than simply present the life of the subject in chronological fashion, *The Quest for Corvo* offers the story of Symons's introduction to Corvo, his enthusiasm for Corvo's works, his determination to find out about Corvo's life, the information he manages to uncover and the people he meets during his search. Thus, the quest itself takes precedent, and biography becomes autobiography, as the life and detective work of the author overshadows the life of the subject, and the text is divided into chapters such as 'The Problem', 'The Clues', 'The End of the Quest'. As Symons's brother wrote in his introduction to the 1966 American edition of the text,

It blows the gaff on biography, as it were, by refusing for a moment to make the customary pretence of detachment. We are

introduced to a biographer who becomes interested in an odd
character, and with a delicate deceptive sleight-of-hand the book
builds up not one picture but two: that of the crab-like Corvo,
hard-crusted, nipping and strange, a self-conscious artist to the
end of his pen nib; and that of his urbane, worldly and elegant
biographer. . . . [The narrative reveals] more about the nature of
Baron Corvo's biographer than it does about Corvo.[84]

In much the same manner O'Nolan conceals a personal archive
within a fictive one, and like *The Quest for Corvo* makes Joyce,
the subject of his/Mick's quest, a pathetic figure of failed ambition
and wasted talent. Inasmuch as Symons worked to uncover the
'truth' of Corvo's life, O'Nolan/Mick uncover the 'truth' of Joyce's,
and as such *The Dalkey Archive* presents a revisionist history of
Irish literature that revives the father/master only to silence him.
Joyce becomes 'nipping and strange', while O'Nolan, through
Mick, becomes 'urbane, worldly and elegant'. Furthermore, in
comparing *The Dalkey Archive* to *The Quest for Corvo*, O'Nolan
not only 'legitimates' his reworking of Joyce through association
with a genuine, if unusual, biography, he also doubly intensifies
his personal involvement, an involvement strengthened by
Myles's earlier claim to have written *The Quest for Corvo*: 'my
book was . . . called – very properly I still think – *The Quest
for Corvo*'.[85] Symons' text is an autobiography masquerading as
biography, about an author who wrote personal histories disguised
as fiction. In comparing *The Dalkey Archive* to *The Quest for
Corvo* O'Nolan highlights the autobiographical elements within
his text, and the novel can be understood as an imaginary version
of a real desire.

In comparing himself – through Mick – to Symons, O'Nolan
pushes Joyce towards Rolfe, and thus the voluntary exile of the man
who became the centre of Irish and European modernist literature
is brought into alignment with the involuntary exile of a failed
ecclesiastic and unsuccessful author. The comparison with the gay,
excluded, publically humiliated and ineffective writer adds another
blow to the ridiculing of Joyce, and yet, Rolfe cannot have been
viewed by O'Nolan as an unambiguously pathetic figure – *Children
of Destiny* was to feature the story of the first Irish pope, Patrick I,
and O'Nolan planned to use *Hadrian the Seventh* for background.[86]
Rolfe's works may not have been commercial successes, but he was

a gifted writer and his work was compared to Joyce's by Stuart Gilbert:

> had the Fates been kinder, that unhappy genius might have moved parallel, if on a somewhat lower plane, to Joyce's [sic]. Nicholas Crabbe, the hero of . . . *The Desire and Pursuit of the Whole*, had a good deal in common with Stephen Dedalus, and . . . the tone of the writing . . . will have a familiar ring for readers of Joyce's early work. . . . Some of Rolfe's cadences and word-patterns are in a Joycean vein . . . [and] Rolfe shared Joyce's fondness for out-of-the-way words.[87]

Rolfe may have been a pitiable figure, but he was also an unfairly neglected and tragic figure. There are thus many interesting resonances between Rolfe and O'Nolan, and as such Rolfe can also be read as an excessive version of O'Nolan, who incorporates the different styles and tendencies of O'Nolan, Flann O'Brien and Myles na gCopaleen. Like O'Nolan, Rolfe employed pseudonyms, played with translations and wrote copious satirical letters. His works included revised and fantastical alternative histories, macaronic neologisms, footnotes, involved stylistic flourishes and esoteric references. He was uncomfortable with women – he is accredited with having said 'there's no more loathsome sight in nature than a pregnant woman'[88] – and, depending on the state of his tempestuous relationships with his friends, was both poorer than O'Nolan and richer than Myles na gCopaleen. He also venomously disliked the Jesuits, claiming that the spurred ring he wore was a weapon to use in the event of a 'second' kidnap attempt made by them and maintaining that

> most of the offers of help and assistance he received could be traced back to a sinister intention to intern him and keep him "safely locked up," and that even those Jesuits who were not bent on thwarting him in subtle unseen ways would not hesitate to "kick a stone in his path".[89]

While O'Nolan's opinions of the Jesuits may have been less hyperbolic and paranoid, the disparaging portrayal of the order is repeated in interview,[90] in *Cruiskeen Lawn* and *The Hard Life* – 'In case of doubt, send for a Jesuit. For your one doubt he will give you twenty new ones and his talk is always full of 'ifs' and 'buts', rawmaish and pseudo-theology' (HL 75). Despite the overriding criticism of the Jesuits implicit in *The Dalkey Archive*, O'Nolan's own casuistry and devotion to minutiae was proudly described as enabling him to gain a point over both the Jesuits and Joyce:

> *None of you – yourself [Timothy O'Keeffe], the Jesuits nor James Joyce* knew that the Holy Ghost was not invented until 381, when a parcel of chancers of the Augustine type assembled at the Council of Constantinople. There is no mention whatsoever of the Blessed Trinity in the New Testament.[91] [Emphasis added]

Rolfe thus acts as a link between O'Nolan and Joyce, and by investing Joyce with Rolfe's negative qualities while taking Rolfe's positive ones as his own, O'Nolan is able to position himself above the father. The abject, inadequate Rolfe debases Joyce, while the romantic, talented Rolfe elevates O'Nolan. O'Nolan also becomes the questing archiver who uncovers the 'truth' about Joyce and writes the legitimate, authoritative biography, reviving the author in order to murder his legacy. Thus, the biographer is shown to possess greater talent and understanding than the subject, and biography turns to autobiography through implied *roman à clef*.

O'Nolan's perceived lack of distance from Mick caused Cronin to suggest that he change the text's first-person narrative to the third person, as

> aspects of the author's own personality seemed to have escaped from their compartments and to be hanging out all over the place. Of course the central character, Mick . . . was not intended to be a self-portrait . . . [but] it is impossible to escape the feeling that Mick and the author are very much the same person.[92]

O'Nolan seemed either unaware or unconcerned about any similarities; in fact, he was concerned that his depiction of his protagonist in the manuscript of *The Dalkey Archive* made him too sympathetic, and so decided to change the narration from first to third on the basis that this would 'materially change . . . the camera angle, and facilitate the job of making him more revolting'.[93] Montgomery's suggestion to remove the first-person narration appears – at least as he expressed it to O'Nolan – to be based on rather more structural concerns. He writes that he presumes that

O'Nolan deliberately chose the first person 'to make the narration dramatic, personal and tense? to make the events assume stature and mystery by reason of the naivety of the narrator?' but argues that in fact it detracts from the work:

> I say m'lud, that the exposition would lose nothing, would gain strength, detachment, clarity if the narration were impersonal. (It would gain in clarity – *oratio recta* soils, weakens irony, exposes it to suspicion of sentimentality (becomes *oratio recti*, of which the afflatus, to irony, is the kiss of death.))[94]

As he summarizes: 'why write 'I' when 'he', 'she' and 'it' makes the writer more godlike, leaves more time for paring fingernails?'.[95] But O'Nolan's mode of shifting the camera angle was to do no more than simply change all relevant pronouns and deictic marks, and thus interrupt what operated, albeit imperfectly – 'the narrator not only changes his personality but also his whole style of writing through the last one-third of the book'[96] – as a monad or microcosm. This shift arguably intensified rather than decreased the text's obvious autobiographical elements.

A text in the first-person absorbs the reader into the protagonist's life, as everything comes from the character's perspective. We are encompassed by an uninterrupted subjective opinion; while the narrator may lie or attempt to obfuscate, we receive only this limited, biased, prejudiced perspective. Which is what gives a first-person narrative its claustrophobic quality, but also its delight. Had O'Nolan chosen to retain this narrative mode, he could have intensified Mick's obnoxious nature and trapped the reader even more within his stifling personality and awkward turns of phrase. Similarly, had O'Nolan crafted a new third persona narrator not only could he have added a voice which humorously, sternly or knowingly reflected on the 'conceited prig'[97] Mick, he could also have clarified the targets of his essay in derision. Instead, he simply changed the grammar throughout from 'I' to 'he', and having stepped outside Mick, landed nowhere. Cut off from its original mooring in Mick, the narrative structure of *The Dalkey Archive* becomes a castrated semi-structure, a lifeless, limping indirect discourse, no longer free. The result of this half-step away from Mick is that the text hovers between modes, unable to commit. Far from having a rounded character to invest in, or a narrator whose perspective to reflect upon, the reader is pushed back towards the author, and the unsatisfying Mick/narrator seem closer to cracked and imperfect masks for O'Nolan himself.[98]

The Dalkey Archive ended a career of masks with a certain slippage, but dropping the veil reveals not a single identity, but a man who, by dint of his own fixation with pseudonyms, is multiple and split. Brian O'Nolan is not a stable origin of a multitude, but the fragmentary host of a fragmentary corpus, at times brilliant, at times prosaic, but worthy of a place among the greats of the twentieth centre, and the acclaim he desired and yet deprecated:

> The writing crowd, it is well known, are only a parcel of dud Czechs and bohemian gulls and if I am seen in that notorious ultimate rigour it will not be in their company, though I can predict that on that day there will be wailed throughout the length (not to say breadth) of this rich and rare land loud cries of "Wisha, he wasn't the worst!"[99]

Notes

1   The substance DMP, a play on Dublin Metropolitan Police, repeats O'Brien's interests in abstract, powerful substances. Not only is it a highly reduced and restricted version of omnium, it also calls to Myles's 'Cruscalon', a 'cosmic vapour . . . designed not to destroy but rather to assist humanity by throwing the earth into neutral', as it has been 'proceeding in too high a gear' (CL 25 January 1950). In a link between De Selby and Myles, a later article details how Myles sends his housekeeper to the chemist for '8 ½ ounces of botulin toxin. . . . I want it for destroying everything in the world' (CL 6 February 1959).

2   Cronin, 228.

3   Jacques Derrida, *Archive Fever: A Freudian Impression*, trans. Eric Prenowitz (Chicago: The University of Chicago Press, 1996), 98.

4   Ibid., 99.

5   Derrida, *Archive Fever*, 94.

6   Derrida, 'Freud', 253–4.

7   Ibid., 12.

8   Andrea Hurst, *Derrida Vis-à-vis Lacan: Interweaving Deconstruction and Psychoanalysis* (New York: Fordham University Press, 2008), 163.

9   Derrida, *Archive Fever*, 10.

10 Ibid., 11.

11 This should not be thought to contradict the reading offered in Chapter 2, but re-fabricate it.

12 Samuel Beckett 'Dante. . . . Bruno. Vico . . . Joyce', *Our Exagmination Round his Factification for Incamination of Work in Progress* (London: Faber and Faber, 1972), 5.

13 James Joyce, *Finnegans Wake* (London: Penguin, 2000), 452.

14 BON to NM 12 January 1964.

15 CL 19 April 1941.

16 CL 5 January 1942.

17 CL 7 August 1958.

18 CL 7 July 1958.

19 CL 9 November 1949.

20 Donohue, 200.

21 *Irish Times* 3 July 1943 – quotation from an article on Myles and Flann by Richard Watts in the *New York Herald Tribune*.

22 BON to TOK, 21 September 1962, SIUC.

23 BON to NM, 12 January 1964, SIUC.

24 CS to BON, 2 January 1964, SIUC.

25 BON to CS, 11 February 1964, SIUC.

26 The only note that strikes out of key is Augustine's claim that the *Confessions* exaggerated his promiscuous past out of pride, but this might not be quite as surprising a claim a he might have thought. As Alan Soble writes, 'I suspect that Augustine's description of his youthful sinfulness (*Confessions* 2) exaggerates the extent of his teenage sexual activity, even if his mental life was dancing with lust'. ('Correcting Some Misconceptions about St. Augustine's Sex Life'. *Journal of the History of Sexuality* 11.4 (2002): 569). In this Soble also argues that there is no solid textual evidence to prove that Augustine engaged in homosexual sex.

27 W. B. Yeats, 'The Scholars'. In *W.B. Yeats: The Poems*, Ed. Daniel Albright (London: Everyman 1995), 190.

28 BON to CS 11 February 1964, SIUC.

29 Cronin, 226.

30 St Augustine, *The Problem of Free Choice,* trans. Mark Pontifex (Mahwah, NJ: Paulist Press, 1955), 234.

31 W. B. Stanford to BON, 21 November 1962, SIUC. The only addition that O'Nolan made to his letter was the addition of the phrase 'yer man'. With this sole amendment, the passage 'The name Petros . . . Annals 11, 4' (DA 35) is included in the text without change from the original letter.

32 O'Nolan might point out that the target in *The Dalkey Archive* is not the finessing or refining of erudite information, but the type of person who engages in such an activity without the self-mocking distance of *Cruiskeen Lawn*. However, the letters show no evidence of self-mockery; in fact, their tone is almost painfully sincere, nor does *The Dalkey Archive* show any real sign of self-reflection.

33 In a letter to O'Keeffe (27 November 1963, SIUC) O'Nolan expresses hope that the book will be banned.

34 BON to TOK 15 November 1963, SIUC.

35 BON to TOK 27 November 1963, SIUC.

36 BON to CS 11 February 1964, SIUC.

37 Ibid.

38 Ibid.

39 BON to MH 28 November 1963, SIUC.

40 BON to TOK 15 November 1963, SIUC.

41 BON to Cecil Scott 11 February 1964, SIUC.

42 Taaffe, *Looking Glass,* 185.

43 Derrida, *Archive Fever,* 67.

44 Ibid., 68.

45 BON to CS 28 July 1964, SIUC.

46 CL 12 February 1951.

47 In *The Dalkey Archive*, one might add, O'Nolan is able to take Joyce, and move the master around as he wishes.

48 CL 27 June 1945.

49 CL 28 December 1957.

50 CL 17 June 1954.

51 CL 20 November 1954.

52 CL 9 May 1947 – According to Taaffe this article was written by Niall Montgomery (See Taaffe, *Looking Glass,* 163–6).

53 CL 16 June 1954.

54 CL 21 November 1949.

55 CL 6 June 1957. See David Powell's 'Annotated Bibliography of Myles na Gopaleen's (Flann O'Brien's) "Cruiskeen Lawn" Commentaries on James Joyce' (*James Joyce Quarterly 9*. 1 (1971): 50–62) for a full list.

56 CL 20 July 1955.

57 BON to MH 6 January 1964, SIUC.

58 BON to NM 12 January 1964, SIUC.

59 CL 7 July 1950.

60 DA MS 202.

61 CL 29 March 1956.

62 DA MS 150.

63 BON to Gerald Gross 10 September 1962, SIUC.

64 Hopper, *Portrait*, 12.

65 CL 20 July 1945.

66 CL 16 June 1954.

67 Ibid.

68 O'Nolan, 'Two in One', *A Flann O'Brien Reader*, 322.

69 O'Nolan, 'Two in One', 326.

70 CL 6 June 1957.

71 This is echoed in an early *Cruiskeen Lawn* article in which Myles speculates if the English would become Irish if they were made to eat only food grown in Ireland (CL 8 December 1944).

72 Sheridan, 39.

73 DA MS 147.

74 Derrida, *Of Grammatology*, 17.

75 Ibid., 35.

76 Derrida, 'Force and Signification'. In *Writing and Difference*, trans. Alan Bass (London: Routledge, 2001), 9.

77 CL 16 June 1954.

78 Ronald L. Dotterer, 'Flann O'Brien, James Joyce and *The Dalkey Archive*'. *New Hibernia Review* 8.2 (2004): 63.

79 Lucas Harriman, 'Flann O'Brien's Creative Betrayal of Joyce'. *New Hibernia Review* 14.4 (2010): 100–1.

80 Harriman, 103.

81 Sigmund Freud, 'Jokes and their Relation to the Unconscious'. In *The Standard Edition of the Complete Psychological Works of Sigmund Freud* VIII, Ed. and trans. James Strachey. London: Vintage, 2001, 115.

82 Slavoj Žižek, *Looking Awry: An Introduction to Jacques Lacan through Popular Culture* (Cambridge, MA: Massachusetts Institute of Technology Press, 1991), 73.

83 BON to TOK 21 September 1962, SIUC.

84 Julian Symons, 'The Author and the Quest', introduction to *The Quest for Corvo: Genius or Charlatan?*, A. J. A. Symons (New York: Penguin, 1966), 9–10. As quoted by Allen Hibbard, 'Biographer and Subject: A Tale of Two Narratives'. South Central Review 23.3 (2006): 23.

85 CL 24 March 1948. On 6 May 1954 he refers to it as a 'really fine book'.

86 Sheridan, 42–3.

87 Stuart Gilbert, *Joyce's Ulysses* (New York: Vintage, 1961), 92–3.

88 A. J. A. Symons, *The Quest for Corvo: An Experiment in Biography* (Harmondsworth: Penguin, 1944), 73.

89 Trevor Hadden to A. J. A. Symons in *The Quest for Corvo*, 108.

90 In an 1964 RTÉ interview, for example, O'Nolan made disparaging remarks about the Jesuits (Taaffe, *Looking Glass,* 200).

91 BON to TOK 22 January 1964, SIUC.

92 Cronin, 227.

93 BON to CS 11 December 1963, SUIC.

94 NM to BON undated, SIUC.

95 Ibid.

96 CS to BON, 2 January 1964, SIUC.

97 BON to CS 11 December 1963, SUIC.

98 Even with the first person narrative of the manuscript the style of narration is highly inconsistent, as the tone of the opening pages, for example, differ strongly from subsequent scenes.

99 CL 7 May 1943.

BIBLIOGRAPHY

(Due to the extent of texts by O'Nolan consulted for this work, only those directly quoted from are listed in this bibliography. A full O'Nolan bibliography can be found at http://www.univie.ac.at/flannobrien2011/bibliography.html)

Agamben, Gorgio. *Homo Sacer: Sovereign Power and Bare Life*, trans. Daniel Heller-Roazen. Stanford: Stanford University Press, 1998.
— *Remnants of Auschwitz: The Witness and the Archive*, trans. Daniel Heller-Roazen. New York: Zone Books, 1999a.
— *The End of the Poem: Studies in Poetics*, trans. Daniel Heller-Roazen. Stanford: Stanford University Press, 1999b.
— *The Open: Man and Animal*, trans. Kevin Attell. Stanford: Stanford University Press, 2004.
Anderson, Simon. 'Pink Paper and the Composition of Flann O'Brien's *At Swim-Two-Birds*'. Unpublished MA thesis, submitted to Louisiana State University, 2002.
Anspaugh, Kelly. *Agonizing with Joyce: At Swim-Two-Birds as Thanatography*. At Swim-Two-Birds by Flann O'Brien: A Casebook. Ed. Thomas C. Foster. Normal, Ill.: Dalkey Archive Press, 2005, 1–28 (each article individually paginated). PDFs at Dalkey Archive Press site: http://www.dalkeyarchive.com/book/?GCOI=15647100481040.
Aristotle. Physics. Ed. and trans. Hippocrates G. Apostle. London: Indiana University Press, 1969.
Asbee, Sue. *Flann O'Brien*. Boston: Twanye Publishers, 1991.
Augustine. *The Confessions of St. Augustine*, trans. E. B. Pusey. London: Everyman's Library, 1966.
Bacik, Ivana. 'Breaking the Language Barrier: Access to Justice in the New Ireland'. *Judicial Studies Institute Journal* 7.2 (2007a): 109–23.
— 'From Virgins and Mothers to Popstars and Presidents: Changing Roles of Women in Ireland'. *The Irish Review* 35 (2007b): 100–7.
Baines, Jennika. 'A Rock and a Hard Place: Sweeny as Sisyphus and Job in Flann O'Brien's *At Swim-Two-Birds*'. In *Irish Modernism: Origins, Contexts, Publics*. Eds. by Edwina Keown and Carol Taaffe. Oxford: Peter Lang, 2010, 145–58.

Bair, Deirdre. *Samuel Beckett: A Biography*. New York: Touchstone, 1990.

Baudelaire, Charles. *Complete Poems,* trans. Walter Martin. London: Routledge, 2002.

Beckett, Samuel. 'Dante . . . Bruno. Vico . . . Joyce'. In *Our Exagmination Round his Factification for Incamination of Work in Progress*. London: Faber and Faber, 1972, 1–22.

— 'Endgame'. In *Samuel Beckett: Complete Dramatic Works*. London: Faber and Faber, 2006, 89–134.

— 'Molloy'. In *Three Novels*. New York: Grove Press, 2009, 3–170.

Benjamin, Walter. 'Critique of Violence'. In *Reflections*, trans. Edmund Jephcott. New York: Schocken Books, 1986, 277–300.

Birmingham, Peg. 'On Violence, Politics, and the Law'. *The Journal of Speculative Philosophy* 24.1 (2010): 1–20.

Blanchot, Maurice. *The Infinite Conversation*, trans. Susan Hanson. Minneapolis: University of Minnesota Press, 1993.

— *The Work of Fire*, trans. Charlotte Mandell. Stanford: Stanford University Press, 1995a.

— *The Writing of the Disaster*, trans. Ann Smock. Lincoln: University of Nebraska Press, 1995b.

Bobotis, Andrea. 'Queering Knowledge in Flann O'Brien's *The Third Policeman*'. *Irish University Review* 32.2 (2002): 242–58.

Boheemen-Saaf, Christine van. *Joyce, Derrida, Lacan and the Trauma of History: Reading, Narrative and Postcolonialism*. Cambridge: Cambridge University Press, 1999.

Bolton, Jonathan. 'Comedies of Failure: O'Brien's *The Hard Life* and Moore's *The Emperor of Ice Cream*'. *New Hibernia Review* 12.3 (2008): 118–33.

Booker, Keith M. 'Science, Philosophy, and *The Third Policeman*: Flann O'Brien and the Epistemology of Futility'. *South Atlantic Review* 56.4 (1991): 37–56.

— 'The Dalkey Archive: Flann O'Brien's Critique of Mastery'. *Irish University Review* 23.2 (1993): 269–85.

— *Flann O'Brien, Bakhtin, and Menippean Satire*. New York: Syracuse University Press, 1995.

— 'Postmodern and/or Postcolonial? The Politics of *At Swim-Two-Birds*.' In *At Swim-Two-Birds by Flann O'Brien: A Casebook*. Ed. Thomas C. Foster. Normal, Ill.: Dalkey Archive Press, 2005, 1–15 (each article individually paginated). PDFs at Dalkey Archive Press site: http://www. dalkeyarchive.com/book/?GCOI=15647100481040.

Breuer, Rolf. 'Flann O'Brien and Samuel Beckett'. *Irish University Review* 37.2 (2007): 340–51.

Brivic, Shelly. '*The Third Policeman* as Lacanian Deity: O'Brien's Critique of Language and Subjectivity'. *New Hibernia Review* 16.2 (2012): 112–32.

Brooker, Joseph. ' "Children of Destiny": Brian O'Nolan and the Irish Ready-Made School'. http://eprints.bbk.ac.uk/172/1/brooker4.pdf. pp 1–18. Also appeared as 'A Balloon Filled with Verbal Gas: Blather and the Irish Ready-Made School'. *Precursors and Aftermaths* 2.1 (2003): 74–98.

— 'Estopped by Grand Playsaunce: Flann O'Brien's Post-Colonial Lore'. *Journal of Law and Society* 31.1 (2004): 15–37.

— *Flann O'Brien.* Tavistock: Northcote, 2005.

— 'The Man in the Hat': Review of Hopper and Taaffe. *Modernism/ modernity* 17.1 (2010): 233–8.

Brooks, Peter. *Reading for the Plot: Design and Intention in Narrative.* Cambridge, MA: Harvard University Press, 1992.

Brown, Terrance. *Ireland: A Social and Cultural History 1922–2002.* London: Harper Perennial, 2004.

Bruford, Alan. *Gaelic Folk-Tales and Medieval Romances: A Study of the Early Modern Irish 'Romantic Tales' and their Oral Derivatives.* Dublin: The Folklore of Ireland Society, 1969.

Burke, Chloe S. and Christopher J. Castaneda. 'The Public and Private History of Eugenics: An Introduction'. *The Public Historian* 29.3 (2007): 5–17.

Camus, Albert. *The Outsider,* trans. Joseph Laredo. Harmondsworth: Penguin, 1981.

— *The Myth of Sisyphus,* trans. Justin O'Brien. London: Penguin, 2000.

Čapec, Josef and Karel. *R. U.R and The Insect Play,* trans. Paul Selver. Oxford: Oxford University Press, 1961.

Carlyle, Thomas. *English and Other Critical Essays.* London: J. M. Dent & Sons, 1900.

Censorship of Publications Act, 1929, Irish Statute Book, http://www. irishstatutebook.ie http://www.irishstatutebook.ie/1929/en/act/ pub/0021/sec0006.html#sec6.

Childs, Donald A. *Modernism and Eugenics: Woolf, Eliot, Yeats and the Culture of Degeneration.* Cambridge: Cambridge University Press, 2001.

Childs, Peter. *Modernism.* London: Routledge, 2000.

Clear, Caitriona. 'Hardship, Help and Happiness in Oral History Narratives of Women's Lives in Ireland, 1921–1961'. *Oral History* 31.2 (2003): 33–42.

Clissmann, Anne. *Flann O'Brien: A Critical Introduction to his Writings.* Dublin: Gill and Macmillan, 1975.

Clune, Anne. 'Flann O'Brien: Twenty Years On'. *The Linen Hall Review* 3.2 (1986): 4–7.

— 'Mythologising Sweeney'. *Irish University Review* 26.1 (1996): 48–60.

Clune, Anne and Tess Hurson ed. *Conjuring Complexities: Essays on Flann O'Brien.* Antrim: W. & G. Baird Ltd., 1997.

Cohen, David. 'An Atomy of the Novel: Flann O'Brien's *At Swim-Two-Birds*'. *Twentieth Century Literature* 39.2 (1993): 208–29.

Comer, Todd A. 'A Mortal Agency: Flann O'Brien's *At Swim-Two-Birds*'. *Journal of Modern Literature* 31.2 (2008): 104–14.

Connor, Steven. *The Book of Skin*. Cornell: Cornell University Press, 2004.

Cornwell, Neil. *The Absurd in Literature*. Manchester: Manchester University Press, 2006.

Costello, Peter and Peter van de Kamp. *Flann O'Brien: An Illustrated Biography*. London: Bloomsbury, 1987.

Critchley, Simon. *Very Little . . . Almost Nothing*. London: Routledge, 1997.

Cronin, Anthony. *No Laughing Matter: The Life and Times of Flann O'Brien*. London: Grafton Books, 1989.

Curran, Steven. 'Could Paddy Leave off from Copying Just for Five Minutes': Brian O'Nolan and Eire's Beveridge Plan'. *Irish University Review* 31.2 (2001): 353–75.

Davison, Neil R. '"We are not a doctor for the body": Catholicism, the Female Grotesque, and Flann O'Brien's *The Hard Life*'. Literature and Psychology 45.4 (1999), accessed via *Literature Online*, no pagination. http://lion.chadwyck.co.uk.ezphost.dur.ac.uk/searchFulltext.do?id=R00 812723&divLevel=0&area=abell&forward=critref_ft.

Deane, Seamus. *Strange Country: Modernity and Nationhood in Irish Writing since 1790*. Oxford: Clarendon Press, 1998.

Derrida, Jacques. *The Ear of the Other: Otobiography, Transference, Translation*. Ed. Christie V. McDonald, trans. Peggy Kamuf. New York: Schocken Books, 1985.

— *Archive Fever: A Freudian Impression*, trans. Eric Prenowitz. Chicago: The University of Chicago Press, 1996.

— *Of Grammatology*, trans. Gayatri Chakravorty Spivak. Baltimore: The John Hopkins University Press, 1997.

— *Monolingualism of the Other, or, The Prosthesis of Origin*, trans. Patrick Mensah. Stanford: Stanford University Press, 1998a.

— *Resistances of Psychoanalysis*, trans. Peggy Kamuf, Pascale-Anne Brault and Michael Naas. Stanford: Stanford University Press, 1998b.

— 'Ellipsis'. In *Writing and Difference*, trans. Alan Bass. London: Routledge, 2001a, 371–8.

— 'Force and Signification'. In *Writing and Difference,* trans. Alan Bass. London: Routledge, 2001b, 1–35.

— 'Freud and the Scene of Writing'. *Writing and Difference*, trans. Alan Bass. London: Routledge, 2001c, 246–91.

— '*Des Tours de Babel*'. (1980) Trans. Joseph F. Graham (1985). *Acts of Religion*. Ed. Gil Anidjar. Routledge: London, 2002a, 102–34.

— 'Force of Law: The "Mystical Foundation of Authority"', trans. Mary Quaintance. *Acts of Religion*. Ed. Gil Anidjar. Routledge: London, 2002b, 228–98.

— 'Aphorism Countertime', trans. Nicholas Royle. In *Psyche: Inventions of the Other II*. Eds. Peggy Kamuf and Elizabeth Rottenberg. Stanford: Stanford University Press, 2008a, 127–42.

— 'Who or What Is Compared? The Concept of Comparative Literature and the Theoretical Problems of Translation', trans. Eric Prenowitz. *Discourse* 30.1–2 (2008b): 22–53.

Dewsnap. Terence. 'Flann O'Brien and the Politics of Buffoonery'. *The Canadian Journal of Irish Studies* 19.1 (1993): 22–36.

Dobbins, Gregory. *Lazy Idle Schemers: Irish Modernism and the Cultural Politics of Idleness*. Dublin: Field Day Publications, 2010.

Docker, John. *Postmodernism and Popular Culture: A Cultural History*. Cambridge: Cambridge University Press, 1994.

Doherty, Francis. 'Flann O'Brien's Existentialist Hell'. *The Canadian Journal of Irish Studies* 15.2 (1989): 51–67.

Donohue, Keith. *The Irish Anatomist: A Study of Flann O'Brien*. Dublin: Maunsel & Company, 2002.

Dotterer, Ronald L. 'Flann O'Brien, James Joyce, and *The Dalkey Archive*'. *New Hibernia Review* 8.2 (2004): 54–63.

Downam, Denell. 'Citation and Spectrality in Flann O'Brien's *At Swim-Two-Birds*'. *Irish University Review* 36.2 (2006): 304–20.

Dunne, J. W. *An Experiment with Time*. London: A. and C. Black, 1929.

— *The Serial Universe*. London: Faber and Faber, 1934.

Eagleton, Terry. *Sweet Violence: The Idea of the Tragic*. Oxford: Blackwell, 2003.

Edelman, Lee. *No Future: Queer Theory and the Death Drive*. Durham, N.C.: Duke University Press, 2004.

Esty, Joshua D. 'Flann O'Brien's *At Swim-Two-Birds* and the Post-Post Debate'. *ARIEL: A Review of International English Literature* 26.4 (1995): 23–46.

Evans, Eibhlín. ' "A lacuna in the palimpsest": A Reading of Flann O'Brien's *At Swim-Two-Birds*'. *Critical Survey* 15.1 (2003): 91–107.

Felski, Rita. *The Gender of Modernity*. Cambridge MA: Harvard University Press, 1995.

Ferriter, Diarmaid. *Occasions of Sin: Sex and Society in Modern Ireland*. London: Profile Books, 2009.

— *The Transformation of Ireland 1900–2000*. London: Profile Books, 2010.

Fink, Bruce. *The Lacanian Subject: Between Language and Jouissance*. Princeton: Princeton University Press, 1995.

Finnan, Joseph P. 'Punch's Portrayal of Redmond, Carson and the Irish Question, 1910–18' *Irish Historical Studies* 33.132 (2003): 424–51.

Flood, Jeanne A. 'Joyce and the Maamtrasna Murders'. *James Joyce Quarterly* 28.4 (1991): 879–88.

Forster, Verna A. *The Name and Nature of Tragicomedy.* Aldershot: Ashgate, 2004.

Foster, Thomas C. 'Flann O'Brien's *At Swim-Two-Birds'.* In *At Swim-Two-Birds by Flann O'Brien: A Casebook.* Ed. Thomas C. Foster. Normal, Ill.: Dalkey Archive Press, 2005, 1–10 (each article individually paginated). PDFs at Dalkey Archive Press site: http://www.dalkeyarchive.com/book/?GCOI=15647100481040.

Foucault, Michel. *The Will to Knowledge: The History of Sexuality Vol. 1,* trans. Robert Hurley. London: Penguin, 1990.

Freud, Sigmund. 'From the History of an Infantile Neurosis'. In *Case Histories II: 'Rat Man', Schreber, 'Wolf Man', Female Homosexuality.* Ed. Angela Richards, trans. James Strachey. London: Penguin, 1981, 227–366.

— 'Beyond the Pleasure Principle'. In *The Standard Edition of the Complete Psychological Works of Sigmund Freud* XVIII. Ed. and trans. James Strachey. London: Vintage, 2001a, 7–67.

— 'The Ego and the Id'. In *The Standard Edition of the Complete Psychological Works of Sigmund Freud* XIX. Ed. and trans. James Strachey. London: Vintage, 2001b, 12–68.

— 'Instincts and their Vicissitudes'. In *The Standard Edition of the Complete Psychological Works of Sigmund Freud* XIV. Ed. and trans. James Strachey. London: Vintage, 2001c, 117–40.

— 'The Interpretation of Dreams, Part 2'. In *Complete Psychological Works of Sigmund Freud* V. Ed. and trans. James Strachey. London: Vintage, 2001d, 339–630.

— 'Jokes and their Relation to the Unconscious'. In *The Standard Edition of the Complete Psychological Works of Sigmund Freud* VIII. Ed. and trans. James Strachey. London: Vintage, 2001e, 159–80.

— 'New Introductory Lectures on Psychoanalysis'. In *The Standard Edition of the Complete Psychological Works of Sigmund Freud* XXII. Ed. and trans. James Strachey. London: Vintage, 2001f, 7–184.

— 'Thoughts for the Times on War and Death'. In *The Standard Edition of the Complete Psychological Works of Sigmund Freud* XIV. Ed. and trans. James Strachey. London: Vintage, 2001g, 273–302.

— 'The Unconscious'. In *The Standard Edition of the Complete Psychological Works of Sigmund Freud* XIV. Ed. and trans. James Strachey. London: Vintage, 2001h, 166–216.

— 'The Uncanny'. In *The Standard Edition of the Complete Psychological Works of Sigmund Freud* XVII. Ed. and trans. James Strachey. London: Vintage, 2001i, 217–56.

Friel, Brian. *Translations. Plays 1*. London: Faber and Faber, 1996.

Gallagher, Monique. 'The Poor Mouth: Flann O'Brien and the Gaeltacht'. *Studies: An Irish Quarterly Review* 72.287 (1983): 231–41.

— 'Reflecting Mirrors in Flann O'Brien's *At Swim-Two-Birds*'. *The Journal of Narrative Technique* 22.2 (1992): 128–35.

— 'Frontier Instability in Flann O'Brien's *At Swim-Two-Birds*'. In *At Swim-Two-Birds by Flann O'Brien: A Casebook*. Ed. Thomas C. Foster. Normal, Ill.: Dalkey Archive Press, 2005, 1–23 (each article individually paginated). PDFs at Dalkey Archive Press site: http://www.dalkeyarchive.com/book/?GCOI=15647100481040.

Galton, Francis. *Inquiries into Human Faculty and its Development*. New York: Macmillan, 1883.

Giebus, Jay. 'Flann O'Brien's at Swim-Two-Bird'. *An Irish Quarterly Review* 80.317 (1991): 65–76.

Gilbert, Stuart. *Joyce's Ulysses*. New York: Vintage, 1961.

Na gCopaleen, Myles. *An Béal Bocht*. Dublin: Mercier Press, 1999.

Gregory, Lady Augusta. (Ed and Trans). *Gods and Fighting Men: The Story of the Tuatha de Danaan and of the Fianna of Ireland* (1904). London: Gerrards Cross, 1970.

Hägglund, Martin. 'Chronolibidinal Reading: Deconstruction and Psychoanalysis'. *CR: The New Centennial Review* 9.1 (2009): 1–43.

Harriman, Lucas. 'Flann O'Brien's Creative Betrayal of Joyce'. *New Hibernia Review* 14.4 (2010): 90–109.

Harrington, T. *The Maamtrasna Massacre: Impeachment of the Trials (with appendix containing report of trials and correspondence between Most Rev. Dr. M'Evilly and the Lord Lieutenant)*. Dublin: Nation Office, 1884.

Henry, P. L. 'The Structure of Flann O'Brien's *At Swim-Two-Birds*'. *Irish University Review* 20.1 (1990): 35–40.

Hibbard, Allen. 'Biographer and Subject: A Tale of Two Narratives'. *South Central Review* 23.3 (2006): 19–36.

Hirsch, Edward. 'The Imaginary Irish Peasant'. *PMLA* 106.5 (1991): 1116–33.

Homer, Sean. *Jacques Lacan*. London: Routledge, 2005.

Hopper, Keith. 'The Dismemberment of Orpheus: Flann O'Brien and the Censorship Code'. *Barcelona English Language and Literature Studies* 11 (2000): 119–31.

— *Flann O'Brien: A Portrait of the Artist as a Young Post-Modernist*. Cork: Cork University Press, 2009.

Howell, Philip. 'Venereal Disease and the Politics of Prostitution in the Irish Free State'. *Irish Historical Studies* 33.131 (2003): 320–41.

Hughes, Eamonn. 'Flann O'Brien's *At Swim-Two-Birds* in the Age of Mechanical Reproduction'. In *Irish Modernism: Origins, Contexts,*

Publics. Eds. Edwina Keown and Carol Taaffe. Oxford: Peter Lang, 2010, 111–28.

Hunt, Roy L. 'Hell Goes Round and Round: Flann O'Brien'. *The Canadian Journal of Irish Studies*14.2 (1989): 60–73.

Hurst, Andrea. *Derrida Vis-à-vis Lacan: Interweaving Deconstruction and Psychoanalysis*. New York: Fordham University Press, 2008.

Imhof, Rüdiger ed. *Alive-Alive O!: Flann O'Brien's At Swim-Two-Birds*. Dublin: Wolfhound Press, 1985.

Jacquin, Danielle. '"Cerveaux Lucides is Good Begob": Flann O'Brien and the World of Peasants'. In *Rural Ireland, Real Ireland?* Ed. Jacqueline Genet. Gerrards Cross, Buckinghamshire: Colin Smythe Ltd, 1996, 223–34.

Johansen, Ib. 'Shadows in a Black Mirror: Reflections on the Irish Fantastic from Sheridan Le Fanu to John Banville'. *Nordic Irish Studies* 1 (2002): 51–61.

Johnson, Barbara. 'The Frame of Reference: Poe, Lacan, Derrida'. *Yale French Studies* 55/56 (1977): 457–505.

Johnston, Adrian. *Time Driven: Metapsychology and the Splitting of the Drive*. Evanston, Il: Northwestern University Press, 2005.

— 'Life Terminable and Interminable: The Undead and the Afterlife of the Afterlife – A Friendly Disagreement with Martin Hägglund'. *CR: The New Centennial Review* 9.1 (2009): 147–89.

Joyce, James. 'Ireland Before the Bar'. In *The Critical Writings of James Joyce*. Eds. Ellsworth Mason and Richard Ellmann. London: Faber and Faber, 1959.

— *Finnegans Wake*. London: Penguin, 2000.

— *A Portrait of the Artist as a Young Man*. Oxford: Oxford University Press, 2008a.

— *Ulysses*. Oxford: Oxford University Press, 2008b.

Joyce, Patrick Weston. *The Origin and History of Irish Names of Places*. Dublin: McGlashan and Gill, 1869.

— *Old Celtic Romances* (1907). Dublin: The Educational Company of Ireland, 1920.

Kafka, Franz. 'In the Penal Colony'. In *The Transformation ('Metamorphosis') and Other Stories*. Ed. and Trans. Malcolm Pasley. London: Penguin, 1992, 127–53.

— *The Castle*, trans. Andrea Bell. Oxford: Oxford University Press, 2009.

Kant, Immanuel. 'The End of All Things' *Religion and Rational Theology*, trans. and ed. Allen W. Wood and George D. Giovanni. Cambridge: Cambridge University Press, 2001, 217–32.

Kemnitz, Charles. 'Beyond the Zone of Middle Dimensions: A Relativistic Reading of *The Third Policeman*'. *Irish University Review* 15.1 (1985): 56–72.

Kenner, Hugh. *A Colder Eye: The Modern Irish Writers*. Baltimore: The John Hopkins University Press, 1983.

Keown, Edwina and Carol Taaffe, eds. *Irish Modernism: Origins, Contexts, Publics*. Oxford: Peter Lang, 2010.

Kiberd, Declan. 'Flann O'Brien, Myles, and The Poor Mouth'. In *Inventing Ireland: The Literature of a Modern Nation*. London: Vintage Books, 1996, 497–512.

— 'Gaelic Absurdism: *At Swim-Two-Birds*'. In *Irish Classics*. London: Granta Books, 2000, 500–19.

Kim, Rina. 'Severing Connections with Ireland: Women and the Irish Free State in Beckett's Writing'. *Samuel Beckett Today* 15 (2005): 57–69.

Kristeva, Julia. *Powers of Horror: An Essay on Abjection*, trans. Leon. S. Roudiez. New York: Columbia University Press, 1982.

Lacan, Jacques. 'Desire and the Interpretation of Desire in Hamlet', trans. James Hulbert. *Yale French Studies* 55/56 (1977): 11–52.

— *Écrits: A Selection*, trans. Alan Sheridan. London: Routledge, 1989.

— *The Four Fundamental Concepts of Psychoanalysis: The Seminar of Jacques Lacan Book XI*, trans. Alan Sheridan. New York: W. W. Norton, 1998.

— 'Aristotle's Dream', trans. Lorenzo Chiesa. *Angelaki: Journal of the Theoretical Humanities* 11.3 (2006): 83–4.

Lacoue-Labarthe, Philippe and Jean-Luc Nancy. *The Literary Absolute: The Theory of Literature in German Romanticism*, trans. Philip Barnard and Cheryl Lester. Albany: State University of New York Press, 1988.

Lambert, Sharon. From 'Irish Women's Emigration to England 1922–1960: The Lengthening of Family Ties'. In *The Irish Women's History Reader*. Eds. Alan Hayes and Diane Urquhart. London: Routledge, 2001, 181–7.

Lloyd, David. 'The Indigent Sublime: Specters of Irish Hunger'. *Representations* 92.1 (2005): 152–85.

— 'Frames of *referrance*: Samuel Beckett as an Irish Question'. In *Beckett and Ireland*. Ed. Seán Kennedy. Cambridge: Cambridge University Press, 2010, 31–55.

Luddy, Maria. 'Sex and the Single Girl in 1920s and 1930s Ireland'. *The Irish Review* 35 (2007): 79–91.

Lyotard, Jean-François. *The Differend: Phrases in Dispute*, trans. Georges Van Den Abbeele. Minneapolis: University of Minnesota Press, 1988.

Macalister, R. A. S. 'The Book of Invasions'. *The Irish Monthly* 44.518 (1916): 500–7.

— (ed. and tr.) *Lebor Gabála Érenn: Book of the Taking of Ireland Parts 1–5*. Dublin: Irish Texts Society, 1938–42.

MacManus, Seumas. *The Story of the Irish Race: A Popular History of Ireland*. New York: The Irish Publishing Company, 1921.

Maslen, Robert W. 'Flann O'Brien's Bombshells: *At Swim-Two-Birds* and *The Third Policeman*'. *New Hibernia Review* 10.4 (2006): 84–104.

Marx, Karl. 'A Contribution to the Critique of Hegel's Philosophy of Right'. *Early Writings*, trans. Rodney Livingstone and Gregor Benton. London: Penguin, 1992, 243–58.

— 'The Eighteenth Brumaire of Louis Bonaparte', trans. Terrell Carver. In *Marx's Eighteenth Brumaire: (Post)modern Interpretations*. Eds. Mark Cowling and James Martin. London: Pluto Press, 2002, 19–112.

Marx, Karl and Frederick Engels. *Ireland and the Irish Question: A Collection of Writings by Karl Marx and Frederick Engels*. Ed. R. Dixon, trans. Angela Clifford et al. New York: International Publishers, 1975.

Mays, J. C. C. 'Brian O'Nolan and Joyce on Art and on Life'. *James Joyce Quarterly* 11.3 (1974): 238–56.

Mazzullo, Concetta. 'Flann O'Brien's Hellish Otherworld: From *Buile Suibhne* to *The Third Policeman*'. *Irish University Review* 25.2 (1995): 218–327.

McMahon, Sean and Jo O'Donoghue. *Brewer's Dictionary of Irish Phrase & Fable* (London: Weidenfeld & Nicholson, 2004).

McKibben, Sarah. 'The Poor Mouth: A Parody of (Post)Colonial Irish Manhood'. *Research in African Literatures* 34.4 (2003): 96–114.

McMullen, Kim. 'Culture as Colloquy: Flann O'Brien's Postmodern Dialogue with Irish Tradition'. *NOVEL: A Forum on Fiction* 27.1 (1993): 62–84.

McNulty, Tracy. 'The Commandment against the Law: Writing and Divine Justice in Walter Benjamin's "Critique of Violence"'. *Diacritics* 37.2–3 (2007): 34–60.

Meaney, Gerardine. 'Race, Sex and Nation'. *The Irish Review* 35 (2007): 46–63.

Mellamphy, Ninian. 'Aestho-Autogamy and the Anarchy of Imagination: Flann O'Brien's Theory of Fiction in *At Swim-Two-Birds*'. *The Canadian Journal of Irish Studies* 4.1 (1978): 8–25.

Menninghaus, Winfried. *Disgust: Theory and History of a Strong Sensation*, trans. Howard Eiland and Joel Golb. Albany: State University of New York Press, 2003.

Merritt, Henry. 'Games, Ending and Dying in Flann O'Brien's *At Swim-Two-Birds*'. *Irish University Review* 25.2 (1995): 308–17.

Mill, John Stuart. *A System of Logic: Ratiocinative and Inductive*, Vol. 1. London: Longmans, 1872.

Murphy, Michael. Index to Macalister's translation of *Lebor Gabála Érenn*. 2008. CELT, the Corpus of Electronic Texts, University College Cork © 1997–2011 Corpus of Electronic Texts (UCC) http://www.ucc.ie/celt/indexLG.html.

Murphy, Neil. 'Flann O'Brien'. *Review of Contemporary Fiction* 25.3 (2005): 7–40.

— 'Flann O'Brien's *The Hard Life* and the Gaze of the Medusa'. *The Review of Contemporary Fiction* 31 (2011): 148–61.

Murphy, Paula. 'Jacques, Jacques and Jacks: The Shifting Symbolic in Derrida and Lacan'. *Textual Practice* 19.4 (2005): 509–27.

Murphy, Peter F. 'Living by his Wits: The Buffoon and Male Survival'. *Signs* 31.4 (2006): 1125–42.

Nally, David. '"That Coming Storm": The Irish Poor Law, Colonial Biopolitics, and the Great Famine'. *Annals of the Association of American Geographers* 98.3 (2008): 714–41.

Nejezchleb, Amy. 'A Saga to Remember: Flann O'Brien's Unfinished Novel'. *Review of Contemporary Fiction* 31 (2011): 205–19.

de Nie, Michael. 'Pigs, Paddies, Prams and Petticoats: Irish Home Rule and the British Comic Press, 1886–93'. *History Ireland* 13.1 (2005): 42–7.

Nietzsche, Friedrich. *The Gay Science*, trans. Josefine Nauckhoff. Cambridge: Cambridge University Press, 2001.

O'Brien, Flann. *The Hard Life*. London: Paladin, 1990.

— *Stories and Plays*. London: Paladin, 1991.

— *The Poor Mouth*. London: Flamingo, 1993.

— *At Swim-Two-Birds*. London: Penguin, 2001.

— *The Third Policeman*. London: Harper Perennial, 2006.

— *Rhapsody in Stephen's Green*. Ed. Robert Tracy. Dublin: Lilliput Press, 2011.

O'Brien, Flann and Myles na gCopaleen. *A Flann O'Brien Reader*. Ed. Stephen Jones. New York: Viking, 1978.

O'Conaire, Breandan. 'Flann O'Brien, 'An Beal [sic] Bocht' and Other Irish Matters'. *Irish University Review* 3.2 (1973): 121–40.

O'Connell, Marc. '"How to Handle Eternity": Infinity and the Theories of J. W. Dunne in the Fiction of Jorge Luis Borges and Flann O'Brien's The Third Policeman. *Irish Studies Review* 17:2 (2009): 223–37.

O'Crohan, Tomás. *The Islandman*, trans Robin Flower. Oxford: Oxford University Press, 2000.

Ó Gráda, Cormac. *Black 47 and Beyond: The Great Irish Famine in History, Economy and Memory.* Princeton: Princeton University Press, 2000.

O'Keeffe, James G. (Ed. and Trans.) *Buile Shuibhne (The Frenzy of Suibhne). Being the Adventures of Suibhne Geilt. A Middle-Irish Romance.* London: David Nutt, 1913. Accessed online UCC's Corpus of Electronic Texts (CELT). Electronic edition compiled by Beatrix Färber 2009

O'Keeffe, Timothy ed. *Myles: Portraits of Brian O'Nolan.* London: Martin, Brian & O'Keeffe, 1973.

Ó Murchadha, Ciarán. *The Great Famine: Ireland's Agony 1845–1852.* London: Continuum, 2011.

O'Nolan, Kevin. 'Homer and the Irish Hero Tale'. *Studia Hibernica* 8 (1968): 7–20.

Ó Nualláin, Ciarán. *The Early Years of Brian O'Nolan/Flann O'Brien/ Myles na gCopaleen*, trans. Róisín Ní Nualláin. Dublin: Lilliput Press, 1998.

O'Toole, Mary. 'The Theory of Serialism in *The Third Policeman*'. *Irish University Review* 18.2(1988): 215–25.

Powell, David. 'An Annotated Bibliography of Myles na Gopaleen's (Flann O'Brien's) 'Cruiskeen Lawn' Commentaries on James Joyce'. *James Joyce Quarterly* 9. 1 (1971): 50–62.

Power, Mary. 'The Figure of the Magician in *The Third Policeman* and *The Hard Life*'. *The Canadian Journal of Irish Studies* 8.1 (1982): 55–63.

Rabaté, Jean-Michel. *Jacques Lacan: Psychoanalysis and the Subject of Literature*. New York: Palgrave, 2001.

Renyolds, Paige. *Modernism, Drama, and the Audience for the Irish Spectacle*. Cambridge: Cambridge University Press, 2007

Richardson, Caleb. 'Transforming Anglo-Ireland: R. M. Smyllie and the Irish Times'. *New Hibernia Review* 11.4 (2007): 17–36.

de Río, Constanza. 'Misogyny in Flann O'Brien's *The Third Policeman*'. In *Gender, I-deology: Essays on Theory, Fiction and Film*. Amsterdam: Rudopi B. V., 1996, 207–24.

Royle, Nicholas. *Telepathy and Literature: Essays on the Reading Mind*. Oxford: Basil Blackwell, 1990.

— *The Uncanny*. Manchester: Manchester University Press, 2003.

Scannell, Yvonne. From 'The Constitution and the Role of Women'. In *The Irish Women's History Reader*. Eds. Alan Hayes and Diane Urquhart. London: Routledge, 2001, 71–8.

Schlegel, Friedrich. 'Dialogue on Poetry'. In *Dialogue on Poetry and Literary Aphorisms*, trans. Ernst Behler and Roman Struc. University Park: The Pennsylvania State University Press, 1968, 51–117.

— 'Athenäum fragments'. In *Lucinde and the Fragments*, trans. Peter Firchow. Minneapolis: The University of Minnesota Press, 1971a, 161–240.

— 'Critical Fragments'. In *Lucinde and the Fragments*, trans. Peter Firchow. Minneapolis: The University of Minnesota Press, 1971b, 143–59.

— 'On Incomprehensibility'. In *Classical and Romantic German Aesthetics*. Ed. J. M. Bernstein, trans. Peter Firchow. Cambridge: Cambridge University Press, 2003, 297–308.

Shea, Thomas F. *Flann O'Brien's Exorbitant Novels*. Lewisburg: Bucknell University Press, 1992.

Soble, Alan. 'Correcting Some Misconceptions about St. Augustine's Sex Life'. *Journal of the History of Sexuality* 11.4 (2002): 545–69.

Stokes, Whitely (ed. and trans.). 'The Voyage of Máel Dúin'. *Revue Celtique* 9 (1888): 447–95.

— (ed. and trans.). 'The Voyage of Máel Dúin'. *Revue Celtique* 10 (1889): 50–95.

Symons, A. J. A. *The Quest for Corvo: An Experiment in Biography*. Harmondsworth: Penguin, 1944.

Taaffe, Carol. '"Tell Me This, Do You Ever Open a Book at All?": Portraits of the Reader in Brian O'Nolan's *At Swim-Two-Birds*'. *Irish University Review* 34.2 (2004): 247–60.

— 'The Pathology of Revivalism: An Unpublished Manuscript by Myles na gCopaleen'. *The Canadian Journal of Irish Studies* 32.2 (2006): 27–33.

— *Ireland Through the Looking Glass: Flann O'Brien, Myles na gCopaleen and Irish Cultural Debate*. Cork: Cork University Press, 2008.

Tennyson, Alfred. *The Major Works: Including* The Princess, In Memoriam *and* Maud. Ed. Adam Roberts. Oxford: Oxford University Press, 2000, 2009.

Tigges, Wim. 'Ireland in Wonderland: Flann O'Brien's *The Third Policeman* as Nonsense Novel'. In *The Clash of Ireland: Literary Contrasts and Connections*. Eds. C. C. Barfoot and Theo D'haen. Amsterdam: Rodopi, 1989, 195–208.

Tóibín, Colm and Diarmaid Ferriter. *The Irish Famine: A Documentary*. London: Profile Books, 2001.

Trotter, David. *The English Novel in History: 1895–1920*. London: Routledge, 2005.

Wäppling, Eva. *Four Irish Legendary Figures in* At Swim-Two-Birds: *A Study of Flann O'Brien's Use of Finn, Suibhne, the Pooka and the Good Fairy*. Uppsala: Studia Anglistica Upsaliensis, 1984.

White, Jerry. 'Irish Literature is not Comparative Literature'. *ESC: English Studies in Canada* 32.2–3 (2006): 115–40.

Westropp, Thomas Johnson. 'The Marriages of the Gods at the Sanctuary of Tailltiu'. *Folklore* 31.2 (1920): 109–41.

Yeats, W. B. *W. B. Yeats: The Poems*. London: Everyman 1995.

— *Synge and the Ireland of His Time and Four Years*. Fairford, Glos.: The Echo Library, 2010.

Žižek, Slavoj. *The Sublime Object of Ideology*. London: Verso, 1989.

— *Looking Awry: An Introduction to Jacques Lacan through Popular Culture*. Cambridge, MA: Massachusetts Institute of Technology Press, 1991.

— '"In His Bold Gaze My Ruin Is Writ Large."' In *Everything You Always Wanted to Know About Lacan (But Were Afraid to Ask Hitchcock)*. Ed. Slavoj Žižek. London: Verso, 1992, 211–72.

— 'Surplus-Enjoyment Between the Sublime and the Trash.' *Lacanian Ink* 15 (1999): 98–107.

— *The Ticklish Subject: The Absent Centre of Political Ontology.*
London: Verso, 2000.
— *The Parallax View.* Cambridge, MA: Massachusetts Institute of
Technology Press, 2006.
— *The Plague of Fantasies.* London: Verso, 2008a.
— *Enjoy Your Symptom!: Jacques Lacan in Hollywood and Out.* London:
Routledge, 2008b.

INDEX

Abbey Theatre   3, 28, 108, 159
academics   29, 96, 108, 124,
    199, 204
    anti-intellectualism   128, 201
    and filth   5
    Joycean academics,   159, 199,
        201, 207–8, 212
Aer Lingus   164–5
aestho-autogamy   32–4, 40–2,
    534–n. 70
afterlife   57, 64, 67–9, 77, 88–9, 91,
    99, 104–5n. 80, 192, 196
Agamben, Giorgio   7, 117–18
alcohol   18, 20, 44, 92, 111,
    115, 152, 157, 180,
    183, 205–6, 210–11
Alice's Adventures in
    Wonderland   129
Amergin   131
Archive   191–2, 200–1, 203–4
    as alternative truth   214–15,
        217
    death drive   192–9
    Joycean archive   191, 204–6,
        208–10, 212
Aristotle,   4, 75, 117, 122–3
At Swim-Two-Birds   1, 6, 9–55,
    129, 203
    aestho-autogamy   32–4, 40–2,
        53–4n. 70
    Athenian Oracle, The,   35,
        53n. 63
    autobiographical
        elements   30–2

character borrowing   114
    fragments   7, 9–18, 22
    gender-relations   152–3, 168,
        173, 182, 184
    Ireland   27–29
atomic theory   81, 104n. 78,
    192, 196, 201
    as contamination   69, 84,
        210, 222n
    and gender   92–5, 97
Augustine of Hippo, St,   184,
    191–3, 198, 201–2, 204,
    217, 220n. 26
autobiography
    as biography   14, 214–17
    At Swim-Two-Birds,   14–15,
        22–3, 30–2, 38
    The Dalkey Archive   7, 213–19
    Gaeltacht autobiographies
        114, 136
    The Quest for Corvo   214–15

Bare Life   7, 117–25, 127, 133,
    136, 138–9
    in relation to Benjamin   130–1
Barnabas, Brother   1, 41
Barnacle, Nora   37–8
'Bash in the Tunnel, A'   205–6, 209
Baudelaire, Charles   171
Béal Bocht, An   1, 7, 107–41,
    142n. 28, 157, 185
    Gaeilgeoirí   113, 124–5, 133
    proper name   116, 125,
        127, 131–8

repetition   107–16, 137,
     140, 142n. 21
tragi-farce   107, 110–14, 116,
     120, 129
women   138, 152–3, 157
Beckett, Samuel, 110, 153,
     170, 207
Endgame   110
Molloy   153
Beelzebub   193
beginnings   10, 17, 21–3, 48,
     57, 79, 89, 97, 109–10,
     112, 159, 187n. 41,
     197, 212
Behan, Brendan   92
Bell, The   151, 159
Benjamin, Walter   130
bicycles   58–9, 71, 76, 79–81,
     84–5, 91–9, 101n. 5,
     124, 210
big Other   72, 83
biography *see* autobiography
biopolitics   117
Bios   117–18, 122–3
Blanchot, Maurice   21, 25, 32,
     76, 109, 112
Blather, Count, 1
Blather   1, 31
Blin, Roger   110
Borges, Jorge Luis   138
*Boy from Ballytearim,
     The*,   152–3
Brecht, Bertolt   12
Broc, An   1, 159
Brothel   168, 175

Camus, Albert   4, 90
Cannibalism   120
     Between *Third Policeman* and
          Dalkey Archive   192,
          204
Čapec, Josef and Karel   99
     The Insect Play   99, 155

Capitalism   43
Carroll, Lewis   3
Carlyle, Thomas   121
Cathleen ni Houlilan   157–8, 167
Catholic Church   48, 181,
     184, 214
     and sex   33, 35, 37, 42
     target   2–3, 154,
          159–61, 166
     Within *Dalkey Archive*   191,
          193, 200, 203, 206,
          211–12
     and women   149–52, 159–61,
          168, 170
Censorship of Publications Act
     (1929)   3, 34–6, 151
censorship   49, 212, 192
     Joyce (character) as
          censor   210–12
Children of Destiny   31–2,
     52n. 44, 207, 215
Comhthrom Féinne   22, 28, 157
conclusions   10, 18–19, 21–5,
     48, 75, 110, 112, 129,
     139, 159, 181–2, 185,
     192–3, 199
contamination *see* atomic theory
contraception   35, 42, 174
     rhythm method   157
Corca Dorcha   109, 112–15, 123,
     125, 133–4, 138, 140,
     142n. 28
Concentration camps   118, 122
Constitution of Ireland, The
     Irish language in
          constitution   127, 130
     and Women the
          constitution   149–50,
          161–3
Constitution, American   185
Corvo, Baron *see* Frederick Rolfe
Cronin, Anthony   5, 13, 170,
     202, 217

Cruiskeen Lawn 1, 3, 45,
  52n. 61, 95, 147n.
  124, 188n. 73, 189n.
  91, 191, 207, 209, 216
  authorship of 31, 160, 164
  fragmentation 13,
    159–60, 178
  and Idealism 107–8, 162–3,
    166–7
  intellectual ambiguity 43,
    199–200, 221n. 32,
    222n. 71
  and Irish language 116, 127–8
  misogyny 156–67, 179–81
  racism 185
Cruiskeen Court of Voluntary
    Jurisdiction, The
    (*Cruiskeen Lawn*) 45,
    127–8
Cruscalon 219n. 1 *see also* DMP
cryptography 77

Dalkey Archive, The 1, 7, 18, 73,
    152–3, 177–84, 191–219
  as autobiography 7, 213–19
  essay in derision 178, 202–4,
    221n. 31
  narration 217–18, 223n. 98
  as revisionist history 209–17
  sexism in, 177–84
  stage adaptations 95, 151,
    176, 184–5, 189n. 93
Danaides, The 58
Dante, Alighieri 57
death drive 7, 60–70, 72–8,
    88–93, 97, 101n. 5,
    102n. 40
  as archive 192–6, 199
  distinction from life drives 60
  and prohibition 78–84
defecation 153, 167–8, 172
Derrida, Jacques 11, 19, 70, 130,
    133, 212

on archive and death drive,
    192–5, 204
fragmentation, 16, 50n. 21
desire 62–6, 68–9, 72–5,
    77–9, 81, 83–5, 87,
    102n. 40
  distinction between desire and
    drive 66–7
  and knowledge 87–90
  and prohibition 78–9, 81
  and sexuality 93–100
Deus ex machina 43, 194
De Valera, Éamon 107–8
Dinneen, Patrick S. 125, 182
disgust 208
  domestic 156
  female body 44–5, 152,
    167–8, 170–7
  male body 44–5, 47, 170,
    173, 176
District Court, The (*Cruiskeen
    Lawn*) 127–8
DMP 191, 199, 219n. 1 *see also*
    Cruscalon
Doe, John James 1
domestic, the
  in *Cruiskeen Lawn* 158–60,
    163–4, 166
  domestic space and
    women 152–8
  domestic violence
    (physical) 158, 163
  in *Hard Life* 174
  legal and constitutional
    positioning of
    women 149–50
doubles 58, 85, 97, 212
Duffy, Matt 1
Dunne, J. W., 18, 73–4, 86,
    103n. 53, 197–8
  *Experiment with
    Time, An* 73
  Serial Universe, The 73

Eagleton, Terry   110
Edwards, Heath   99
Eliot, T.S.   9–10, 41
Engels, Friedrich   49
Eros   60, 91, 97, 100, 171
eternity   57, 65, 67, 70–5, 77,
        84, 99, 198
ethics   26
    authorial   36, 42
    by numbers   18–21
eugenics,   35, 38, 40–4, 141
    psycho-eugenics   40–3

failure   32, 43, 45, 62, 66–7, 89
Fallon, Gabriel   155–6
famine   118–22, 127, 143n. 52,
        144nn. 54, 56, 67, 182
farce   107, 109–10, 113, 120,
        127, 129, 139
fathers   26, 29, 33, 41, 48, 78,
        87, 91, 158
    absence of   114–15, 137–8,
        152–3, 174
    Church fathers   193, 200–1
    Joyce   204, 208, 210–12,
        215, 217
Faustus Kelly   152
fragments   9–32, 45, 193,
        203, 219
    anonymous/pseudonymous   31
    autobiography   30–2
    beginnings and endings   21–5
    contradiction   25–7
    Cruiskeen Lawn   159–60, 178
    German Romantic   11–13,
        15–16, 19, 31–2, 50n. 11
    in relation to Ireland   26–9
    modernist   9–11
Freud, Sigmund   60–1, 67, 69–70,
        102n. 40, 192–5, 204,
        207, 213
    O'Nolan on Freud and
        Psychoanalysis   27, 59–60

filth   170
footnotes   1, 77, 88, 216
form and formlessness   9–10,
        12–13, 15–17, 19, 21,
        25–6, 31–2, 36, 43–9,
        65, 68, 82
Foucault, Michel   117
Friel, Brian   135
    Translations   135

Gaeilgeoirí   113, 124–5, 133, 159
Gaelic League   27–8, 40, 55n. 82,
        108, 113, 127, 133
Gaelic Revival   2–3
Galton, Francis   40–1
Gate Theatre   99
gaze
    the gaze (Lacan)   83–4
    male gaze   45, 172
God
    absence of God and religion in
        Third Policeman   68–9,
        71, 89
    Catholic   157, 194, 197–8,
        201, 203–4, 207, 211–12
    Greek gods   58, 90, 130
    God-like narrator/author   33,
        48, 82, 218
    and numbers   37
    and omnium   65–6
    Roman gods   118
goddesses (Irish)   131
Goethe, Johann Wolfgang von   61
    Faust   61, 87
gombeen bourgeoise   43
Gregory, Lady Augusta   28,
        111, 114
Gregory clause, the   122
gynandromorphism   95

Hard Life, The   4, 7, 152–4,
        156–7, 167–71, 173–6
Hades   57, 90

heaven 5, 20, 68–9, 71, 73, 193–4
Hegel, Georg Wilhelm Friedrich 19, 75, 107
hell 48, 57–9, 68–70, 73, 75–7, 82, 89–90, 192, 199
homo sacer 118
homosexuality 46, 51n. 32, 91–5, 99–100, 118, 178, 214, 220n. 26
homunculi 86
Hyde, Douglas 133

Immram Curaig Máel Dúin 114–15
incest 34, 37–8, 94, 138, 158, 173
Irish
  artist 205–6
  identity 122, 149, 206
  language 116, 123–38, 141n. 12
  language and speakers and the law 126–38
  place names 125
  speakers as animals 123–5, 145n. 77
Irish Censorship Board, The 35–6, 156, 203
  as 'smut board' 157
Irish Colleen 150, 152, 158, 162–3
Irish Countrywoman's Association 149
Irish Housewives Association 149, 163–4
Irish Poor Law 122
Irish Times 31, 201
  letters to 95–6, 159
infidelity 40, 55n. 82, 153, 181–2
infinity
  of afterlife 72, 81
  as series of the finite 75

of subject in artistic production 30
Ixion 58

Jesuits 201–2, 208, 212–14, 216–17, 223n. 90
Jouissance 63–4, 66–7, 73, 77–8, 98–100
Joyce, James 37–8, 124, 127, 205
  as catholic 206, 211–12
  as censor 210–12
  denying authorship 206–7
  Dubliners 207, 211
  Finnegans Wake, 13, 197, 206–7, 210
  as Irish Artist 205–6
  and the Jesuits 202–3, 212–13, 217
  Joycean archive 191, 204–5
  Joyce and Rolfe 215–17
  mistaken identity, 208–10
  parodied in O'Nolan's works 177–8, 191–3, 200, 203–4, 207–8, 210–13
  Portrait of the Artist as a Young Man 33, 41–2, 216
  Ulysses, 176, 188n. 73, 206–7, 210
  Work in Progress 13
Joyce, John and Bridget 125–6
Joyce, Myles 126–7
Joyce, Patrick Weston 114, 125
Judas 191, 200–1
justice 49, 80, 110, 116, 123, 127–9, 132

Kafka, Franz, 59, 132, 176
  Castle, The 176
  'In the Penal Colony' 132
  Trial, The 129
Kant, Immanuel 5, 170, 172–3

Keats and Chapman   59,
    103n. 53, 199–200
Keats, John   169
Kiberd, Declan   29, 133
Knowall, George   1
knowledge   4–5, 7, 26–7, 43–4,
    81, 85–90, 193–4,
    200–7, 211
    God as knowledge   201
Kristeva, Julia   154, 172

Lacan, Jacques   59–63, 78, 83, 87
    gaze   83–4
    imaginary   75
    real   73, 75, 83, 88
    symbolic   66, 72–3, 75, 83,
        85, 88
landscape   55n. 81, 58, 68,
    113, 196
Lang, Fritz   72
law   93
    and language   116, 123,
        127–32, 136
    and bare life   123, 127, 130–1,
        136, 139
    and desire   78–85, 89, 97
    and mechanics   82, 84
    and mythical violence   130–1
    Policemen in Third
        Policeman   64, 68, 73,
        78–9, 81, 85, 97
    Poor Law   122
    Roman law and Homo
        Sacer   118
    and the state of
        exception,   121, 127
    and women   150, 152–3
Laverty, Maura   159
Lebor Gabála Érenn (Book
    of the Taking of
    Ireland)   131–2
Leonard, Hugh   95, 184–5,
    189n. 93

Lethe, 90
Leventhal, Con   184
libido   37, 65, 73, 91–2, 97
Literary and Historical Society,
    UCD   28–9, 54n. 74
Lucifer   57, 193
lumpenproletariat   43

Maamtrasna Murders   125–7
MacDonagh, Donagh   31
MacNamara, Brinsley   133–4
Madame Bovary   45
Máel Dúin (also Maoldún,
    Maeldoon,
    Maildun)   114–16,
    139–40, 142n. 29
Máire (see Séamus Ó
    Grianna)   134
marriage, 2, 35, 39–40, 42, 54n. 70,
    113, 150, 152–3, 156–8,
    161, 164, 173, 175,
    181, 211
'Martyr's Crown, The'   154–5
Marx Brothers   110, 213
Marx, Karl   13, 107
Mary, Rose of Tralee   162
Mary, virgin   151–2, 181
masturbation   33–7, 40, 170
Maugham, Somerset   167
McClelland, Alan   176
McCool, Finn (also Fionn
    MacCumhaill)   15, 22,
    24, 29, 40, 114–15
mechanisation   58, 64, 73, 82,
    84, 86
memory   35, 40, 69, 89–90, 98,
    140, 193–6, 199, 209
menstruation   167, 172
Mephistopheles   61, 87
Mill, John Stuart   132
modernism   9–11, 13, 26, 28,
    30–1, 43–4, 47–8, 57,
    96, 141 208, 215

Mollycule theory *see* atomic theory
Montgomery, Niall
  in *At Swim-Two-Birds*, 30
  Blather 31
  Cruiskeen Lawn 31, 160, 164,
    187n. 43, 221n. 32
  Dalkey Archive 177–8, 180,
    182–3, 201, 217
  'The Pathology of
    Revivalism' 173
mothers 138
  absent mothers 33, 36,
    91–2, 152–4
  idealisation and parody 108,
    154–8
  legal position 149–52

na gCopaleen, Myles 7, 52n. 61,
  59, 128–9, 139, 142n. 28,
  178, 185, 185n. 4, 188n. 73,
  215–16, 219, 222
  contradiction 1, 13
  Dublin and Ireland 2–3,
    108–12, 114, 124,
    140, 206
  Joyce 204, 206–9, 212
  misogyny 95, 156–67,
    179–81, 187n. 44,
    189n. 94
  on erudition 5, 199–200
  woman as authors of 180–1
narration 78, 179, 217–18,
  223n. 98
Nietzsche, Friedrich, 19
Niobe 130–1

O'Brien, Flann 1–8 see also
  Myles na gCopaleen;
  Brian O'Nolan
O'Brien, Kate 166
Objet petit a 62–4, 74, 83
O'Connor, Lir 96
O'Connor, Luna 96

Ó Criomhthainn, Tomás (also
  Tomás O'Crohan)
  110–11, 142n. 21
  t-Oileánach, An 110,
    129, 142n. 21
O'Faoláin, Sean (also Sean
  O'Faolain) 162, 199
Ó Grianna, Séamus 134
Ó Laoghaire, Fr Peadar 111
omnium 64–5, 72–3, 87–9, 97,
  99, 219n. 1
O'Nolan, Brian
  absence of heroes 114–15,
    131–2, 139
  intellectualism 3–6, 24, 100,
    191–204
  Ireland 2–3, 10, 27, 29,
    107–11, 116, 124
  Joyce 203–17
  pseudonyms 1–2, 7
  racism 184–5
  sexuality 92–3, 95–6, 99–100
  translation 133–4
  women 38, 94, 97, 138, 149,
    151–8, 161, 166–83
O'Nolan, Ciarán (also Ciaran Ua
  Nuallain) 22, 31
O'Nolan Gearóid 6
O'Nolan, Evelyn 134, 180
Origin of Species, The 42

paradox 4, 11, 15, 26, 45, 61–2,
  74–5, 152, 203
Parnell, Charles Stewart 91
parody 33, 159–60, 212
  of Ireland 27, 111, 113–14,
    116, 127, 136, 170,
    140, 141n. 12
  of sex 100
  of sexism 166, 181
  within *Cruiskeen
    Lawn* 159–60
  within *Dalkey Archive* 204, 212

'Pathology of Revivalism, The'
      116, 132, 189n. 86
pedantry,   5, 200–2
Peel, Sir John   121, 144n. 63
pigs   123–4, 138, 157
      Ambrós as metaphor for
         Ireland   124
Playboy riots   151, 184
pleasure principle   35, 60, 63,
      71–2, 93
Plain People of Ireland   26, 43,
      46, 128, 164, 200–1
pneuma   197–8, 206, 211–12 *see
      also* Ruach
Poor Mouth, The see *Béal Bocht, An*
Pope, The   193–4, 214–15
Pornography   210
postmodernism   9, 13, 110
power   36, 43, 46, 58, 219n. 1
      authorial power   23, 66, 68
      biopower and bare life   117,
         122, 130–1
      death drive   61, 65, 66, 72–3,
         78, 81, 88, 90
      doubles   85, 212
      proper name   133, 146n. 104
Power, P. J.   119, 134, 145n. 77
Preformationism   74
pregnancy   33–4, 39, 53n. 64, 98,
      151–6, 169, 174, 177,
      181–2, 216
Prometheus   58
proper name   7, 20, 47, 54n. 75,
      91, 102n. 40, 104n. 80,
      125, 127, 181, 189n. 91,
      202, 207
      Jams O'Donnell, 116, 131–8
      namelessness   59, 77–81,
         85–7, 196
      pseudonyms   1, 7, 31, 96,
         158, 160
      surname   29, 54n. 71, 175,
         177, 183
      translation   132–7

prostitution   154, 168, 170,
      174–6, 183
psychobiography
      avoidance of   7, 194
psycho-eugenics *see* eugenics
Pythagoras   19

queer   44, 46, 55n. 83, 109, 201
      Divney and narrator   64, 77,
         91–4, 97–9
Quidnunc, 206

racism, 79, 122, 125, 140, 183–5
rape, 24–5, 33–4, 36, 39–40,
      53n. 68, 54n. 78,
      58, 91, 151, 176
realist novel, 9, 26, 43, 48, 111,
      153, 178
religion   89, 153, 203–4, 212, 214
      see also Catholic Church;
         God
repetition   7, 192
      An Béal Bocht   107–16, 137,
         140, 142n. 28
      At Swim-Two-Birds   15, 19
      between *Dalkey Archive* and
         Third Policeman   194–9,
         204, 210
      Third Policeman   57–8, 60, 62,
         66, 69–71, 74–9, 88–90,
         97–8, 104n. 78
Rhapsody in Stephen's Green   99,
      152, 155–6
Rolfe, Frederick   214
      *Desire and Pursuit of the
         Whole*   216
      Hadrian the Seventh   214–15
      In relation to Joyce   215–17
      In relation to O'Nolan   215–17
romance   156, 178
      Celtic romance   114
Royal Myles na gCopaleen
         Institute of Archaeology
         (*Cruiskeen Lawn*), 180–9

Ruach 206, 211–12 see also
  Pneuma
Russell, Lord John 121, 144n. 63

saints, 108, 168, 198, 201, 211
Saints Go Marching In, The 151
satire 9, 136, 165, 201, 203
Sayers, Peig 51n. 35, 110
'Scenes in a Novel' 41, 54n. 78
Schlegel, Friedrich 11, 15, 19,
  31–2, 50nn. 10, 19,
  21, 24
Schmitt, Carl 118
Scott, Cecil, 177, 185, 201,
  203, 207
serialism 74
sex 91, 184, 201, 220n. 26
  female sexual pleasure 86,
    93–4, 100, 152, 155, 167
  pleasure/procreation
    tension 33–8, 41–2,
    53n. 68, 154–7
  queer sex 55n. 83, 92–100
sexual identity and gender
    confusion 46–7, 95–6,
    177–8, 181–2
sexually transmitted disease 151,
    170, 174, 183, 185,
    185n. 4
Shakespeare, William 100
  Macbeth 140
Sheehy-Skeffington, Andree 164
Shelley, Mary 125
Sheridan, Niall 13, 18, 30–2,
    52n. 44, 59, 160,
    187n. 43, 207, 210
Sisyphus 4, 58, 61, 90
Slattery's Sago Saga 152–3, 177,
    182–3, 185
Smut Board *see* Censorship Board
soul 20, 22, 39, 47–8, 71, 74,
    84–6, 197, 211
stage Irishman 3, 28, 108–9, 111,
    158, 166

state of exception 118–22, 127
suicide 36, 100, 205
Summa 200
Sweeny 13, 15, 20, 24, 48, 54
Symons, A. J. 214–15
  Quest for Corvo, The 213–15
Synge, John Millington 28, 41,
    111, 114, 151

Taaffe, Carol 53n, 153, 187n,
    204, 221n. 42, 52,
    223n. 90
*Táin Bó Cúailgne (The Cattle Raid
    of Cooley)* 39
Tantalus 58
Tartarus 57–8, 90
Tennyson, Alfred 142n. 29
Thanatos 60, 77, 91, 97, 100,
    171, 192, 194, 196
  thanatography 77, 196
Third Policeman, The 1, 5, 7,
    18, 57, 105n. 91,
    113, 152–3
  atomic theory 69, 81, 84,
    92–5, 97, 104n. 78
  black box 58–9, 63–8, 72, 76,
    78–9, 81–9, 97
  omnium 64–5, 72–3, 87–9,
    97, 99, 219n. 1
  rejection of 170
  sexuality 91–9
Th'oul Lad of Kilsalaher 152
time
  countertime 18, 22, 24, 107–8
  De Selby 75, 104n. 80
  and Dunne 18, 73–4, 197–8
  God 198
  oxygen 193, 197–9
  repetition 15–16, 109
  time within narrative 14, 16,
    18–19, 22, 26, 48,
    50n. 18
  unconscious 57–9, 61–2,
    64–5, 67, 69–72

toilets   5, 93, 95, 168–70, 205
torture   14–15, 23–4, 32, 40,
        47–8, 50n. 18, 54n. 81,
        57, 99
tragedy   90, 107, 110, 112, 116,
        120, 129, 196, 214, 216
tragi-comic   110, 169
tragi-farcical   107, 110–14, 116,
        120, 129
translation   109, 115, 129, 134–6,
        145n. 77, 211–12, 216
Trevelyan, George   126–7
trial
   An Béal Bocht   116, 122,
        125–7, 131–2, 137, 139,
        146–7n. 105
   in An t-Oileánach   129
   Cruiskeen Lawn trails   128–9
   and Language   129
   of Myles Joyce   125–7, 80
   Third Policeman   8
   of Trellis   16, 24, 36, 40, 49
truth   4, 13, 82, 89, 162, 180
   alternative truths   200–2,
        209–10, 212–13, 215, 217
   archive   191, 193, 200
   and numbers   19, 21, 46, 48
   unconscious   195
Tweedy, Hilda   164
'Two in One'   209

unconscious   41, 59, 64
   archive   195
   jokes   213

and negation/death   67–8
and time   69–70
University College
        Dublin   28–9, 199
urination   153, 167–9, 172–3

venereal disease see sexually
        transmitted diseases
Vico, Giambattista   196–7, 206
violence   114, 116, 131,
        196, 209
   as art   48, 53n. 68
   in relation to women   91,
        154, 158, 163, 166–7,
        175, 179
   mythical violence   130,
        146n. 100
virgin/whore   40, 151, 175
vomit   44, 46, 76, 167, 170–1,
        173, 175–6, 210

watches   23–4, 51n. 37, 64–5, 86
wish fulfilment   71–3, 75
women and intellectual
        inquiry   179–81, 201
Woolf, Virginia   41, 180

Yeats, William Butler   28, 41, 111,
        114, 151, 202

Zeno   61–2, 74–5
Žižek, Slavoj   60–3, 66, 78, 213
Zōe   117
Zōon Politikon   117, 123